The War Diary of William

1916 – 1

A Soldier in Africa

By his granddaughter
Shirley Jean Day

Published by Daylinks Publications

ISBN 978-1-8384663-0-5

Preface

This family history is prompted by the sight of my grandfather's pocket diary - just 3 inches by 5 inches - which he kept during the year 1916 when he fought for the British Empire against Germany in German East Africa (now Tanzania) and British East Africa (now Kenya) in World War One. This small notebook is hard to read because of the tiny writing in pencil and the nibbling by insects on some pages and it needed to be transcribed.

It provides insight into the writer, his values and his time. It is not so much a war diary but more a companion and confidante that helped him make sense of the hardship where the "real enemies were the deadly climate, the wild regions and the swamps and forests and scrub" causing "appalling losses on both sides as men and animals succumbed to tropical diseases and starvation." [1]

That William did his duty is in no doubt for he was mentioned in a Despatch by General J.C. Smuts in 1916 and awarded the Distinguished Conduct Medal [2] in 1917 because: "This Warrant Officer, by his untiring energy and devotion to duty, has set an excellent example to the NCO's and men of the regiment." [3]

The diary recorded William's final year of military action but there were earlier wars in Africa for this woodworker from Yorkshire, England and something of that is described here.

---

[1] Brown, J.A. page 309

[2] London Gazette 25 May 1917

[3] Monick, S. page 185

Acknowledgements

My thanks go to Gail Ellis and Brenda McSweeney for loaning me the diary which was given to their mother, Olive, William's youngest daughter and to my mother, Toody, William's eldest daughter, for her recollections about Watson family life and to David Hayden for a photograph of William's war medals. I owe special thanks to John Day not only for the detective work in locating elusive bits of family history but also for his help in compiling the diary and for arranging the publication.

This book is dedicated to John, Mark, Shannah and Gordon and also to Christina and Hannah.

Table of Contents

1. Early Years

What prompted William Robert Watson in 1899 to leave his hometown of Hull in the East Riding of Yorkshire England at the age of 23 and answer the call for volunteers to fight the Boers in South Africa?

Kingston upon Hull

The Watson family had lived in Yorkshire for many generations. William's grandfather had been a soldier until his marriage in 1843 when he joined the police force rising to be Superintendent of Police. William's father, Robert Lawson Watson, had married Elizabeth Salmon while stationed at the Preston Sussex Army Barracks but left the army to set up business as a builder in Hull where he taught his three sons their woodworking skills and encouraged William to join the Volunteer Battalion. Here, Wiliam learnt how to shoot a rifle well enough to earn a medal for marksmanship at Bisley.

2. The Anglo Boer War 1899 - 1902

When William was growing up, he would have read newspaper accounts of the conflicts in South Africa between the two British Colonies of the Cape and Natal and the two Boer Republics of the Transvaal and the Orange Free State.

Events there came to a head in October 1899 when the Boer Republics declared war on Britain.

In the first three months of the year, the Boer Republics had the upper hand. Their commandos invaded northern Natal and besieged the town of Ladysmith, invaded the Cape Colony and attacked the British garrisons in Kimberley and Mafeking (now named Mafikeng). The British fought back with victories at Elandslaagte and Talana Hill but sustained serious defeats at Magersfontein, Colenso and Stormberg during December 1899.

Over the following year, the British brought in reinforcements under the command of Lord Roberts with Lord Kitchener as Chief of Staff. The town of Kimberley was relieved on 15th February 1900, closely followed by the relief of Ladysmith on 28th February 1900. By mid-March, Lord Roberts had taken Bloemfontein, capital of the Orange Free State and the besieged town of Mafeking was relieved.

These events must have inspired William for he enrolled with the 2nd East Yorkshire Regiment on the 19th March 1900 and No. 7024 Corporal W. R. Watson took the long sea voyage to Durban South Africa where he joined other British Regiments.

By mid-1900, the war was well under way. Britain occupied all major centres including Bloemfontein (the capital of the Orange Free State), the Rand Goldfields (real cause of the interest) and Pretoria (capital of the Transvaal).

On 28th May the Boer Republic of the Orange Free State was annexed and renamed the Orange River Colony. On 31st May British troops entered Johannesburg and on 5th June Pretoria was taken.

At this time, William was in the Orange Free State, near to the border with Basutoland and where he would earn the clasp "Wittebergen" for the various engagements and assaults that took place between 1st and 29th July 1900 in the magnificent setting of the Brandwater Basin.

> *"The country to which the Boers had now retired may be described as a huge horse-shoe formed by the Wittebergen range, which extends from Commando Nek opposite Ficksburg, by Moolman's Hoek, Nelspoort, and Witnek to Slabbert's and Retief's Neks on the north, and then by the Roodebergen range, which continues from Retief's Nek in a south-easterly direction through Naauwpoort Nek and Golden Gate to Generaal's Kop, a magnificent mountain mass which connects the main Drakensberg ridge with the Roodebergen; the circumference of the horse-shoe measured this way is roughly seventy-five miles (120 km). The base-line of the horse-shoe, about forty miles in length (64 km), is formed by the Caledon River, separating the Free State from Basutoland.*
>
> *The principal gates of this great citadel are four - Commando, Slabbert, Retief and Naauwpoort Neks; but there are also a few posterns, such as Witnek and Nelslpoort, Bamboeshoek and the Golden Gate, by which at need scouts could steal out or an enemy could creep in.*

Inside this well-guarded enclosure the land is again cut up into deep chines and valleys by the fantastic cleavings of the plateau and by the three rivers - the Brandwater, the Little Caledon, and the Caledon - which generously water this favoured country, named after the river which runs through the central valley, the Brandwater Basin." [4]

Lord Roberts sought to encircle the Boers in the Brandwater Basin where the Boers had retreated after various engagements and assaults including the Battle of Bakenkop and the attack and capture of Bethlehem.

The fighting culminated when 3000 Boers under command of General Prinsloo formally surrendered at Surrender Hill on 30th July followed by more at the Golden Gate soon after, but many weeks followed before the remainder, who had hidden away in the caves and alleys of the surrounding mountains, finally gave up.

The British had gained the upper hand. The Transvaal was annexed in October 1900 and it seemed that the war was over. Lord Roberts returned to England in triumph at the end of November 1900.

From his service record, it shows that William was discharged and returned home to England in June 1901 after fighting in the South African Campaign 1900-1901 and being awarded the Queen's South African Medal 1901 with three clasps – Wittebergen, Transvaal and Cape Colony.

However, things did not settle down in South Africa. The Boers changed their tactics, abandoned the British style of warfare and increased their reliance on small mobile units.

---

[4] The Times History of the War, Vol IV, edited by Leo Amery

This mobility enabled them to capture supplies, undertake raids and disrupt communication on the army of occupation.

It seems that William could not settle down either. He resented taking orders from his older brother Frederick who had led a quiet life in the family building and joinery business while William was overseas and seven months after returning home - in January 1902 - he joined the 27th Battalion Imperial Yeomanry as 38347 Corporal Watson.

The Imperial Yeomanry was a unit raised specially for the Boer War. It did not come under the regular army. The idea was to form a unit that could match the Boer at shooting and riding and mobility. Many of the volunteers were from the nobility with their hunting and shooting background. William had first-hand experience and was a crack shot and he sailed again for South Africa.

South African Campaign Medal and Queens South African Medal

The British response to the guerilla tactics of the Boers was a scorched earth policy to deny supplies to the fighters. Many farms were burnt and movement restricted with blockhouses and wire fencing.

Refugees were sent to concentration camps around South Africa. Such measures were largely responsible for bringing the Boers to the negotiation table to end the War on 31st May 1902.

William's tour of duty expired on 2 January 1903 and he decided to stay in South Africa and No 38347 Sc Sergeant W.R. Watson took his discharge in Stellenbosch giving his address as GPO, Cape Town. He was awarded the Queens South African Medal 1902.

In November 1903 he joined PWO Cape Peninsular Rifles until 10 July 1906 when he was transferred/joined the Kimberley Regiment of Volunteers Corps as No 2098 Sergeant W. R. Watson and was discharged two years later.

3. Family 1907 - 1914

On 5 June 1907, William married Susan Jane Smith (known as Jane) in Kimberley. Jane maintained she was a true Cockney having been born in the East End of London where she had trained as a nurse. When she was 18, she was advised to move to a warmer climate for her health and managed to secure a passage as a child nurse on board a ship bound for Cape Town where she gained employment as a cook and parlour maid for the wealthy Harry Struben at his home 'Strubenheim'.

Jane wrote to her sister, Emma, in London saying that she could hear lions roaring at night but Emma did not believe her. However, it was true. Cecil John Rhodes lived nearby at 'Groote Schuur' where he kept wild animals and Rudyard Kipling [5]wrote about taking his family to his parents home that was next door to 'Strubenheim' and how his children would take "flying barefoot visit to our neighbours the Strubens" and he recalls that "uphill lived the lions, Alice and Jumbo, whose morning voices were the signal for getting up".

After their son William was born, the family moved up to the Transvaal where William worked on the Modderfontein Gold Mine becoming Foreman Carpenter and where he met the Foreman Blacksmith, John Semple whose son would marry William's eldest daughter. William built his own house in Benoni with the help of four friends who took it in turns to complete a house for each of them.

William was chosen as the representative of the Witwatersrand Rifles Regiment to go to the Coronation of King George V in 1911 taking his wife, Jane and his two young sons, William Robert and Charles Frederick.

[5] Kipling, R. page 126

Two years later, Enid Ruth (known as Toody) was born in December 1912 in Benoni. Enid's nickname arose from the fact that her mother had named her daughter after Enid Struben - daughter of Harry Struben for whom she had worked.

Jane had been christened Susan Jane but hated being called Suzie which she said sounded 'common'. William had little time for such pretensions and teased Jane by calling Enid Suzie which her brother pronounced as Toody and the name stuck.

Witswatersrand rifles: Contingent to Coronation King George V 1911. Sgt. W R Watson: front row 3rd from left

Monick, S. , A Bugle Calls, page 68

In 1910, the merger of the Cape Colony, Natal, the Orange Free State and the Transvaal formed the Union of South Africa with a Boer - Louis Botha - as its first Prime Minister. Britain continued to maintain a military garrison of considerable strength in the Union as well as a naval base at Simonstown.

When Britain declared war on Germany in 1914, the Union of South Africa offered to take on responsibility of the British garrison situated there, thus releasing British forces for duty in Europe and leaving the newly-formed Union Defence Force to face the German Imperial Protectorate of German South West Africa (now Namibia) on its northern border.

The Union

"further pledged themselves to dispatch a military expedition against the enemy forces in German South West Africa in order to secure the seaports in that territory and the powerful wireless installation at Windhoek."

It was decided to

"occupy Luderitz Bay while the wireless station and landing equipment at Swakopmund were to be destroyed by naval bombardment, and to take pressure from the Luderitz Bay expeditionary force, a Union force was to be landed at Port Nolloth to operate against the enemy's southern frontier while another force was concentrated at Upington to threaten his eastern border." [6]

This operation was under the joint command of General Louis Botha and General J.C. Smuts. It is interesting to note that many of the volunteers who responded had fought against each other in the Boer War which had concluded in 1902 with bitter feelings of hatred and resentment but now joined ranks against a common enemy.

---

[6] Collyer, J.J. page 27

4. World War 1 – German South West Africa Campaign

For William, the call came on 15th August 1914, when the South African Government ordered F Company (Benoni and Brakpan) of 10th Infantry Battalion (Witwatersrand Rifles) to assemble at the Railway Station in Benoni and to carry the following: -

> *"All ranks: record book and jack knife.*
> *Officers: Field glasses, field service pocket book, notebook, Pencil, whistle and lanyard.*
> *All ranks in kitbag: housewife 1, spare boot laces, two pairs socks, one tin dubbin, towel and soap, two shirts, shaving kit, toothbrush and paste, hair brush and comb, black leather cleaning kit, brass cleaning kit, knife, fork and spoon, six yards of sash line or box cord for roping blankets and kit. One day's rations should be carried by all ranks.*
> *Absentees from mobilization will be treated as deserters under the Defence Act."*

The 751 men left by train for Johannesburg and then marched to Booysen's Camp for training. Ten days later the "Warlike Wits" as the *Rand Daily Mail* called them, were given a grand send off by family to the pipes of the Transvaal Scottish on 24 August 1914.

They were part of a larger contingent of 2420 men in Force A under the command of General H.T. Lukin and sailed in the Galway Castle to Port Nolloth which was situated in the north of the Union of South Africa and near to the border with German South West Africa.

The German garrison in South West Africa (SWA) was small – some 9000 men. Colonel Botha had 43,000 men but the terrain and logistics presented major problems. SWA is protected on three sides by desert – Kalahari Desert in the East, the desert wastes of Namaqualand in the South and the Namib Desert on the west coast.

The Germans commanded the one railway and as they withdrew, they destroyed the railway lines as shown here. This picture shows how arid the region is and how important water would be. Water had to be brought by rail all the way from Cape Town and stored in a reservoir.

As the Germans destroyed the railway line, one of the first jobs was to rapidly construct a railway line in Cape gauge along the west coast and this was completed by February 1915.

Railway demolition during the S.W.A. Campaign - Alamy

However, before Botha could enter the German West Africa region, he had to contend with a rebellion from one of his own commanders. Lt. Col. Maritz of B Company led a rebellion against Botha and refused to enter German territory, resigned and with 700 men went into open rebellion, crossed the SWA border in October and betrayed those of his men who did not support him to the Germans. Maritz declared the independence of South Africa and war on Britain. It seemed that Maritz had not accepted the result of the Boer War and saw an opportunity to overthrow the British.

However, the Germans did not trust Maritz and gave him no support in his claim, and, by early December 1914, the rebellion had been crushed and Maritz fled to SWA and then to Angola.

Three precious months had been lost before Botha could continue the war in SWA. On 13 December 1914, 5864 men of 1st Infantry Brigade (of which Witwatersrand Rifles formed a part) arrived at Luderitz Bay in SWA.

The object was to cross the desert in several stages and finally to confront the enemy at Aus. The first stage was to march 72 km to Tschaukaib in the intense heat at a demanding pace with very little water.

The total water supply was carried in water bottles by the troops and could only be replenished with hot, brackish water from waterholes.

The march was extremely exhausting and the heat was 53 degrees Centigrade in the shade when they arrived there on 15 December. Despite the heat, the Wits. Rifles managed the following marching song whilst tramping through the desert of SWA. William loved a sing-song and I am sure he knew the words of this song.

We are the Wits Rifles bold
We're worth our weight in gold,
And every Sunday morn,
When we're upon the lawn
The Ladies come from near and far
To see our uniform –

Chorus:
So we're going, going very well
Going, going, going to merry hell.
So ladies don't you fret
We'll catch the Kaiser yet
For our hearts are full of courage
And our socks are full of sweat.

At Tschaukaib, they remained for ten weeks before marching 9km to Kieshohe and three days later, they arrived at Garub where there was a major advantage – water. Although the water tanks had been destroyed by the Germans, new boreholes could be sunk and when completed, reinforcements arrived in March in preparation for the advance into Aus.

The town of Aus was guarded by a 700 ft high rock belt and was approached via a narrow gorge – Aus Nek. The Wits. Rifles led the advance on Aus on 1 April 1915 and found that the Germans had evacuated it so as not to be cut off by the encircling forces.

This photo outside Aus is of the Oryx (Gemsbok). These horse-like antelopes can go without water for months by regulating their temperature as well as evaporation rate.

Aus, South West Africa - Alamy

At this time, Smuts was busy in the south of the country trying to push the German forces from Kalkfontein to Gibeon but they overcame the resistance on the railway line and escaped north, hotly pursued and leaving casualties and prisoners behind.

On 29 April 1915, the main force returned by rail to Luderitz Bay and sailed on the Galway Castle to Walvis Bay. The troops arrived on 12 May 1915 at the town of Swakopmund. It must have been rather surprising to find this town with its Bavarian architecture in the hot, arid desert.

The war in SWA was ending – the capital city of Windhoek was captured in May and on 9th July, the last German forces surrendered at Tsumeb. The casualties were not heavy. Out of over 100,000 men, 246 had been killed, 181 died of disease and 560 were wounded.

Swakopmund Railway Station - Alamy

The Witwatersrand Rifles returned from the "land of sand, sun, sorrow and sore eyes" in the deserts of SWA to an unusual fall of snow in Johannesburg on 20 July 1915 and marched from Park Station to the Wanderers grounds where a civic welcome was laid out and then onto Milner Park where they were demobilised and could return to their homes and families. William held the rank of Colour Sergeant in 10th Infantry (Wits. Rifles).

The campaign in German South West Africa was over and a great success but only a "small side-show" [7] in comparison with Europe where fighting continued and men from all over South Africa volunteered for service over there including some of those who had served in German South West Africa.

---

[7] Collyer, J.J. page 173

South African army in South West Africa 1914 - Alamy

5. World War 1 - German East African Campaign

In November 1915, the South African government again called for volunteers – this time to fight the Germans in East Africa and William re-attested as a private for service in this campaign. William would be promoted to Regimental Sergeant Major and subsequently commissioned as a Lieutenant and awarded the Distinguished Conduct Medal.

Most of the volunteers had had no military training and, whereas in the past, Kitchener had insisted on 6 months training as a minimum, the recruits received only six weeks training.

Initially, Britain thought that some 8,000 troops would be sufficient to conquer the German East African Protectorate. Further, that the comparatively easy victory in SWA could be repeated and casualties would be similarly low. These illusions were rudely shattered.

A month later, the number of troops was increased to nearly 19,000 and by November had risen to a staggering 111,731 men. The engagements with the enemy showed that the German force had been seriously underestimated.

It was the area itself that provided the most problems. From the coastal plain, the country rises gradually to a plateau bordered on the east by mountains that bend to the north of Lake Nyasa. The plateau falls sharply to the west to Lake Tanganyika. The Great Rift Valley extends inland across the plateau from Lake Lukwa in the south to Lake Naivasha in Kenya. The greatest rivers in the territory all flow into the Indian Ocean, cannot be forded and are infested with crocodiles.

In the area where most of the battles took place, the coast region and hills bordering the eastern side of the central plateau are dense bush with limited visibility. Elephant grass, long and tough, grew in profusion near rivers. The heat is invariably intense. "Roads" were winding tracks and the dry soil turned to liquid mud in heavy rain.

The rainfall pattern is important because of its influence on wildlife and the road conditions. Upon the rains, any roads become flooded or muddy and are impassable. The rainy season is divided into two periods: the long rains fall between March and June, whereas the short rains take place between October and November. In general, temperatures are higher during the months corresponding to the boreal winter, i.e., January, February and March.

Such conditions caused profound communication problems which aided the enemy and hindered the army who had some 23,300 South Africans in the theatre of war and a need for an enormous quantity of supplies to be distributed. The Germans had few troops but relied heavily on local Africans or askaris who were used to the environment.

On top of this, there was the continuous threat of endemic tropical diseases, which killed most of the troops, such as a severe strain of malaria, dysentery, hookworm disease, jigger flea and blackwater fever. One must not forget that thousands of horses and oxen were brought by ship as part of army supplies and they died within six weeks of being bitten by the tsetse fly. Then, of course, there are the wild animals.

Perhaps a good illustration of the danger and disruption which wild animals could cause is illustrated by the 1966 film *The Ghost and the Darkness* which is based on fact about when Britain was building a railway - called the

Lunatic Express - across Africa from Mombasa to Nairobi in 1898.

Colonel Patterson was the military commander in charge of building a bridge over the river Tsavo for the railway and had recruited some 13,000 workers to lay the railway sleepers which were made of steel because termites ate the timber.

However, work was hampered by lions. Lions in this region are unusual in that they do not have a mane. Two lions, in particular, performed nightly raids into camps pulling workers from their tents and devouring them.

The workers developed such a fear of these beasts that they named one of them 'Ghost' and the other 'Darkness'. Eventually, Colonel Patterson managed to kill these two lions and complete the bridge in 1901 but only after at least 28 Indian workers and an unknown number of locals had been eaten.

William mentions lions several times, as well as getting a cheetah skin, in his diary.

The area that was to be the theatre of operations for his unit, the 7th SA Infantry, lay between Kilimanjaro and the foothills of the south. The dominant physical feature was the huge mountain of Kilimanjaro that totally barred all movement save on the lower extremities of the foothills.

To the south flowed the Lumi River crossed by the only road and leading to Taveta. The river, combined with the mountain range, fever infested swamps and dense bush produced a formidable obstacle to movement in the south as did Kilimanjaro in the north.

It is interesting to note how different are the words used by William and those read by the British public about the war in Africa. For example, the war correspondent covering the progress of the war with General Smuts for *The Times* edition of the 23rd May 1916 wrote :

> *"10th April 1916 - New Moschi: We campaign in Wonderland, a land of surprising beauty, deep dark forests, rushing snow-cooled torrents radiating from the mountainous mass that stands upon the marches of British and German East Africa: ... But this tropical terrain is as poisonous as it is beautiful.... "This place", complained a cockney chauffeur, "is a blooming Zoo, and they don't lock the animals up at night."'*

William wrote:

> *"Monday 10th April 1916: On the move to New Moschi. We left Himo this morning at 11am. We had only got about 5 miles out when it started to rain and we are all drenched through. The roads are terrible. We camped for the night about 2 miles out of Moschi about done up. We did about 15 miles and New Moschi is about 17 or 18. Had no tent and blankets wet through very likely."*

Mount Kilimanjaro - Alamy

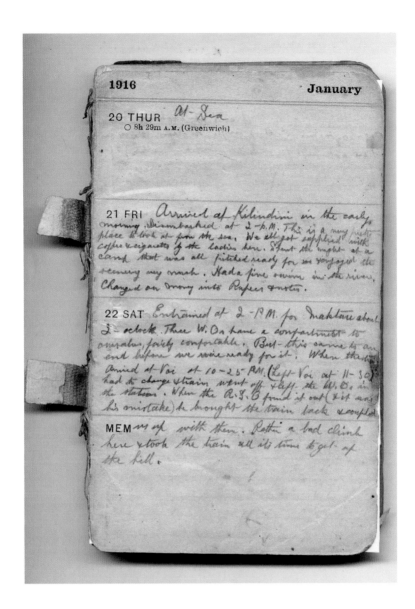

20 THUR At Sea
○ 8h 29m A.M. (Greenwich)

21 FRI Arrived at Kilindini in the early morning. Disembarked at 2-P.M. This is a very pretty place to look at from the sea. We all got supplied with coffee & cigarettes by the ladies here. Spent the night at a camp that was all pitched ready for us & enjoyed the scenery very much. Had a fine swim in the river. Changed our money into Rupees & notes.

22 SAT Entrained at 2-P.M. for Maktare about 2-oclock. Three W.Os have a compartment to ourselves, fairly comfortable. But this came to an end before we were ready for it. When the train arrived at Voi at 10-25 P.M. (Left Voi at 11-30) had to change & train went off & left the W.O. in the station. When the R.S.C found it out (& it was his mistake) he brought the train back & coupled

MEM us up with them. Rather a bad clinch here & took the train all its time to get up the hill.

6. The War Diary of W.R. Watson Jan 1916 to Feb 1917

Thursday 20 January 1916
At Sea

Friday 21 January 1916
Arrived at Kilindini harbour in Mombasa in the early morning. Disembarked at 2 pm. This is a very pretty place to look at from the sea. We all got supplied with coffee and cigarettes by the ladies here. Spent the night at a camp that was all pitched ready for us, enjoyed the scenery very much. Had a fine swim in the river. Changed our money into Rupees and notes.

Saturday 22 January 1916
Entrained at 2 pm for Maktau about 2 o'clock. Three W.O's have a compartment to ourselves fairly comfortable. But this came to an end before we were ready for it. When the train arrived at Voi at 10.25 pm. (Left Voi at 11.30) had to change and train went off and left the W.O. in the station. When the A.D.C. found it out (and it was his mistake) he brought the train back and coupled us up with them. Rather a bad climb here and took the train all its time to get up the hill.

Sunday 23 January 1916
Arrived at Maktau at 10.00 a.m. Pitching camp today. We have got very fine tents (Indiana pattern). I have a small officers tent to myself.

Monday 24 January 1916
At Maktau. General …. and Headquarters are here on one side and the 6 Regiment on the other.

Tuesday 25 January 1916
At Maktau. Parades and cleaning camp.

Wednesday 26 January 1916
At Maktau. Usual parades.

Thursday 27 January 1916
At Maktau. A couple of our aeroplanes went up this morning and looked fine overhead. Didn't they get a cheer. It was quite a change not to have to dodge bombs when the planes were above us.

Friday 28 January 1916
At Maktau.

Saturday 29 January 1916
At Maktau.

Sunday 30 January 1916
At Maktau. The balance of our regiment arrived at camp today. B Company that came before us having been at ... & D Coy. & details who sailed after us.

Monday 31 January 1916
At Maktau. Regiment Parade at 9 a.m. I am taking the regiment with bayonet practice today. They can do with it too.

Tuesday 1 February 1916
At Maktau. Regiment Parade 9 am. Bayonet Practice at 4 pm

23 SUN—3 aft Epiph Arrived at Maktau at 10-30 A.m. Patchey Camp, to day. We have got my fine tents (Indian pattern) I have a small affairs tent to myself.

24 MON At Maktau. General Revue Held gtrs are here on one side with 6th Regt on the other.

25 TUES At Maktau, Parades
Conversion of St. Paul
& cleaning Camp

26 WED At Maktau, Usual parades

27 THUR At Maktau, A couple of our Aeroplanes went up this morning & looked fine overhead. Didn't they get a cheer. It was quite a change not to have to dodge bombs when the planes were above us.

28 FRI At Maktau.
☾ 0h 35m A.M. (Greenwich)

29 SAT At Maktau

MEM

Wednesday 2 February 1916
At Maktau. Regiment Parade at 9 a.m. A lecture this afternoon by Col. Keene of the staff on local conditions. It was very interesting.

Thursday 3 February 1916
At Maktau. Saw Ian Smith and Rishton. They are looking fit.

Friday 4 February 1916
At Maktau

Saturday 5 February 1916
Left Maktau. Very hot today. Had orders to move to Mbuyuni – the first of the next station up the line.

Sunday 6 February 1916

Preparations to move to Mbuyuni. Busy packing up. Struck tents at 1 pm. Loaded baggage on motors at 2 pm. Regiment marched out at 5.30 pm. I went by train with Adjutant.

Monday 7 February 1916

At Mbuyuni. We reached here about 1 pm. The Regiment marched in at 3 pm.

Tuesday 8 February 1916

At Mbuyuni. Struck .... camp this morning ....

Wednesday 9 February 1916

At Mbuyuni. Reveille ...... Marched ... yds of Salaita Hill. Arrived at 9.30. .... Left for camp at 10... Marched ...…
Had a bit of a rest after... there at 5.30. Very hard trek.

Thursday 10 February 1916

At Mbuyuni. Nothing doing today. Having a rest and a clean up.

Friday 11 February 1916

Left Mbuyuni for Serengeti camp at 8.30 a.m. Arrived at 11. Rained hard at 1 o'clock – only a shower. Of course, we have no tents here so we got pretty wet.

Saturday 12 February 1916

Left Serengeti at 4.30 am. Reached Salaita about 8 am. I was in charge of ammunition .... About 8.30 as my motor came out of cover the first shot was fired from the hill and before very long it was warm I can tell you. All the bush was cut into lanes and as we showed ourselves in these openings, we got a shot. We were laid down under ...... and a shot struck the ......

of a tree in front of me and covered me with earth. One flank of ours line got forward with a bayonet rush and got the trenches there. We couldn't hold it as the fire was too hot without support and we were ordered to retire. This was about 2 o'clock. Arrived at Serengeti at 2.30. Our casualties - 8 killed + 51 wounded and 27 missing at 6.15 pm.

Sunday 13 February 1916
We buried two more of our chaps this morning at 12 noon. They were Ingram and Hans Gosch. Left Serengeti at 3 and arrived at Mbuyuni at 4.30 am and camped on the site that we occupied before.

Private J.H. Gosch 1122 and Private J.B. Ingram 3812 are buried at Taveta Military Cemetery

Monday 14 February 1916

We got our tents up today and drew our kits again that we packed away here when we left last Friday.

Tuesday 15 February 1916

Regiment parade this morning. We returned to camp at 1 pm.

Wednesday 16 February 1916

Regiment parade again this morning. ....duties today.

Thursday 17 February 1916

No parade today as we are on Brigade duties. Our chaps came back today from Mashoti that we left in reserve. It will take them all to make up the strength again. Had a concert tonight and invited the 5th regiment over as our guests. A fairly good do.

Friday 18 February 1916

Parades at 9 am today and general fatigues as usual. Capt Ormond took charge as all the big bugs were out watching artillery practice etc. Concert in 8th Regiment lines tonight.

Saturday 19 February 1916

Parade at 9 as usual. Nothing much doing today. Had Tom Canning over to see me he came over with another chap and I didn't for the moment recognise him. He looks very well indeed.

Sunday 20 February 1916

No Parades. Gen Smuts arrived today at 9.30 and left again at 3. We supplied guards of honour etc. Our strength now in 1010.

Monday 21 February 1916
On Brigade duties today. All our pay staff has left today for Nairobi so I suppose they will remain there. We got a lot of transport today. Indian drivers & oxen in small A.T carts.

Tuesday 22 February 1916
Regiment out on Tactical exercises and covering fire by artillery today. Two companies under Major Thompson went out to ... Hill on patrol expects they will be back tomorrow.

Wednesday 23 February 1916
A & D Companies out on parade this morning. Major Thompson went back for water for his patrol. Sent out a motor lorry with water at 11.15. The patrol reached camp about .... pretty well done in.

Thursday 24 February 1916

One company went out on patrol today as far as Makta Hill at 7 am. They returned about 2.55 pm. I had remainder of regiment on parade.

Friday 25 February 1916

No parade today. We are doing Brigade duties, guards etc. I have to give them bayonet exercise this afternoon at 4 pm.

Saturday 26 February 1916

Had a very heavy rain last night and this morning. Most of the chaps were marched out. We generally have no parade on a Saturday afternoon but I have bayonet fighting on today and I suppose one idiot will keep on at it.

Sunday 27 February 1916

Reveille at 3.30 am. We moved out at 6 am in a northerly direction for K.... and T... Hills. We left ....all along the way. Arrived. 10.30 and as one had to remain all night we dug in at 5.30 and bivouacked as we had no blankets or tents. 3 lorries came out with rations and sheets.

Monday 28 February 1916

Stood to arms at 4.30. About 8 am one of our chaps brought in a German sergeant and 2 Askaris. One of my chaps spotted them and we went out and captured them. Saw some fine Lions today. The 8 Regiment relieved us at 2.30 and we set off back for Mbuyuni; arrived there 6 pm.

Tuesday 29 February 1916

Brigade duties today. Nothing doing

Wednesday 1 March 1916

No regiment parades today as we are remaining on Brigade duties.

Thursday 2 March 1916

Parade in marching order at 9 am. No water bottles to be carried. This is to make the men get used to doing without water on the march. Had a very nice concert in the 5th Regiment lines.

Friday 3 March 1916

Paraded today for Generals inspection at 5 am. Returned to camp at 7.30 and were dismissed for the day.

Saturday 4 March 1916

No parades today. L. Cpl Wilde died of wounds received at Salaita. We are trying different ways of rolling the coats into bundles to go on the A.T. carts.

Sunday 5 March 1916

Nothing much doing today. I had all the N.C.O's out this morning and demonstrated the best method of packing greatcoats in A.T. carts.

Monday 6 March 1916

Left Mbuyuni at 3 pm for Serengeti; arrived about 5. Bivouacked for night after digging in reporting outposts.

Tuesday 7 March 1916

All day at Serengeti. Very hot today. Drew Reo lorries and more transport. Left Serengeti at 6.30. Marched all night. We were.........guard of the brigade.

Wednesday 8 March 1916

Arrived at Ridge overlooking Lumi River at dawn. Marched onto river and camped there at 7.30 for breakfast. Moved off and camped about 11 am. About 3.30 we were rushed out to intercept a party of Askaris about 200 coming in our direction. Had two men wounded. One sniper in a tree fired on me 3 times and each time his shot struck the ground between my legs.

February   1916   1916   February

20 SEPTUAGESIMA SUN

21 MON

22 TUES

23 WED

24 THUR
St. Matthias, Ap.

25 FRI

26 SAT
☾ 9h 21m A.M. (Greenwich)

MEM

Thursday 9 March 1916

There has been firing going on all the blooming night. The enemy are concealed in trees here and keep letting us have it. There were tremendous heavy rains. We are all about washed out. Heavy thunder and lightning.

Friday 10 March 1916

We are like drowned rats this morning. We are to march to S.E. corner of Lake Chala today. Left camp at 4.30. We are rear guard. Arrived about 6.15. Raining again.

45

Saturday 11 March 1916

Chala Lake. Went to see the lake this morning. Fine sight. The water is about 200 feet down in the centre of the hills. Left Chala at 1 pm and arrived at Taveta at 4.15. Very hot indeed. At 7.30, we got orders to move out to support the attack on the Nek. Got orders to move through and attack the Nek. We advanced in rushes and spurts of fire right up to the Nek. I was with Ammunitions.

Gen. Tighe withdrew the regiment at 2 am to a line further back. Received orders to return to Taveta at 4 and retired under cover of darkness. Arrived at Taveta about 7 am very done up. Major Thompson and a party were left on Reata. Freeth was also missing reported to be on Latema which was held by the Rhodesians. Freeth came in about 9 a.m. Thompson came back about 5pm.

Monick, S. (1989). A Bugle Calls. pg 177
The War Diary of 7 South African Infantry Regiment
Saturday 11.3.16. Chala Lake. Camped on slope of Chala Hill around Chala Lake. Climbed hill in the morning. Very fine sight. Force Reserve left Chala at 1 pm and moved on Taveta. Very hot march. Arrived Taveta at 4.15 pm. Filled water bottles, carts, and dug trenches. Received orders at 6.30 pm to move bivouac to other side of camp and hold Regt. in readiness to proceed to support the 5th Regiment under Lt. Col. Byron. Orders received to attack the neck between Reata and Latema with rushes with the bayonet and bursts of rapid fire. Regt reached Nek under heavy machine gun fire. Line broken in right centre. Gen Tighe withdrew the Regt to a line further back.

Feb & March — 1916

27 SEXAGESIMA SUN

28 MON

29 TUES — Brigade duties to day. Nothing doing.

1 MARCH WED St. David

1916 — March

2 THUR

3 FRI

4 SAT — 3h 58m A.M. (Greenwich)

MEM

Sunday 12 March 1916

I had an awful job this afternoon offloading the dead from the lorries for burial. Buried 4 this afternoon. Buried Lt. Lowden and 15 other chaps at 9.45 pm. We lost 23 killed, 46 wounded and 6 missing.

Lt. J.H. Lowden buried in Taveta Military Cemetery

Monick, S. (1989). A Bugle Calls. pg 177
The War Diary of 7 South African Infantry Regiment Sunday 12.3.16. Taveta. Gen. Tighe gave orders that Regt would retire on Taveta and leave the Ridge under cover of darkness. Regt returned and reached Taveta at about 7 am. It was reported that Major Thompson and 200 men had been cut off on Reata.

Lt Col. Freeth was also missing. Adjutant reported to Gen Beves that Col. Maj + 265 men were missing but he was sure that Reata Hill had been taken. .... Buried 4 men at 6.15 pm ....

Monday 13 March 1916

Left Taveta at 10 am for Himo Reim. Arrived German border at 11.10 am. Arrived at Himo at 5 pm. A few Askaris surrendered. Jan Benas read letter of thanks from G.O.C. for our fight at Reata-Latema.

Tuesday 14 March 1916

Had a grand bath in river. It was beautiful. A mail came up today. A letter from them for one. Rained very hard. Camped in a coffee plantation and the mud is terrible.

Wednesday 15 March 1916

We moved the camp to a new site today on better ground. Dug ourselves in and got down to it. Our blankets were scarcely dry yet but that made very little difference.

Thursday 16 March 1916

During night Germans fired over camp but we did not reply. No casualties. Fergie takes over as Q.M. I think he has been strafed. Some of our fatheads went hunting for honey. They got something else instead. The blooming bees nearly sent the chaps mad.

Friday 17 March 1916

Received word from Headquarters that Freeth and Thompson had been awarded D.S.O. and Fulton of the 5th the M.C. Whatever for no body seems to know for none of them deserve it darn sure.

5 QUINQUAGESIMA SUN Nothing much doing to day. I had all N.C.Os out this morning & demonstrated the best method of packing greatcoats in A.T. Carts.

6 MON Left Mbuyuni at 3 P.M. for S'engete; arrived about 5. Bivouaced for night after digging in reporting outposts.

7 SHROVE TUES All day at Serengeti. Very hot to day. Drew Pos Lorries & more transport. Left Serengeti at 6-30. Marched all night. We were advanced guard of the brigade.

8 ASH WED Arrived at Ridge overlooking Lumi River at Dawn. Marched on to River & camped there at 7-30 for breakfast. Moved off & camped about 11 A.M. About 3-30 we were rushed out to intercept a party of Arkaris about 200 coming in our direction. Had two men wounded. One Sniper in a tree ___ me 3 times reach time his shot struck the ground between my legs.

9 THUR There has been firing going on all the blooming night. The enemy are concealed in trees here & keep letting us have it. There were tremendous heavy rains. We are all about washed out. Heavy thunder & Lightning

10 FRI We are like drowned rats this morning. We are to march to S.E. Corner of Lake Chala to day. Left Camp at 4-30. We are Rear Guard. Arrived about 6-15. Raining again.

11 SAT Chala Lake. Went up to see the ☽ 6h 33m P.M. (Greenwich) lake this morning. Fine sight. The water is about 300 ft down in the centre of the hills. Left Chala at 1 P.M. arrived at Taveta at 4-45. Very hot indeed. At 7-30 we got orders to move out to support the attack on the mk. Got orders to move through & attack the mk. We advanced in rushes & short of fire light up

MEM to the mk. I was with ammunition. Gen Tighe withdrew the Regt at 2 A.M. to a line further back. Received orders to return to Taveta at 4 and retired under cover of darkness. Arrived at Taveta about 7 A.M. Very done up. Major Thompson & a party men left on Rista. Fraett was also mining supposed to be on Lateime which was held by the Rhodesians. Fraett came in about 8-00 A.M. Thompson came

---

Saturday 18 March 1916

Marched out to attack Unterre Himo at 9.am. 5 Battery shelled hill all morning. the Enemy cleared out and 8th Regiment occupied hill at 4 o'clock. Our regiment returned to Himo camp at 5 am. We reached camp about 7 pm. Capt Westbrook and Hazeldene and Lt Allen came back from hospital. They were wounded at Salaita. They look fairly well.

Sunday 19 March 1916

We left camp for Unterre Himo with the battery at 7 am. Reached them about 8.30. Got orders to advance on Rusthaus and went forward until about 5 then retired to Unterra Himo. Bush awfully thick.

Monday 20 March 1916

Heavy firing last night. Germans attacked one night. Nothing doing. 1 Brigade relieved us and we returned to Himo. 5 , 6 and 8 regiments are joining General Sheppard's forces. They are giving us a rest.

Tuesday 21 March 1916

Very heavy firing during night. Received news that Germans attacked 8th regiment and Sheppard's force. Many casualties in 8 regiment. Dave Smith was wounded in arm. Our Adjutant must go into hospital today – pretty bad with dysentery.

Wednesday 22 March 1916

Roll call and .... Drill this morning. Went for a swim in river. General clean up.

Thursday 23 March 1916 to Wednesday 29 March 1916

The page for this period is missing from the diary

Thursday 30 March 1916

Still another new camping site. I wonder when they will be satisfied. This site is certainly a better one and I hope they will leave us alone for a bit now. Strafing the recruits today.

Friday 31 March 1916

Clearing bushes from new site and getting things ready to stand the floods, they talk about. Heath went away sick today.

Saturday 1 April 1916

Still busy with the bushes and drains for the camp in view of heavy approaching rains. The skies are very much overcast nowadays and you would think we were going to be flooded out any minute now.

12 SUN—1 in Lent (Ember Week) back about 5 PM. I had an awful job this afternoon offloading the dead from the Lorries for burial. Buried 4 this afternoon. Buried Lt Lowden & 15 other chaps at 9-45 PM. We lost 23 killed 46 Wounded & 6 missing

13 MON Left Taveta at 10 AM for Himo. Crossed German border at 11-10 AM. arrived at Himo at 5 PM. A few Askaris surrendered. Gen Bonar had letter of thanks from G.O.C. for our fight at Rata Latema.

14 TUES Had a grand bath in river. I was beautiful. A mail came up to day. A letter from the Mammy for one. Rained my hard. Camped in a Coffee Plantation & the mud is terrible.

15 WED (Ember Day) We moved the camp to a new site to day on better ground. Dug ourselves in & got down to it. Our blankets were scarcely dry yet but that made very little difference.

16 THUR During night Germans fired over camp, but we did not reply. No casualties. Fungie takes over as C.M. I think he has been strafed. Some of our patrials sent sniping for hours. They got something else instead. The blooming fools nearly sent the chaps mad.

17 FRI (St. Patrick, Bank Holiday, Ireland. Ember Day) Received word from Headquarters that Freeth & Thompson had been awarded D.S.O. & Fulton of the 5th the D.C.L. Whatever for one body seems to know; for none of them deserve it I am sure.

18 SAT (Ember Day) Marched out to attack Muhure Hma at 9 AM. 3rd Battery shelled hill all morning. Enemy cleared out & 8th Regt occupied hill at 4 o'clock. Our Regt returned to Himo camp at 5 AM. We reached camp about 7 PM. Capt Westbrook & Hawldane

MEM & A Allen came back from Harford. They were wounded at Salaita. They look fairly well.

Sunday 2 April 1916

Himo. No parades today. Several voluntary church services.

Monday 3 April 1916

Adjutant returned from sick hospital today. General fatigues as usual and parade for recruits under me.

Tuesday 4 April 1916

At Himo. Nothing fresh going on today. Usual fatigues and recruit strafing parades. Had a fine swim today. The brains are having a Boma built to take afternoon tea in.

Wednesday 5 April 1916

At Himo camp. 500 of our chaps are out today road making and getting ready for the heavy rain that is expected any time now. Had a swim after which had to transfer the reinforcements.

Thursday 6 April 1916

At Himo Camp. Good news today. Van den Venter has captured 2 companies of the enemy at Lolkissale and 2 machine-guns about 35 miles S.W. of Arusha. There is an order today about leave but as it only refers to troops who have been 6 months in the field, it does not affect me, so I am not worrying about it.

Friday 7 April 1916

At Himo Camp. An order out today that no one is to work in the sun between the hours of 11 and 4 as so many men are getting parched out with the sun. One road working party (same as Wednesday) had to return early on that account.

Saturday 8 April 1916

At Himo Camp. Had a nice swim before breakfast this morning. Received 2 letters today – 1 from Mother and 1 from you. Pleased to hear that all is well. I wrote to you today. Also to Mother. I just got them finished in time, as we are to move off tomorrow. We have had all kinds of tales told us that we were to remain at this camp for about 5 or 6 weeks whilst the rains are on but it has turned out otherwise.

Sunday 9 April 1916

We have made all kinds of preparations for heavy rains and have to leave them now.

19 SUN—2 in Lent
☾ 5h 27m P.M. (Greenwich)

20 MON

21 TUES

22 WED

30 THUR

31 FRI

1 APRIL SAT

MEM

Monday 10 April 1916
On the move to New Moschi. We left Himo this morning at 11 am. We had only got about 5 miles out when it started to rain and we are all drenched through. The roads are terrible. We camped for the night about 2 miles out of Moschi about done up. We did about 15 miles and New Moschi is about 17 or 18. Had no tent and blankets wet through very likely.

Tuesday 11 April 1916
On the move this morning at 6 am. And after about one hour, we reached New Moschi. This is the first German town we have reached. The troops are pretty much done up with the heavy roads and all getting so wet. Received orders to move off at 6 am tomorrow towards Arusha. Saw Forsyth and Willie Widman today.

Wednesday 12 April 1916

At Moschi. Raining hard. Not moving until later. Left Moschi at 9.30...............4 o'clock. There will be a..........getting over the river with the transport as ....get over until the morning.

Thursday 13 April 1916

Had a terribly wet night. No sleep. Left Kikafu at 1 pm after struggling with the transport and the rain. Arrived at Sanja River about 4.30. Just getting blankets out to dry when the rain came on again, so it will be wet blankets tonight.

Friday 14 April 1916

Sanja River. Rigged a bit of shelter up and had a few hours sleep last night. It rained hard too. Expected to go off at 6 am but are not doing so. Remaining here until tomorrow now so we are off to have a bathe.

Saturday 15 April 1916

Left Sanja River at 11 am and marched until 2.30. The roads are terribly bad here and have to get the chaps to shove behind the wagons. Made tea and were ready to move off again at 4 pm. Owing to have to shove each wagon over the drifts we did not get away until 6 pm and struggled on pushing behind wagons. .... until about 8 pm when we halted for the night. Before we could get the tents up the rain was on and most of us got wet through in a few minutes. After my tent was up, I was all right and had a pretty good sleep.

April   **1916**   **1916**   **April**

2 SUN—4 in Lent
● 4h 21m P.M. (Greenwich)

3 MON
Cambridge Lent Term ends,
Quarter Sessions Week

4 TUES

5 WED
Dividends due at Bank

6 THUR

7 FRI

8 SAT
Fire Insurances expire

MEM

Sunday 16 April 1916

Up again this morning at 4 am to get the water carts out but turned in again until 6.30. We moved off about 11 am in teeming rain but had to get out of this place as the ground is so bad. Had a rotten time until we halted about 3.30 as we could not cross the river – it was in flood.

Monday 17 April 1916

1.1/2 miles east of Rusthaus We left here this morning about 12 as the river was down again. The roads are terrible and we could only go about 6 miles then the men and mules were done up. We halted and pitched tents and as usual, it rained hard during the night.

Tuesday 18 April 1916

Off again this morning about 8.30 and halted for the day about 2.30. You can guess the state of the roads when I tell you that we only did 3 miles. The wagons sank over the tops of the front wheels in mud and we had to put 40 oxen in them to move along.

Wednesday 19 April 1916

Did not move off until about 2 o'clock as we were rear guard and had to wait until the ox-wagon got through. Up to 7 o'clock at night, we had only done about 2 miles so that speaks for itself.

Thursday 20 April 1916

Moved off this morning about 9.15 am. We did a little better today and I think we covered about 4 miles halted about 4.30 pm. It is thundering and lightning a lot tonight so I think it means rain.

Friday 21 April 1916

Good Friday and no hot X buns. Instead, we are still on half rations. 1½ biscuits per day and several days without that too. I am about half dead with a cold. I think it is with getting wet. There are such a lot of rivers here and we have to walk right through them and if the sun does not come out there is no means of getting dry again. I shall be glad when we reach Arusha. We are rear guard today and did not get off until about 12 o'clock. Went about 3 miles then halted for the night at about 3 o'clock.

9 SUN—5 in Lent

10 MON
☽ 2h 36m P.M. (Greenwich)

11 TUES

12 WED.

13 THUR

14 FRI

15 SAT
Oxford Lent Term ends

MEM

Saturday 22 April 1916

Advance guard this morning so we packed up and were off about 7 'clock. We have about 4.1/2 miles to do to Arusha and as the roads are worse in this part, we shall do well to get there today. No rations today so shall have to manage on sweet potatoes and mealies. Got off about 9.20 on trek and reached Arusha at 12.30. We are staying here for tonight but I expect we shall go on tomorrow. Saw Charlie Davies as we went in; he has been in hospital here.

Sunday 23 April 1916

We are staying at Arusha for today. It rained tremendously last night and the rivers are too high to pass through. We expect to go on tomorrow towards Kumbulum. I wrote you a post card today. I have not been able to smile for a fortnight now we have had no letters.

Monday 24 April 1916

We left Arusha this morning about 10 o'clock and halted for the day about 2.30 to wait until the transport got up to us. We have no rations and are living on the sweet potatoes in the fields. In some of the swamps we had to come through the mules were nearly level by their backs in the mud.

Tuesday 25 April 1916

We set off this morning at 9.15 and reached Kumbulum about 12.30. We are camped now on the side of the hills and it is the nicest places we have had to camp in since we landed. I hope we stay here a few days to get a clean up.

Wednesday 26 April 1916

Not moving on for three or four days. We badly need a rest to wash and mend our clothes as everybody is nearly in rags and boots are nearly worn out.

Thursday 27 April 1916

Having a parade this morning and this afternoon too. One idiot of a C.O. cannot let men rest for a day to save his life. He is absolutely daft. Looks like more rain tonight. Received good news today about German Squadron (15 battle cruisers) captured off Lowestoft and 8 destroyers after 20 minute engagement.

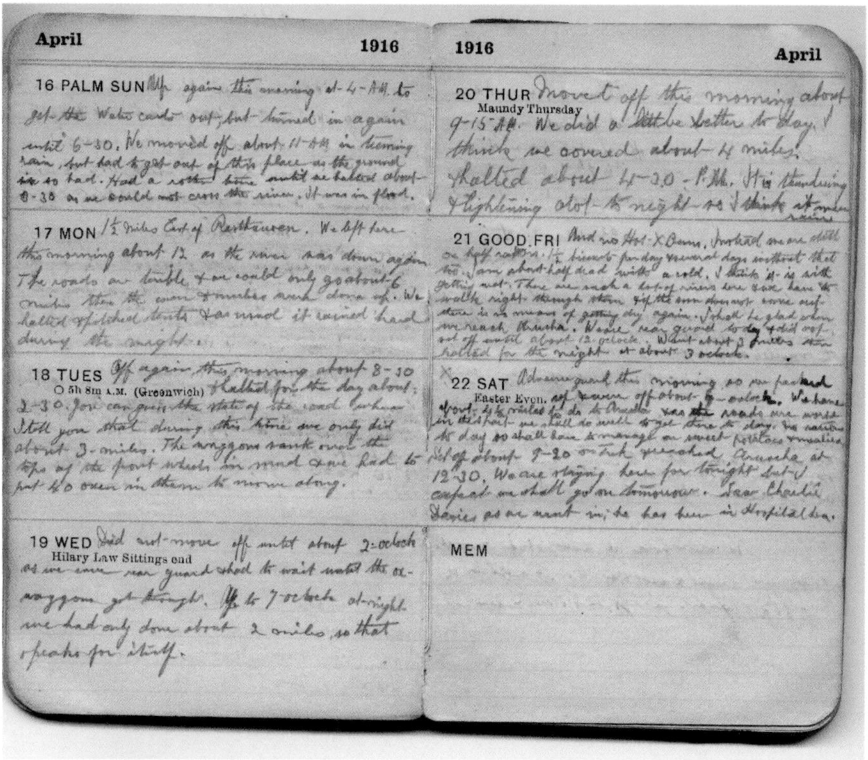
April
1916
16 PALM SUN
17 MON
18 TUES
5h 8m A.M. (Greenwich)
19 WED
Hilary Law Sittings end
1916
April
20 THUR
Maundy Thursday
21 GOOD FRI
22 SAT
Easter Even.
MEM

Friday 28 April 1916

At Kumbulum Camp. It rained hard last night and continued until about 11 o'clock this morning. No parade too wet. Am busy repairing shirts and pants today. Busy instructing the new men that arrived with the draft.

Saturday 29 April 1916

At Kumbulum. Another rainy night last night. It is a very good thing that we have our tents as we shall be gone in. Not very well today. I think I have got a cold in the stomach. We have no parade today so I am taking it easy.

Sunday 30 April 1916

At Kumbulum. Raining nearly the whole day. Still out of sorts. Am keeping in bed as much as possible. Have sent a party back to Arusha for mails; hope there is one for one. Haven't had one for nearly a month now.

Monday 1 May 1916

The party arrived back to camp this afternoon with nothing. It was all a rumour there was no mail at all. A miserable drizzle day.

Tuesday 2 May 1916

At Kumbulum. Rations are getting very short here. We are only on half bread and jam and meat. If the convoy comes in things will be different we hope. The General left today for Moschi. I don't know where we are for now – seem to be stranded.

Wednesday 3 May 1916

Nothing fresh to record today. It is still wet and miserable. It rains every night and until about 11 o'clock in the morning and .... during the day.

Thursday 4 May 1916

At Kumbulum. The Colonel and Major Thompson went over to Arusha today. They will be there for about a week we expect. We got a message today about the rebellion in Ireland. I hope they all get sorted out; they deserve it this time.

Friday 5 May 1916

At Kumbulum. Major Hazeldene came back today. He was wounded at Salaita Hill. Has been at Nairobi Hospital up to now. We expected letters up today but none came.

23 EASTER DAY We are staying at Aruscha
St. George
for the day. It rained tremendously last night
the rivers are too high to pass through. We expect
to go on tomorrow towards Kuhmbulum. I wrote
you a post-card to day & have not been able to write
for a fortnight, even we have had no letters.

24 EASTER MON We left Aruscha this morning
☾ 10h 38m P.M. (Greenwich) about — 10 o'clock, & halted
Bank Holiday
for the day about — 2—30. to wait until the
transport got up to us. We have no rations here
living on the sweet potatoes in the fields.
In some of the swamps we had to come through
the mules were nearly level by their backs in
the mud.

25 EASTER TUES We set off this morning at
St. Mark, Evan, Cambridge Easter — 15 & reached
Term begins
Kumbulum about — 12·30. We are camped
now on the side of the hills & it is the nicest
place we have had to camp in since we
landed. I hope we stay here a few days to
get a clean up.

26 WED Not arriving on for three or four days. We
Oxford Easter Term begins
badly need a rest to mend our clothes as
everybody is nearly in rags & boots are nearly worn
out.

27 THUR Saving a parade this morning & this
afternoon too. One idiot of a C. O cannot
let men rest for a day to save his life. He is
absolutely daft. Looks like more rain to night.
Received good news to day, about German squadron
(15 Battle cruisers) captured off Lowestoft & 8 destroyers
after 20 min engagement.

28 FRI At Kumbulum Camp. I rained hard last
night & continued until about 11 o'clock this morning
No parade too wet. Am busy repairing shirt & pants
to day. Busy instructing the new men that
arrived with the draft.

29 SAT At Kumbulum. Another rainy night
last night. It is a very good thing till we
have our tents as we should be gone in. Not
very well to day. I think I have got a cold
in the stomach. We have no parade to day
so I am taking it easy.

MEM

Saturday 6 May 1916

At Kumbulum. A fine morning for a change. The 8th are shifting camp today and we go tomorrow. It rained hard about midday for a couple of hours.

Sunday 7 May 1916

At Kumbulum. We are moving our camp across the swamps this morning to the other hills about a couple of miles away. I don't know why but the brains have arranged it so it must be all right.

Monday 8 May 1916

At Kumbulum New Camp. We are camped on the slopes of a kopje. The grass here is as high as your armpits and in places it is over your heads. All round the bottom of the hill are swamps; so I suppose we shall have a lot of the chaps down with fever.

Tuesday 9 May 1916

At Kumbulum New Camp. All are busy cutting down the grass round about the tents. Several chaps have been out shooting and have brought in buck and wild boar. There are a lot of lions about here. They stampeded our cattle last night so we shall have to be without meat today. We have got an issue of soap and matches today. They were very badly needed.

Wednesday 10 May 1916

At Kumbulum. Regiment parades and drill for recruits as usual. I have to take the recruits each day until passed by the Colonel.

Thursday 11 May 1916 to Wednesday 17 May 1916

The page for this period is missing from the diary.

Thursday 18 May 1916

Reveille at 4.15 moved to the other side of river at 6.30. Left the drift about 7.15. Halted for midday at 10 at Sima-La-Kuim. Moved on again at 4 and halted at Ufiome at 8 pm. We did about 18 miles finishing up the 95 miles.

Friday 19 May 1916

We are remaining here at Ufiome until 4 o'clock this afternoon when we move on for Kondoa-Irangia about 45 miles S.E. I wrote home to you today. Marched out of camp at 4.00. Halted for the night at 8 o'clock. It has been one long climb up for the whole 4 hours. It would have been very pretty in daylight.

Saturday 20 May 1916

Cannot see many yards in front of you for fog this morning. Caught up with the Tenth Regiment when we halted last night. We had trouble with some of our wagons and they have only come in this morning so we shall not move out so early as we thought to have done. Left at 1 o'clock and halted for the night about 6 o'clock

Sunday 21 May 1916

Left this morning at 6 am but only went about 3 miles up to the water. Halted for the whole day to give the animals a rest. Had a clean change and it makes a change too.

Monday 22 May 1916

Off again this morning at 6.30 and marched until 10 o'clock. Moved on again at 11. Marched until 1 when we halted for 3 hours to give the animals a rest as they are about done up. Off again at 4 and halted for the night at 5.45 as the animals are finished.

Tuesday 23 May 1916

Moved off this morning at 9 am and halted for 3 hours at 12 0'clock. Could not get any further today owing to the poor state of our cattle so had to rest and expect to move on again at 7 am tomorrow. Saw Jackson today that went home on the ship with me he is a Lieut. in the Motor Cyclist Corp.

Wednesday 24 May 1916

Moved off this morning at 7 am. We are getting near the enemy now as we heard their big guns start about at 2 o'clock. Halted for an hour and a half at 9 am. Moved off again and reached Kondoa-Iranga at 12.30 and halted in the ....for an hour. This turned out to be all right, as we are pitching our tents here for tonight.

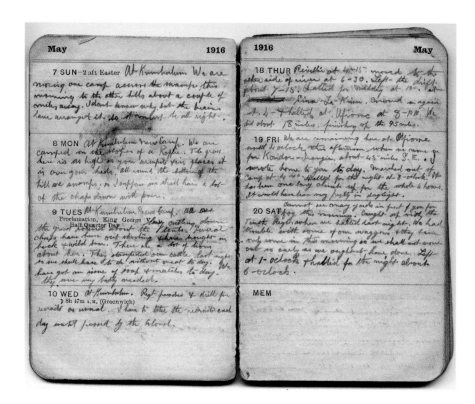

Thursday 25 May 1916

The squareheads made us a present of a few shells this morning but did not do any damage. We are not moving out until dark tonight. Left Kondoa-Irangi at 6.30 pm and marched until 9.30. Took up our position on the kopjes about 6 miles out S. East. It was very cold so as we have no tents up for tonight I think we shall feel it.

Friday 26 May 1916

Woke this morning about 4.30 nearly frozen through. As soon as the sum came up it was alright. A good breakfast of porridge, sausages and tea and homemade bread and feel OK. They shelled us pretty heavily about 3.30 pm. No damage done.

Saturday 27 May 1916

Had a fine nights rest last night. Got my little tent up and turned in about 7.30 and did not wake until daylight. Busy today digging trenches and making shelters for protection from shellfire. Have got a slight touch of dysentery but think a few doses from the doctor will fix it up alright. The squareheads gave us a few hours shelling this afternoon but did not do any damage here. A report from the town says that 10 men were injured and one killed at this hospital by yesterday's Bombardment. We were camped on the ground that was shelled when we entered the town and the natives had carried the information to the enemy but fortunately, we had moved onto the kopjes before they started shelling or we should have caught it hot.

Sunday 28 May 1916

Oelefsen's sentence (75 days) expires today. Went down to the river for a bathe this morning – feel much better today. Had a good dinner too. There is a report of a mail being on. Hope it is correct.

Monday 29 May 1916

A quiet morning this morning. Only two or three shells fired and quite a long away off us. Been baking bread this afternoon. We get only flour issued here so we have to make the best of it. Turned out some jolly fine bread through not quite as good as the Mammy's.

21 SUN—1 aft Easter

22 MON

23 TUES

24 WED
(5h 16m A.M. (Greenwich).
(Empire Day)

25 THUR

26 FRI
Queen Mary born, 1867

27 SAT

MEM

Tuesday 30 May 1916

Received a letter today from you dated 25 April. This is the first for two months. I don't understand it as there is a lot in it that I know nothing whatever about. You say that you have sent photos; parcels etc. and I have not got any of them so I suppose I shall be receiving some letters that ought to have come before. I wrote home today. The squareheads shelled the artillery horses rather heavily this afternoon but no damage done.

Wednesday 31 May 1916

Still on Battery Hill as they call the kopje where we are stationed. The usual daily shelling was indulged in by both sides. As far as we know, no damage was done to our forces and we could not see the damage done to our squarehead friends.

Thursday 1 June 1916

A party of our chaps arrived today that we left behind at Kumbulum. They brought a few pairs of boots and pants etc with them so we shall be able to fit out a few of the men. We hear today that as the result of our shelling 6 whites and 10 Askaris were killed. We have good hopes of giving them a good doing shortly. Very interesting artillery duel this afternoon. Good shooting on both sides.

Friday 2 June 1916

Nothing much doing today. The enemy did not worry us much today. I suppose they are saving themselves for tomorrow as we expect to have a pretty heavy shelling match tomorrow.

Saturday 3 June 1916

The strafing match that we expected did not come off today. Being King's birthday, everyone seemed to expect a big shelling affair. Only about 20 or 30 shells were fired. The Bishop of Pretoria visited us today and gave a short address to some of our chaps.

Sunday 4 June 1916

This is a red-letter day. 2 letters and the Mammy's photo. The letters are dated 4th April and 18 April. I think the photo is grand though the Mammy is still very thin and staring hard. Toody is excellent.

Monday 5 June 1916

Quite a bit of shelling today but so far no one is any the worse for it on our side. The Wedding Anniversary and having to spend it apart is rotten; I don't know what you think about it. I wrote home to you today.

May   1916   1916   June

28 ROGATION SUN

29 MON Rogation Day

30 TUES Rogation Day

31 WED Rogation Day (Greenwich) ● 7h 37m P.M.

1 THUR Ascension Day

2 FRI

3 SAT King George V. born, 1865.

MEM

Tuesday 6 June 1916

Had quite a busy day today. The shells have been dropping pretty thickly too. Expected to go out to occupy another post today but instead we sent out about 150 men at 8 o'clock tonight as reconnoitering patrol. About 80 of the chaps that we dropped along the way here have rejoined us tonight.

Wednesday 7 June 1916

Been up observing the greater part of the day today. That consists of getting up to the highest part of the kopje and watching through the glasses the result of the bursting of our shells and spotting the enemy's guns. Quite an enjoyable times as long as the enemy don't spot you.

Thursday 8 June 1916

The day started rather quiet but made up for it later. A fairly stiff fight is going on our left flank. Sgt. Knoll went out with rations to our patrol at 10 am. The enemy shelled our hill terrifyingly this afternoon the shells bursting very close.

Friday 9 June 1916

Had news today that Wilson of ours is killed and Sgt Mallott and Cpl Brud (both of ours) severely wounded. Knoll not yet returned. Taylor gone out on the same errand today. Things quiet up to noon. Knoll got back this evening and off again one hour later. Nothing much doing here, though plenty on our flank.

Saturday 10 June 1916

Very little shelling today and things quiet on our left. Hope the squareheads have got strafed. A party of our wounded came out today on their way to hospital. There were only slight wounds and some had to retire from the firing line owing to sickness.

Very bad news about Kitchener and Staff – hope it is not true; but afraid it is only too true. He will be very much missed but we shall strafe the squareheads all the same.

On 5 June 1916, Kitchener, Secretary of State for War, was making his way to Russia on HMS Hampshire to attend negotiations with Tsar Nicholas II when the ship struck a German mine 1.5 miles west of Orkney, Scotland, and sank. Kitchener was among 737 who died.

Sunday 11 June 1916

Great good luck today. Two letters for me from the Mammy. One from Mother and Willie and one from you (dated 9th May). Our reconnoitring party are expected back tonight as we are getting coffee ready for them.

Monday 12 June 1916

The party got back about 2 am and our horses are about a dozen killed and wounded. They had a very rough time and could not get scoff through for 50 hours or more. Nothing much doing today.

Tuesday 13 June 1916

A change today, it is very cold and cloudy very much like rain. The squareheads made up for their silence of yesterday and put about 60 shells all around in very short time. Did not do any damage but got very close to the......for they are...

Wednesday 14 June 1916

Had a not very nice job to do today. Had to march into town (a distance of about 11 miles return) to bury one of our Corporals who died from fever last night. I took the firing party in and conducted the funeral. Had to wait about 2.1/2 hours for the parson. Eventually 2 of them turned up. Got back to camp about 8.30.

Thursday 15 June 1916

A quiet day today and taking advantage of it too. Having a lazy day. Managed to get a bag of tobacco today so I shall be alright for a few more days. No signs of the parcels yet. I begin to think that somebody has strafed them.

Friday 16 June 1916

Another unthankful job today again. Have to go to town to bury Sgt Mallett of ours. He was wounded in the scrap last week (in the calf) and owing to gangrene setting in they had to amputate and he has died from the effects.

Good news on the board today – the Russians are doing remarkably well. Hope it will soon finish.

Sergeant G Mallett 2090 grave moved to Dar es Salaam Cemetery in 1968

11 WHIT SUN Ember Week. St. Barnabas, Ap. *[handwritten diary entry]*

12 WHITSUN MON Bank Holiday *[handwritten diary entry]*

13 WHITSUN TUES *[handwritten diary entry]*

14 WED Ember Day *[handwritten diary entry]*

15 THUR ○ 9h 42m P.M. (Greenwich) *[handwritten diary entry]*

16 FRI Ember Day *[handwritten diary entry]*

17 SAT Ember Day *[handwritten diary entry]*

MEM *[handwritten diary entry]*

Saturday 17 June 1916

We heard yesterday that our troops on the Tanga line had captured Karanga and in the hospital there, they found one of our chaps who was captured at Tapeta. I'll bet he will not be sorry to be in our hands again. A very quiet day today. The squareheads seem to be having a rest. Had the aeroplane over this morning but he only seemed to drop a few bombs as far as we could learn.

The Howitzer Guns that are on the hill with us here turn out to be all Hull chaps. They call the Battery "the Hull Battery" I have been..............that with them and their news is quite fresh as no news of any sort gets through the papers. They were giving me a lot of details about the Air Raids etc and the Sunk Island ford.

Sunday 18 June 1916

Nothing doing today. A very quiet day. Chiefly reading and sleeping is what we are doing. I wrote home to you today.

Monday 19 June 1916

Another very quiet day today and nothing doing. Went up to mind the Hullites today for a chat. They are very broad. You might fancy yourself at Cottingham or listening to group at Martin... time.

Tuesday 20 June 1916

Got our first bit of comforts up today. They were rationed at 3.1/2 men to 1 bag and you see how they run out. Very quiet day today.

Wednesday 21 June 1916

The squareheads gave us a ....today. No damage done. They have not got our range and a jolly good job too.

Thursday 22 June 1916

Very few shells today. Our aeroplane went over and strafed the Huns a bit today for a change. Our troops on the Tanga line have had a stiff go. 18 killed and 70 wounded chiefly the 5 regiment.

Friday 23 June 1916

Received two letters today from you dated 24 and 30 may. Awfully sorry about you being ill. We got an issue of tobacco and matches today. We are killing one pig tonight ready for Sunday.

Saturday 24 June 1916

Very quiet day today. We gave the squareheads a few shells; but they did not reply. I wrote home to you today. Had a sweepstake on the weight of our pig. I guessed 32 lbs and I won it. There were two us at 32 so we divided the stake. Attacking the enemy positions tomorrow so the story goes. Heard today that Andy Smith of the 8 Regiment had died in Kondoa-Irangi from fever and dysentery.

Sergeant A A Smith 7814, 8 Regt. grave moved to Dar es Salaam cemetery in 1968

Sunday 25 June 1916

I am up observing today. It is very cold. The troops on our left and right attacked the enemy position at dawn this morning. The 8th got possession of South Hill and another post. Don't know what was the result on our left.

Monday 26 June 1916

All quiet today. The Huns have cleared out from the position in front of us so what will be the next move I cannot say. Expect one shall shift on shortly.

Tuesday 27 June 1916

Received orders to be in readiness to move at short notice, so we are getting things into shape. Lent Chinky a £1. Got a letter today from you dated 16 May. I am getting them backwards now. I hope the next will be the parcels. We are to move tomorrow at 8 am.

Wednesday 28 June 1916

We left Battery Hill this morning at 8 o'clock. We marched into Kondoa-Irangi and are camped there I don't know how long it is for but it looks like garrison duty.

Thursday 29 June 1916

In camp Kondoa-Irangi. Klinky repaid 10 Rupees. Back to the old game – parades etc and shaving like peacetime. Heard today that Dave Smith has had his arm off. Hope it is not correct. Had Allen Booth Ler... to see us today – looks very fit.

25 SUN—1 aft Trin

26 MON
Quarter Sessions Week

27 TUES

28 WED

29 THUR
St. Peter, Ap.

30 FRI
● 10h 43m A.M. (Greenwich)

1 JULY SAT
Dominion Day, Canada

MEM

1916   June & July

Friday 30 June 1916

Regiment parade today at 9 am Also parade at 2.30 which I have to take. Rotten, it does not give us much time for anything else.

Saturday 1 July 1916

All kinds of rumours going round today. I hope they turn out to be correct. I am properly fed up with the worms we have here as officers. They have just … left school some of them and the airs that they put on are absolutely it. Roll on the finish of it all. Lent Old Mac a quid.

Sunday 2 July 1916

No parades today. We are surrounded with churches today, R.C., C of E and all kinds. Getting ironed out with new Webb equipment today. This is how they let me rest on the Sundays.

Monday 3 July 1916

Parades today and fitting new uniforms. 1 small mail today but nothing for me. All very quiet here today. We sent .... duck shooting on the lakes ....

Tuesday 4 July 1916

Had a couple of eggs for breakfast this morning – must record this as they are the first I have tasted since ... at Durban. Visited a few friends in Town at the Gaol. Not prisoners by the way.

Wednesday 5 July 1916

Parades today for inspection by the C.O. I am just fed up with parades. I got 3 letters today. 1 dated 12 ... and 24 April and 1 dated 6 of June. Fancy getting these three dates on the same day. I ... Sunday for April.

Thursday 6 July 1916

Having a busy day today answering letters. I wrote home to Mother and to you today. Nothing particular doing today.

Friday 7 July 1916

We are to have a route march or something of the kind tomorrow. I have got a slight touch of fever and if I am no better I shall remain in camp.

Saturday 8 July 1916

Had a draught of new chaps out today also a lot of our chaps returned from hospital. The Regiment are out on route march. I am remaining in camp. Got two letters today. One dated 26 March and the other 1 May. The letters appear to be coming along now but still .... up a great deal. The two dates I mention are quite a long way apart.

Sunday 9 July 1916

We got orders today to get packed up ready to move tomorrow. Where we are going we do not know.

Monday 10 July 1916

The orders to move are cancelled for the time being. There are all kinds of rumours about as to where we are going but no one seems to know anything.

Tuesday 11 July 1916

We got about 50 more chaps up today. Some that had been sick and left behind in hospital, some new chaps of the draught. That makes up to 797 men now so we are creeping up again.

Wednesday 12 July 1916

We are back again on our old game of parades now that we are not moving for some time. Had a chap over today taking cinema photos of our lot on parade and drilling. Got a fine ....today. It was a treat. Though I hadn't a lemon to squeeze over it.

Thursday 13 July 1916

Parades again as usual. We are getting very short of rations here. I don't know why but there seems to be very little supplies coming up. The Ninth Regiment moved further over today also a battery of mountain guns.

Friday 14 July 1916

Parades today as usual. Nothing particular to report. Arthur Rishton (Lt A.H. Rishton) came over to see me today. He brought me some tobacco and matches. Just the things I was wanting badly.

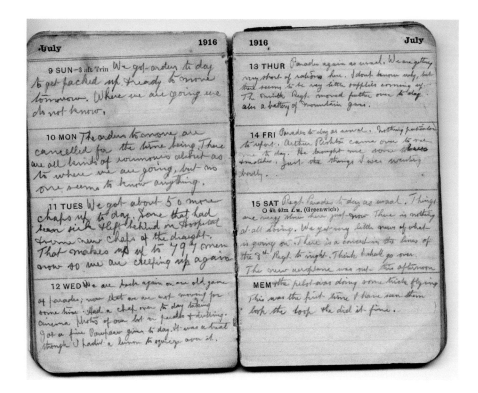

Saturday 15 July 1916

Regiment parades today as usual. Things are very slow here just now. There is nothing at all doing. We get very little news of what is going on. There is a concert in the lines of the 8 regiment tonight. Think I shall go over.

The new aeroplane was out this afternoon and the pilot was doing some trick flying. This was the first time I have seen them loop the loop. He did it fine.

Sunday 16 July 1916

No parades today. Voluntary Church services. Have to find a firing party today of guns for one of the 9 regiment who has died in hospital here.

Monday 17 July 1916

Parades today as usual. Another Firing Party today for one of our chaps. He was one of the new draft and died of fever as soon as he got here.

Tuesday 18 July 1916

Parade is changed a little today. Having a kind of Field Day ......the attack on one of the officers............... Returned to camp about 1.30. A fairly good affair. No casualties.

Wednesday 19 July 1916

Parades as usual. Got a letter today from you dated 14 June. I answered it today also.

Thursday 20 July 1916

On parade today as usual went down to the Town today for a look round. All troops appear to be leaving. Got orders to be ready to move at short notice. Got another letter today from you dated 22 June.

Friday 21 July 1916

No date or time for moving as yet. Still carrying on with parades. Fancy the orders to move are going to be knocked on the head again.

Saturday 22 July 1916

Went down to Town last night to see some chaps (Ben Johnston and I) got back about 10 o'clock. We are getting paid out today. I shall not take any money as I have plenty to last me I think.

16 SUN—1 aft Trin No parades to day. Voluntary Church services. Have to found a Firing party. A day of sorrow for one of the 8th Regt who has died in Hospital here.

17 MON Parades to day as usual. Another Firing Party to day, for one of our chaps. He was one of the most chaff-edied of few as soon as he got here.

18 TUES Parade is changed a little to day. Having a kind of Field day. Practice the attack on one of the Hills close by. Returned to Camp about 1-30. A fairly good affair. No Casualties.

19 WED Parades as usual, Got a letter to day from you dated 14th June. I answered it to day also.

20 THUR On parade to day as usual. Went down to the Town to day for a look round. All Troops appear to be leaving. Got orders to be ready to move at short notice. Got another letter to day from you dated 22nd June.

21 FRI ☾ 11h 33m P.M. (Greenwich) No date on time for moving given as yet. Still carrying on with Parades. Fancy the orders to move are going to be knocked on the head again.

22 SAT Went down to Town last night to see some chaps (Ben Johnson & I.) got back about 10 o'clock. We are getting paid out to day. I shall not take any money as I have plenty to last one I think.

MEM

Sunday 23 July 1916
Church parades this morning or rather services this morning as we do not have parades for church. Nothing much doing.

Monday 24 July 1916
Parades as usual this morning. Rumours of moves etc are very persistent today. I wonder if it is coming off this time. We have had orders about a dozen times or more to move and nothing has come of it.

Tuesday 25 July 1916
Company parades this morning. We are not to move out now the 8th are going instead. Our C.O. is in a deuce of a bad temper over it. He thinks he ought to do the lot. He never studies the men, as long as he is all right that all that matters.

Wednesday 26 July 1916

Parades as usual. The 8th Regiment moved out this morning towards ....Post. 100 of our chaps have gone with them also machine guns & 2 field guns.

Thursday 27 July 1916

No parades this morning. We are changing the site of our camp. Not going far only just up to the top of the rise. In fact, I am not moving my tent at all.

Friday 28 July 1916

Parades as usual. Putting a hedge round the Headquarters to keep off the wind and make the Q. Room more private.

Saturday 29 July 1916

Klinky arrived back today from Moschi. Didn't bring any stuff back not room in car. Went down to the Town today. Very deserted now that the majority of the troops are away. Another rumour today. Supposed to be going back to Sanja river shortly to entrain for another part of the .... of operations. Hope it is so as we are about fed up with staying at Kondoa so long.

Sunday 30 July 1916

No parades for companies today. Writing letters today. I wrote home to you this afternoon. Went down to the Gaol to see some pals. Not convicts.

Monday 31 July 1916

Parades as usual today. Having a few more fresh oxen to make up for what we have lost to sickness and disease. Things are awfully slow here now. Heard today that the 9 regiment had a few casualties.............

Tuesday 1 August 1916

Parades under Coy arrangements this morning. Mail up today. 1 letter for me dated 8 June. The Provost Staff are moving on today to Dodoma that has been in our hands for the past week or so. I suppose will be our turn one of these days.

Wednesday 2 August 1916

Company parades today as usual. ....of rumours are going about as to ....negotiations but I don't think there is any truth in them.

Thursday 3 August 1916

Parades under Coy arrangements this morning. Our chaps are busy breaking in oxen for the wagons. There is some sport too watching them. Heard today that we are moving off in a day or two's time as soon as transport arrives in the direction of the railway to the East of Dodoma.

Friday 4 August 1916

Parades as usual. We are to move off to Kwa Nfarolbo tomorrow. That is about 80 or 90 miles and about 15 miles off the railway. We have orders to cut down our kit as low as possible. The orders allows 6 officers to carry 800 lbs between them and 6 men are only allowed 84 lbs.

Saturday 5 August 1916

Left Kondoa Irangi this morning at 7.45. Marched about 7 or 8 miles then halted above Dodoma Nek at 12 o'clock for the day. The roads so far are very thick with dust and if the rains get into it will be terribly hard dragging for the animals that are in a very poor state.

Sunday 6 August 1916

Reveille at 4.30 this morning, marched off at 6 o'clock and expect to reach.......today. Halted at 9.30. Sent the tents back from here as the oxen are done in and we cannot get along with them. Had a terrible job getting them ....Had a bathe this afternoon, as we are not moving on today.

30 SUN—6 aft Trin
2h 15m A.M. (Greenwich)

No parades for Company to-day. Writing letters to-day. I wrote home to you this afternoon. Went down to the jail to-night to see some pals. Not convicted.

31 MON *Parades as usual to-day. Having a few more field ... to make up for ... Things are awfully slow here now. Heard to-day that the 9th Regt have had a few casualties ahead.*
Trinity Law Sittings end

1 AUG TUES *Parades under lug arrangements. On mail day ... to day. 1 letter for me dated 28th June. The Provost staff are moving on to-day to Dodoma which has been in our hands for the last week or so. I suppose it will be our turn one of these days.*
Lammas Day. Scottish Quarter.

2 WED *Company parades to day as usual. All kinds of rumours are going about as to peace negotiations being on but I don't think there is any truth in them.*

3 THUR *Parades under Coy arrangements this morning. One chap are busy breaking in oxen for the waggons. There is some spot ... them. Heard to day that we are moving off in a day or two's time as soon as transport arrives; in the direction of the railway to the East of Dodoma.*

4 FRI *Parades as usual. We are to move off to-morrow. That is about 80 or 90 miles ... about 15 miles off the Railway. We have orders to cut down our kit as low as possible. The order allows 6 officers ... 500 lbs between them & 6 men are only allowed 84 lbs ...*
War declared between Great Britain and Germany, 1914

5 SAT *Left Kondoa Irangi this morning at 7-45. Marched about 9 or 8 miles then halted at Dodoma. Such at 12 o'clock for the day. The roads so far are very thick with dust; ... the ... will be terribly hard dragging for the animals who are in a very poor state.*

MEM

Monday 7 August 1916

Set off this morning at 4.40, marched until 9.30 had a cup of tea then off again at 12. Went for about 2 hours then halted until 7 pm. Did about 4 miles then camped for the night at 9 pm. The roads are terribly dusty and it rises in clouds and chokes you nearly and the water is terribly scarce.

Tuesday 8 August 1916

Reveille this morning at 6 am moved off at 8 am marched until 11 then rested for 2 hours then marched again until half past 3. The heat was terrible and no water. When we got to the water our C.O. was going to move on again without water but the men refused so we halted here for the night.

Wednesday 9 August 1916

Off this morning at 6 am and marched until 8 am then halted until 11.30. Our rotten Colonel set off at this hour of the day and marched us in the heat of the day until 6. We reached Tchenee where there is a little ……. and halted. About half of the regiment had fallen out on the way here owing to the heat and the dust which was terrible. This part of the journey is infested with lions, which are as plentiful as horses in Serengeti, but they seem more afraid of us than we of them.

Thursday 10 August 1916

Having a rest today. Had a bath last night and enjoyed it. What with the dust and the perspiration, we were black as sweeps. Expect to move off again this evening. Left Tashenere at 3.30 this afternoon. Marched until 7.30 and halted for 2.1/2 hours. Got off again at 10 and marched until 2 am. We covered about 20 miles. A very hot and dusty march all the way to Meia Meia

Friday 11 August 1916

Did not wake up this morning until 8 o'clock. Rested all day until 4 pm. We marched until 7 o'clock and halted for 2 hours. Off again at 9 and marched until 11 and reached Makutapora in pretty good condition. Had a pipe and off to sleep.

Saturday 12 August 1916

Woke up this morning at about 8. Practically had breakfast in bed. I do not know how long we remain here at Makutapora but expect we shall get orders some time today. In the meantime we are resting. Moved off at 4 pm. Marched until 6.30 then halted for two hours. Off again at 8.30 and reached Dodoma on the Central Railway at 10.30. Bivouacked for the night on the square opposite the Railway Station.

Sunday 13 August 1916

Our Colonel has taken over the town of Dodoma as Camp Commandant and I am Garrison Sgt. Major quartered in the Bahn Hotel. There is no rolling stock in our possession yet but the pioneers have constructed one of the Reo cars so that it runs on the rails; and it gets along too.

Monday 14 August 1916

Reveille 6 am. Bath ready to get into as soon as I get out of bed. I haven't slept in a bed since I left home and enjoyed it immensely. I wrote home today. Nothing much on today.

Tuesday 15 August 1916

Post came in today. It generally seems to come as soon as I have written. I got two letters date the 6 and 12 of July. Had a great job this afternoon. I had to send out 150 porters onto the next town about 43 miles and an escort of about 50 men too. It was a tough job to get them out as they do not want to do any work.

Wednesday 16 August 1916

Reveille 6 breakfast 7.15. We are to send onto Mpwapwa about 100 of our regiment this evening. This will mean an alteration of duties so I shall be pretty busy. Had a hard day today so I am having a good peg of German Whiskey and turning in early. It helps to keep the fever down.

Thursday 17 August 1916

Quite fit this morning. Heard last night that the aeroplane had blown up the line further east and cut off several trains. Hope it is so it will help us immensely. Had a funeral on today. Had to find Firing Party and bearers for one of the Field Ambulance Staff ....

Friday 18 August 1916

Nothing much doing today. It is getting very hot now during the day. The room I have is fine and lofty which makes it cool so I can have a sleep in the afternoon when not busy. We are not doing at all badly here now though rations are short.

Saturday 19 August 1916

I saw Tom Canning today. He rode round to see me. He is quite fit again and like the rest of us is about fed up with things. We are sending another party out today up the line about 50 miles. Also expect to send out posts tomorrow all along the line at intervals of about 50 miles. This looks like being our line of communications for the remainder of the war.

Sunday 20 August 1916

Nothing much doing today. Had a great treat today and got hold of some vegetables. Had cabbage, spinach and tomatoes for dinner today. And a cigar to finish of with. We have had no vegetables for months and the continual meat diet is telling on me.

Monday 21 August 1916

Several cases on today before the O.C. Saw young Pattison of Benoni today. He is going back with prisoners. He has had a bad attack of fever and is terribly run down. Expects to go to Wynburg Hospital.

Tuesday 22 August 1916

Pretty busy today; not much time to myself. Sometimes the blooming place is like a police court with cases on all the day. A few of our details arrived up today. They have been pretty badly off for scoff on the way up.

Wednesday 23 August 1916

Not doing too bad just now. Getting a fair amount of vegetables brought in by the natives. Had a concert this evening. We got a Piano out of one of the houses here and have some very good talent too. Ben Johnson was the stage manager and organizer. It went off quite alright.

Thursday 24 August 1916

Had venison and eggs for breakfast this morning. It was great too. Of course, these luxuries are what we have to buy ourselves and are glad to do so when one can get the chance of them.

Friday 25 August 1916

A few strafing today. That is cases for the Camp Commandant but the idiot doesn't know how to weigh them off at all. But he thinks he does so that's all that matters.

20 SUN—9 aft Trin
(0h 53m P.M. (Greenwich)

21 MON
Black Game Shooting begins

22 TUES

23 WED

24 THUR
St. Bartholomew, Ap.

25 FRI

26 SAT

MEM

Saturday 26 August 1916

Things are about the same today. Rumour has it that we can expect to hear good news within a few days. Well we got good news this afternoon. That was an issue of jam and tobacco and matches. We haven't had jam for months in fact we have not been in full rations since we left Mbanie.

Sunday 27 August 1916

Nothing extra special to record today. Roast venison, pumpkins and sweet potatoes and jam roll for dinner. So it is necessary to have a lay down this afternoon to sleep off the effects.

Monday 28 August 1916

Good news this morning. Smuts in Morogoro. This should help to shorten the campaign quite a bit unless the Bosches clear off south of the line if they can get there which I hope not.

Tuesday 29 August 1916

Nothing much doing this morning. A few cases of natives for lashes etc. A small mail up. Nothing for me. Have not had a letter for a fortnight now. Must have got stranded somewhere.

Wednesday 30 August 1916

Busy day today. A mail going out I believe. Must try to get a letter off. I have written home today so I suppose there will be a mail come in now.

Thursday 31 August 1916

Have nothing of interest to put down today. Am spending a bit of time trying to mend my vests as they are in rags.

Friday 1 September 1916

Got heaps of papers up today but nothing for me. Still the papers are farmed around so it makes something to pass the time with to read the news though it is old.

Saturday 2 September 1916

Expect to move away shortly. Our chaps are coming in here that we left along the road also the platoons that went with the 8th to Kilimatinde are expected in tomorrow or the next day. Don't know where we are going but hope it is homeward but afraid it will be otherwise.

Sunday 3 September 1916

A very hard day today. I think I have been off the bed about twice so you can see how hard I am worked. It is very hot today outside but all right in my room that is very cool.

Monday 4 September 1916

Got funeral on today. Sergeant of the 10th SAI died in hospital here. A mail in and two letters for me dated 19 and 25 July. Sorry to hear that you have measles in the house. Two platoons B Company came in today from M .....

Tuesday 5 September 1916

Much as usual today. The pioneers have got another tractor on the line today so I suppose that will make things better for us. Heard that some rolling stock had been captured but I think it is almost too far gone.

Wednesday 6 September 1916

It was confirmed last night about Dar es Salem being in our hands but the rumour about rolling stock is not confirmed.

Thursday 7 September 1916

Nothing much doing today. Reading most of the day. We have lately been passing our evenings with dominoes. Ben Johnson, Alf Butt, Alex Black and myself.

Friday 8 September 1916

Blow paid up his 5 Rupees. We got paid out today. I drew £2, that is 30 Rupees. Of course we are always paid out in rupees and they weigh a bit too.

Saturday 9 September 1916

We are having a concert tonight and we had a bit of a rehearsal last night. We got the piano over to our rooms (Ben and I) and had a champion nights entertainment. We have some really fine singers in our lot and if last nights rehearsal is anything to judge by we ought to have a fine concert tonight. 10.30 pm. The Concert has been a huge success everything went off swimmingly. I was in the chair for about an hour until the Colonel came.

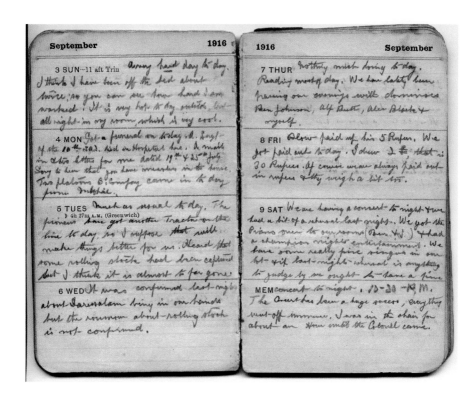

Sunday 10 September 1916

We have got orders to move. We expect to move on Morogoro at 4 am today. I wrote home today. Having a great day today. Ham and eggs for breakfast. Chicken and plum pudding for dinner and a cigar to finish. Left Dodoma at 4 pm. Marched until 7 o'clock halted until 9 then marched to 4.

Monday 11 September 1916

Got down to it about 12 last night and left about 7 this morning. Had to leave about 20 chaps behind with bad feet.
We moved off again about 3.30 then marched until 8 pm. Halted until 10 then marched on until 12.

Tuesday 12 September 1916

Arrived at Nyangolo at 9.30 after about 1.1/2 hours marching. Marched off again at 4 pm, halted at 7 until 9 pm and marched until 12. Very trying march. Dust is very bad and no water for animals; they take of bit of getting along.

Wednesday 13 September 1916

Remained at this halt all day until 4 pm marched until 6 pm, rested for 2 hours, off again at 8 and marched until 9.45 pm.

Thursday 14 September 1916

Water very scarce here and men and mules are about done up. Transport moved off about 2.30 pm. We left at 4 marched until 6.15. On account of the condition of the animals had to remain here until 10 pm. Arrived at Mpwapwa at 12.45. A Coy. Had hot tea ready for us and it went down all right.

Friday 15 September 1916

Did a good move this morning. Saw the C.O. bath just alongside where I slept so I had a fine hot bath before breakfast. Left Mpwapwa at 4 pm. Halted at the Giant Baobab Tree at 7.30 pm and moved on again at 10 pm and halted for the night at 12.15.

Saturday 16 September 1916

Slept until about 8.30 had a bath in a cup full of water this time, moved off at 3.30 and marched until 7, halted until 10.30 and reached Kidete at 12.30 pm. Very fine station and pumping plant here also waterborne sewerage all very up to date. From here to Kilosa is a tsetse fly hell of 15 miles through which we shall have to pass during the night. So that will mean a long night trek when we leave here.

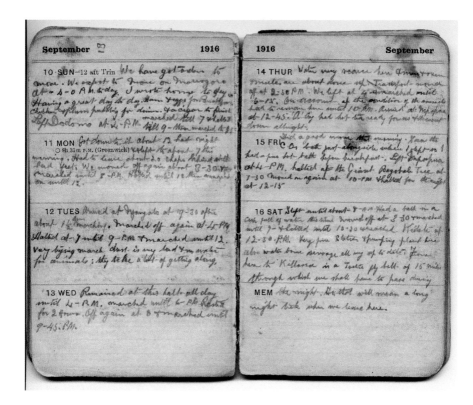

Sunday 17 September 1916

Had a fine cold shower his morning. It was a treat to.. Also had a bowl of tomatoes. We moved out at 3.45 for Kilosa. Just before we left I bought a tin of tomatoes to take with us. We halted at 8 until 2.30 had a sleep during the interval with lions and jackals for a chorus. Halted at 6.15 am having done 21 miles.

Monday 18 September 1916

Am remaining here for a little while as the town of Kilosa is very full of sickness. The river is close here and it is a treat to have plenty of water to wash with. We are moving fresh camp to the other side of the river tomorrow.

Tuesday 19 September 1916

Shifted camp this morning. The site is a bit better for the C.O. so I suppose that is alright it doesn't matter about anyone else as long as he is all right. The chaps are busy putting up huts to live in with the pampas grass as the sun is terribly hot.

Wednesday 20 September 1916

On duty room this morning. The C.O. is chucking it out well today. Expect to move on again tomorrow or the following day.

Thursday 21 September 1916

Left this morning at 4.30 for Kilosa. It rained a little during the night and also early morning. It was not as bad as it kept down the dust as we marched. We reached Kilosa about 8.30 and marched about two miles the other side. We had just got halted when it commenced to rain again and it teemed down the whole day. We have no tents or covering of any sort so you can guess the state we are in. It slowed off a little about 5 pm and we rigged up a bit of shelter.

Friday 22 September 1916

It was fine this morning with the exception of a shower or two. We managed to get all our things dry again. The lions were very close to us last night. We could hear them roaring throughout the night but everyone was pretty tired and didn't think the lions worried us much. We had one of our mules taken by them also. We traced the spoor and the blood for some distance. We left the camp at 4 o'clock and marched until 6.30 and halted for the wagons to catch up as the roads are bad. They never turned up and it commenced to rain and rained the whole night so we were wet through again.

September   1916 | 1916   September

17 SUN—13 aft Trin
Ember Week

18 MON

19 TUES
☽ 5h 35m A.M. (Greenwich)

20 WED
Ember Day

21 THUR
St. Matthew, Ap.

22 FRI
Ember Day

23 SAT
Ember Day

MEM

Saturday 23 September 1916

Have spent a wretched night in the rain without any covering so we were in a pretty rotten state this morning. Very little scoff yet as the wagons are stuck fast further up the road. Had a cup of oxo and some biltong so I suppose I shall manage until the food turns up. It is very showering this morning. Took off our shirts and dried them at the fire but as soon as they are dry it comes onto rain again so they are not much better. The wagons got up to us about 12 o'clock and we moved off at 2 o'clock. We marched until about 4 then halted for the night at the water. Had just got our sheet up to keep off the dew when it commenced to rain again and rained hard for hours.

Sunday 24 September 1916

Moved off this morning at 6 am. The roads are awful and after some hours had to halt for another hour to enable the wagons to catch us up. Set off again after another hour and we had 5 halts until 3 pm as cattle and mules are done. Marched until 6.45 and halted for the night. We are on half rations of mealie meal no bread flour or biscuits and have to carry great coats.

Monday 25 September 1916

Off this morning at 5 pm and marched until 9 and halted until 4.15. There was a grand river here and enjoyed a fine bath. I am remaining behind for a little longer with the Ammo Columns. Expect to leave about 5. Only marched about 3 miles but it took nearly two hours to do it.

Tuesday 26 September 1916

Moved off this morning at 5 and then marched until 8.30 then halted again at 5.15 Only marched about 4 miles then halted for the night. Did not make any provision for rain as it looked like being a fine night. However it rained hard about midnight but did not disturb me much.

Wednesday 27 September 1916

Moved off the morning at 5, marched until 7.30, and halted at another river about 5 miles out of Morogoro. Had a fine swim and shave for a change. Left again at 3 and marched into Morogoro. This place is very pretty on the slopes of a mountain among rubber plantations.Of course, our C.O. could not halt us close to the Town and he marched us out of the town about 2 miles before we halted. Whilst I was busy rigging up for the night Heath and Mick ...... arrived with a tin of coffee and biscuits which was a God send.

Thursday 28 September 1916

We are busy today erecting shelter from the sun and rain out of the rubber trees and grass. You can make quite decent huts out of them too. We expect to remain here for a few days to get rigged out with clothes and boots etc. Got full rations today for a change. We have been most of our time on half or even quarter rations along the way here.

Friday 29 September 1916

Very little rain last night. Busy again getting huts and lines into shape. Heard today that the whole of our Brigade are coming back here to reorganize etc in a few days. I hope it means that we are going to get out of the country and back to the Union but I don't suppose it will be our luck. A mail in today but there is nothing for me.

Saturday 30 September 1916

We are starting parades again today. They ....us too much time to ourselves. We are all badly in need of clothing and boots etc. but I think there are no stores here yet so I suppose we shall get them shortly. Killed the chicken tonight ready for tomorrow's dinner. We intend to feed ourselves up here if we can.

Sunday 1 October 1916

Nothing much on today. Am having an extra hour on the blankets. Raining a good deal today. The chickens are grand and with paw paw for a vegetable go down immensely.

Monday 2 October 1916

Busy today enlarging the dining room and creating a larger bedroom. These are grass huts but they make very fine shelters. We must have cut down hundreds of pounds worth of rubber trees.

Tuesday 3 October 1916

Morning parade this morning and recruits drilling. I wrote home this morning. Am getting on fine .... and expect to be able to sleep ... tonight.

Wednesday 4 October 1916

We are shifting again today and going back to Kilosa. Everyone is in the dumps and marched out at 4 pm leaving some of our fellows sick that could not move with us.

1 SUN—15 aft Trin
Cambridge Michaelmas Term begins

2 MON
Pheasant Shooting begins

3 TUES

4 WED
) 11h 1m A.M. (Greenwich)

5 THUR
Dividends due at Bank

6 FRI

7 SAT

MEM

Thursday 5 October 1916

Off again this morning at 5 am. Marched until about 8.30 halted at Blue Bean Camp until 3.45. Marched until 6.15 then halted for 2 hours. Left again at 8.15 and marched until 10.30. Men about all done in.

Friday 6 October 1916

No Reveille this morning and got up when we felt inclined. Went to the river and had a fine swim before breakfast. Had a good feed of mielie meal and a can of biscuits. Wagons moved off across the river about 3 pm. The regiment left about 4 pm and marched until about 8 pm. We got caught in a shower of rain and it made it very hard work as all this area is a swamp and your feet sink in over the bootlaces.

Saturday 7 October 1916

We moved off this morning at 5.30 and marched until 9 am. The C in C passed us on his way to Morogoro. I gathered some lucky beans at that halt. They will mix nicely with the blue beans that I got at the other halt. We fell into march about 5 pm but owing to the wagons getting stuck in the river we did not get away until 7.10. We marched until about 9.30 then halted for the night.

Sunday 8 October 1916

Left this morning at 6 am, marched through Kilosa about 3 miles the other side, and camped on the slopes of the hills at about 10.30. It is very nicely situated but a long way to fetch water and wood. A party of our chaps that we left behind have joined us again this afternoon.

Monday 9 October 1916

We expect to remain here a few days to get boots etc., as we are very much in need of them. Got a few pairs of boots up but not sufficient to go round.

Tuesday 10 October 1916

Rained a little last night but today is terribly hot. A mail came in today. There was nothing for me. I cannot understand it. Six weeks and no letter.

Wednesday 11 October 1916

Very overcast this morning looks like more rain. Orderly Room this morning. Usual parades. I wrote home today. Our story of a few days has soon come to an end. We have orders to move off tomorrow about 40 miles south. We are not very pleased at the idea.

Thursday 12 October 1916

Off this morning at 5 am and marched until 8.30. Halted until 4 then marched off. Halted from 6 to 8 then marched to 10. Halted at Ulaya. This is as far as we can go with wheeled transport. We are to take porters from here.

Friday 13 October 1916

We remained here at Ulaya until 4 pm. I met ....of the 9th regiment here. The 9th, 10th , 11th and 12th regiments are here. Saw Charlie Davis he is to be sent home invalided. Saw Percy Hindle, and ... Horton and Mendoza. And heaps of others. We are … tropical scenery now. The road from here … through mountain forest .... We got orders that we are not to move until tomorrow morning. Saw Fatty Burroughs – he is in the 9th regiment.

Saturday 14 October 1916

Left this morning at 5 marched until 9.30 through some fine country. The track is only wide enough for one to walk along and is through the heart of dense forest then again through swamps with hordes of mosquitoes and grass 12 foot high. Wild elephants ……….. in grass ………… ahead are …………… Then it changes and we get ……mountain passes with the path along the side of a slope and the precipice below……………….. We halted at 9am in the middle of a tropical forest. The foliage is really ………here and ………. ripe ……………….. here but his is a bit ……. without. We ………… and marched until 7.30 and halted in a ……….. game hut. All the ripe fruit had been taken by the Germans.

Sunday 15 October 1916

Off this morning at 6 am and marched until 9 am and halted until 4 and nearly got burnt out as a grass fire sprang up and if the wind had not changed we should have had a hot time. Left at 4 pm and marched until 6.30 at the foot of the Pass through the mountains.

Monday 16 October 1916

Marched off this morning at 5.45 started up the mountain. It took us until 8 o'clock to get up but the scenery is lovely. We camped just over the highest point on the road ………………… I spotted a tree with the large lucky beans and got some. Moved off at 11 and marched until 2. Had a fine bathe in the river and halted for the night.

Tuesday 17 October 1916

Moved off this morning at .... 8.15, halted until 3.30. While we were halted here our cook made us a jam roll pudding and with chicken broth and boiled beef and dumplings we managed to make a decent meal. In fact it was painful to move after. Left at 3.30 and marched until 6.30. Halted at the D.A.H. camp at the Drift.

Wednesday 18 October 1916

We are not moving on today. Expect to be here two or three days then to move on to Iringa. A string of porters are going back to Ulaya today. I have written to you today.

Thursday 19 October 1916

Have got a decent shade put up so we are sure to leave it soon. Our scoff is about run out so if we don't get any by tomorrow we shall be all out. Have got orders to push through to Iringa at once so we expect to go off tomorrow. Rations came in tonight so we shall be all right for another week.

Friday 20 October 1916

Moved out this morning at 6 am. Had to cross the river this took us about an hour and we marched until 11 am. Our C.O is a lunatic so we expect these things. He has about killed half the men. We halted for the night and have orders to push on again tomorrow morning at 3....

Saturday 21 October 1916

Reveille at 2 and moved off at 3 am. Halted at 5.30 for an hour then marched until 9. Halted at the mountain pass for the day until 3.30. All the chaps are just about done up and if things go on like this much longer then there will be trouble among us.

We left a lot of chaps behind at the River and there are a lot more now that are unfit to go on. Myself I feel about all in but it is no use throwing up the sponge here as it would only mean pegging out. We got in truck with the first party of Montys Force at the last halt.

Marched off at 3.30 halted at 5.30 in the Nek of the mountain. Staying here for the night. A lot the men will not be able to go on so we shall have to leave them here. There is plenty of water and shade.

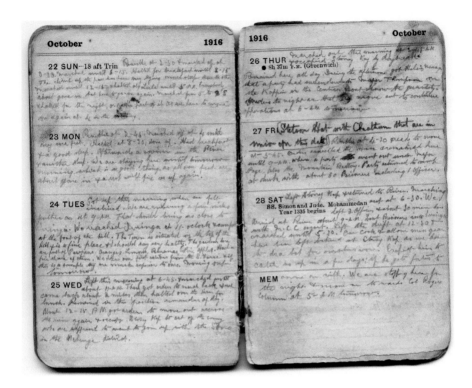

Sunday 22 October 1916

Reveille at 2.30 and marched off at 3.30. Marched until 6.15. Halted for breakfast until 8.15. The climb up the pass has been very trying......and steeper than the other. Marched until 12.15 and halted at Lugalu. Until 5 pm. Everybody about gone in but gave to go on again. Marched from 5 to 8 and halted for the night or part of it as we have to go on again at 4 in the morning.

Monday 23 October 1916

Reveille at 2.45 and marched off at 4. Very sore feet. Halted at 8.30, done up. Had breakfast and a good sleep.Afterwards a swim in the river and another sleep. We are staying here until tomorrow morning which is a good thing as all our feet are about gone in and a rest will fix us up again.

Tuesday 24 October 1916

Marched out this morning at 2.45 am and occupied Stoney Kop by daybreak and remained here all day. During the afternoon got Hales' message that a party had surrendered to Major Thompson on the kopje in the Centre. Don't know the quantity. Orders tonight are that we move out to continue operations at 6 am tomorrow.

Wednesday 25 October 1916

Left this morning at 6.45 and marched until about 11. Then got orders to march back and we came back about 2 miles then halted over the .....for lunch. Remained in this position for the remainder of the day. About 12.15 pm got orders to move out ....again and occupy Stoney Kop to ... the way when....suffered to ....

Thursday 26 October 1916

Marched out this morning at 2.45 am and occupied Stoney Kop by daybreak and remained here all day. During the afternoon got Hales' message that a party had surrendered to Major Thompson on the kopje in the Centre. Don't know the quantity. Orders tonight are that we move out to continue operations at 6 am tomorrow.

Friday 27 October 1916

Reveille at 4.30 ready to move at 5.45. Orders cancelled the move and...........here until.........when a party went out under Major Page with the Mountain Battery. Party returned to camp at dark with about 60 prisoners including 1 officer.

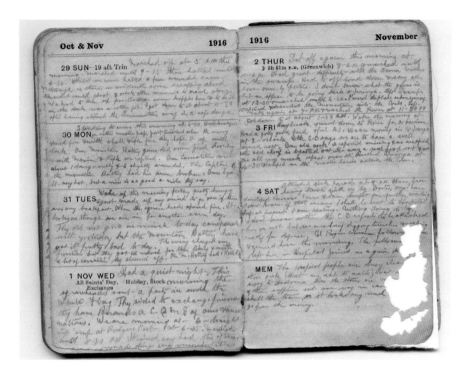

Saturday 28 October 1916

Left Stoney Kop and returned to River. Marching out at 6.30. We left 2 officers and about 30 men here. Arrived at River about 9 am. Sent prisoners into Iringa with M.C.C. escort. Left the drift at 12.30 and marched until 5.30. Our cook and all our main gear have been left behind at Stoney Kop as we have ....for a .... Expect him to catch up in a few days ....porters to. We are stopping here for the night and move on towards Col. Rogers column at 5 am tomorrow.

Sunday 29 October 1916

Marched off at 5 am this morning. Marched until 9.15 then halted until 4.30. Whilst we were halted a few wounded came through so there is evidently some scrapping ahead. Marched along until 8 o'clock and then crawled along. We had to take up positions on some kopjes here and to do this in the dark was a rotten job. I got down to it about 11.30 after having stowed the Ammunition away in a safe donga.

Monday 30 October 1916
Standing to arms this morning at 4.30. Had breakfast or rather mielie pap. Just finished when the enemy opened fire and with shell and rifle fire kept it up until dark. Our Mountain Battery guns did some good shooting...with .... And rifle ... replied. Our casualties were about 1 dangerously and 6 slightly wounded. The Captain of the Mountain Battery had his arm broken. One got it very hot but a miss is as good as a mile they say.

Tuesday 31 October 1916
Woke up this morning feeling pretty hungry and just made up my mind to go see if there was any breakfast when the squareheads opened fire. It looks as though we are in for another warm day. They did not go on as much today compared with yesterday but the Mountain Battery have got it pretty bad today. The enemy charged our position but they got too much for their liking and with a bit of casualties they cleared off. The M. Battery had 1 killed.

Wednesday 1 November 1916
Had a quiet night. This morning the squareheads sent a party in under the white flag. They wished to exchange prisoners they have Brands a C.O.... S. Africans.... natives. We are moving at 6 tonight. Left camp at Rogers Post at 6.45 Marched until 11.30pm. It rained very hard this afternoon and made things more uncomfortable.

November   1916

5 SUN—20 aft. Trin
Gunpowder Plot

6 MON

7 TUES

1916   November

9 THUR
O 8h 18m P.M. (Greenwich)
King Edward VII. born, 1841

10 FRI

11 SAT
Martinmas. Scottish Quarter Day.
Half Quarter Day

MEM

Thursday 2 November 1916

Set off again this morning at 8 am and marched until 11 am. Had great difficulty with the Ammo. Mules in the swamps. Had to offload them and carry all boxes over by porters. I don't know what the game is but we appear to be going back to Iringa. Left swamps at 12.30 and marched until 4.30. Passed the place where convoy captured and descended the mountains into the Nek. Left Nek again at 7 pm and reached the river at 11.30 pm. Got down to it about 1.20 am.

Friday 3 November 1916

Woke this morning at daybreak and went down to river for a swim. Had a jolly good feed and feel A.1. We are moving into Iringa at 2 o'clock and the C.O. says we are to have a well-earned rest. Our old cook is reported missing and we are afraid that the old chap is blotted out. He was a real good sort and we are all very much upset over it. Reached Iringa at 4.30 and camped on the mealie lands outside the town.

Saturday 4 November 1916

Attended sick parade at 8 am. Have .... Having trouble with my leg. Doctor says I have developed varicose veins and I am ..... from further marching. I don't know if that means I shall be sent to hospital but at present I am resting.

Nothing doing today. I don't know whether the C.O. expects to be attacked here or not but we are busy digging trenches and making ready for defence. Col. Rogers columns following....and arrived here this morning. The fellows we left here in hospital joined us again. The hospital people are busy clearing their sick out on way to Dodoma. Also the stores are ..... and their supplies ... our way.... Left the town so it looks very much......go from the enemy.

Sunday 5 November 1916

A mail is going out via Dodoma today at 4 o'clock and I shall try to get a letter off. I haven't had a letter myself since 5 July. I wrote home to you today. Nothing particular to note today.

Monday 6 November 1916

Busy improving defences today. The aeroplanes arrived here today. This is the first time they have been over in this part and they expect great things from it.

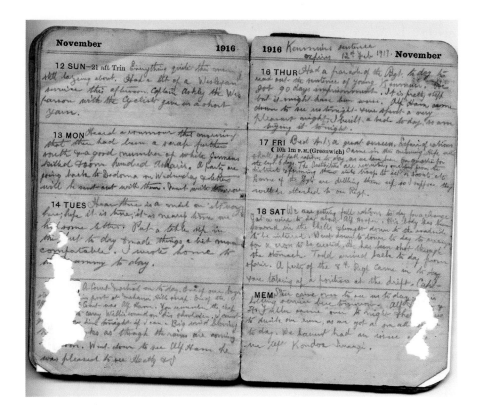

Tuesday 7 November 1916

Nothing doing today. Taking it easy trying to get fit as we are all about along. Aeroplane had an accident and wings are damaged. Another one expected up tomorrow.

Wednesday 8 November 1916

Went to the village today. Called at the ..... to see Jack Harrison who is laid up...........foot. He is getting along all right. Aeroplane arrived tonight.

Thursday 9 November 1916

Nothing much doing today. Got the boys on building a Banda so expect we shall shift as soon as finished as we usually do. .... rations today so it looks as though supplies are getting short again.

Friday 10 November 1916

Still waiting at Iringa. Nothing at all doing. All we do now is to lay about all the day in the shade of the bandas. I suppose there will be another move on of these days but at present it appears as though everything is at a standstill.

Saturday 11 November 1916

Sent a party of boys out with the conductor to pick up the rations that are coming in from Dodoma. At present, we are on quarter rations and expect to be so until the 16 so that will not pull men together. Got a report this morning that some native women had found the body of a white man in the bush where the convoy was attacked. I think it is ....sure that it is our old cook who was blotted out there. A party have gone .... miles to see if they can identify .... and to bury it decently.

Sunday 12 November 1916

Everything quiet this evening still lazing about. Had a bit of a Wesleyan service this afternoon. Captain Ashby Wes parson with the Cyclists gave us a short yarn.

Monday 13 November 1916

Heard a rumour this morning that there had been a scrap further south and a good number of white Germans killed and some hundred Askaris. A party are going back to Dodoma on Wednesday and letters will be sent out with them. Must write tomorrow.

November   **1916**   **1916**   **November**

19 SUN—22 aft Trin *[handwritten diary entry]*

20 MON *[handwritten diary entry]*

21 TUES *[handwritten diary entry]*

WED *[handwritten diary entry]*

23 THUR *[handwritten diary entry]*

24 FRI *[handwritten diary entry]*

25 SAT *[handwritten diary entry]*

MEM *[handwritten diary entry]*

Tuesday 14 November 1916

Hear there is a mail on its way here; hope it is true; it is nearly time we had some letters. Put a table up in the ....today and made things a bit more comfortable. I wrote home to Mammy today.

Wednesday 15 November 1916

A Court Martial on today. One of our boys ....his part at Maharin Hills scrap. One of the … Court was Alf Harm. You remember the chap.. he used to carry Willie around on his shoulder. I must … him tonight if I can. Big wind blowing …. looks as though the rains are coming soon. Went down to see Alf Harm he was pleased to see Heathy and I.

Thursday 16 November 1916

(Kensmuirs sentence expires 12 Feb 1917.)

Had a parade of the regiment today to read out the sentence of young Kensmuir. He got 90 days imprisonment. It is pretty stiff but it might have been worse. Alf Harm came down to see us tonight and we spent a very pleasant night. I built a bed today so am trying it tonight.

Friday 17 November 1916

Bed A.1. a great success. ....of rations came in this morning.

Hope we shall get full rations today as we have been on quarter for the last 6 days. The Authorities are recruiting natives from the district and forming them into troops to act as scouts etc. Some of the Sergeants are drilling them up so I suppose they will be attached to our regiment.

Saturday 18 November 1916

We are getting full rations today for a change. Got a wire today about Alf Hooper. His body has been found in the hills and brought down to the roadside to be interred. Went down to town today to arrange for a cross to be erected. He has been shot through the stomach. Todd arrived back today from .... A party of the 8 Regiment came in today and are taking up a position at the drift.

Capt. Steen came over to see us today.... Holding review here tomorrow. Alf....Lt. Fuller came over tonight....to drink our rum as we got a ...all today. We haven't had an issue....we left Kondoa Irangi.

26 SUN—23 aft Trin *[handwritten diary entry]*

27 MON *[handwritten diary entry]*

28 TUES *[handwritten diary entry]*

29 WED *[handwritten diary entry]*

30 THUR
St. Andrew, Ap. *[handwritten diary entry]*

1 DEC FRI
Queen Alexandra born, 1844 *[handwritten diary entry]*

2 SAT
☽ 1h 56m A.M. (Greenwich) *[handwritten diary entry]*

MEM *[handwritten diary entry]*

Sunday 19 November 1916

Attended church service this morning. There was a good attendance too. Steen is very popular in our regiment. Had Wesleyan parson to tea tonight as we are doing well. It rained very hard this afternoon and our roof was not waterproof so we got a good deal of water in.

Monday 20 November 1916

We are trying to make our home a little more weatherproof. Col. Rogers's column moved out about 15 miles today to Morogoro. Got a nasty attack of diarrhoea today, so am taking this easy a bit.

Tuesday 21 November 1916

A bit better today but very little. I got three rupees engraved in Iringa for the kiddies. I got them back today. They look very well indeed and I think the youngsters will like them.
The rain threatened very much today and it blew over again after a few drops.

Wednesday 22 November 1916

Nothing much doing today. The Padre .....back to Dodoma today. Lt. Rice is .....K.A.R. He left us a bag of tobacco which was very acceptable.

Thursday 23 November 1916

Looks like rain today. Jack Bernards came back today. He escaped from the Germans. He is very thin and he had a rough time with them. The Doc. sent him into hospital. Got a ring made today by one of the Indians out of a piece of copper band off the shell. The Indian came and .... us while we were in bed.

Friday 24 November 1916

Quite a slack day today. Nothing much to record. Took it easy all day.

Saturday 25 November 1916

A real top-hole day today. The mail came in and I got five letters and more to be mailed so I may get more. What an awful time the Mammy has been having. I hope you are not overdoing yourself dearest. Very pleased to hear that Toody is better, I sincerely hope she will regain her sight. I would be awful for anything to happen to her eyes; she had such lovely eyes too. It was four months since I had a letter so you can guess I was getting anxious to hear from you. However, alls well that ends well and let me hope all will end well.

Sunday 26 November 1916

More letters today. I have got three more. Two from you and 1 from somebody I don't know asking for a V.C. Two more letters this afternoon that is 10 altogether so I am nearly up to date. We had a general service tonight conducted by Capt. Ashby.

Monday 27 November 1916

Nothing much doing today. There are a few papers knocking about now the mail has arrived so we can ....a few hours reading.

Tuesday 28 November 1916

Another of our rotten C.O.'s tricks. He has taken a tent belonging to one of the Companies to cut up to make caps for his nigger regiment. Not his own tent of course. A funeral party today. Lt Bridges of the 8 regiment. He used to be the R.S.M. before he got his commission so I went to pay best respects. The firing party was alright.

Wednesday 29 November 1916

A change of programme today as I am instructing the caps in drill and bayonet fighting, another fad after 12 months in the field.

Thursday 30 November 1916

I wrote home to you today. Busy with instructing parade.

Friday 1 December 1916

Parade as usual. Nothing much doing at present. Composing verses for a concert that we are having on Monday night.

Saturday 2 December 1916

Some good news on the ...... today. Quite a large number have surrendered to Monthys Force here . Hope it will help to bring things to a finish soon.

Sunday 3 December 1916

Ferguson expires – all (3) My prisoners finish up today. Had the Wesleyan parson down to dinner today and went to service this evening.

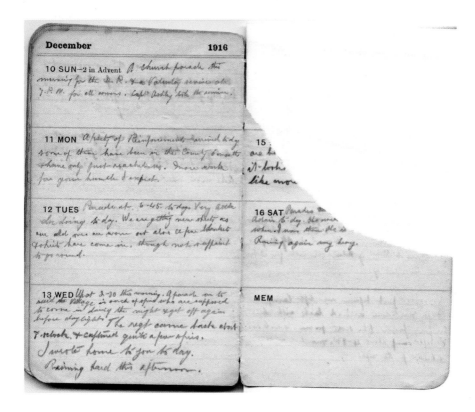

Monday 4 December 1916

A Court Martial today but as the evidence was not correct the boy got off. We had a concert this evening and everything has gone off first rate. We held it in Iringa inside the Boma wall. The German ladies were present and seemed to enjoy it as much as us.

Tuesday 5 December 1916

Harry Hall called round to see me this morning. We were taking it easy in bed when he came round. Nothing much doing today.

Wednesday 6 December 1916

Instructional parades today. It gets very hot here after 9 am so all parades have to be finished before that hour.

Thursday 7 December 1916

Batt. Parade this morning instead of the normal Company's. I am busy with the cross for Old Alf's grave. It will look very well.

Friday 8 December 1916

Batt. Parade this morning. A mail in today and 2 letters for me (21 Sept and 26 Oct.)

Saturday 9 December 1916

Nothing much today. Harry Hall came down to see us this afternoon. Many happy returns to the Mammy.

Sunday 10 December 1916

A Church parade this morning for the D.R. and a voluntary service ....for all ...... Capt Ashby took the service.

Monday 11 December 1916

A party of reinforcements arrived today some of them have been in the country 6 months ...only just reached us. More work for your humble......

Tuesday 12 December 1916

Parade at 6.45 today. Very little doing today. We are getting new sheets as the old ones are worn out also. A fine blanket and sheets have come in though not sufficient as normal.

Wednesday 13 December 1916

.....2.30 this morning. A parade on to aid the village in search of spies who are supposed to come in during the night and got off again before daylight. The regiment came back about .....
and captured quite a few spies. I wrote home to you today. Raining hard this afternoon.

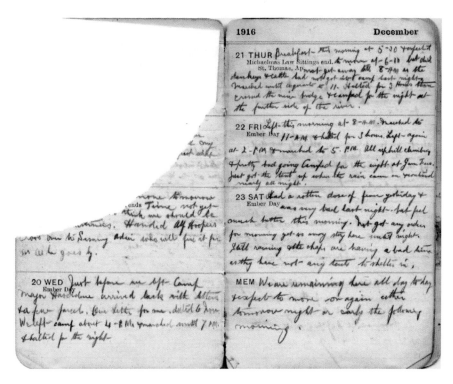

Thursday 14 December 1916

....

Friday 15 December 1916

.............it looks................like more....................

Saturday 16 December 1916

Parades......................He.............when I was there. He is.............
Raining again very heavy.

Sunday 17 December 1916

....

Monday 18 December 1916

....

Tuesday 19 December 1916

..........none tomorrow. ......Time not yet ....think we should be............ Handed Alf Hoopers cross over to Sammy Ad.... Who will fix it for us as he goes by.

Wednesday 20 December 1916

Just before we left camp Major Hazeldene arrived back with letters and a few parcels. One letter for me dated 6 Nov. We left camp at 4 pm and marched until 7 pm and halted for the night.

Thursday 21 December 1916

Breakfast this morning at 5.30 and ....tomorrow at 6.30 but did not get away till 8 am as the donkeys and cattle had not got into camp last night. Marched until quarter to 11. Halted for 2 hours then crossed the new bridge and camped for the night at the further side of the river.

Friday 22 December 1916

Left this morning at 8 am and marched to 11 am and halted for 3 hours. Left again at 2 pm and marched to 5 pm. All up hill climbing and pretty bad going. Camped for the night at Gum Trees. Just got the tent up when the rain came on ..... nearly all night.

Saturday 23 December 1916

Had a rotten dose of fever yesterday and was very bad last night but feel much better this morning. Not got any orders for morning yet so may stay here until night. Still raining and the chaps are having a bad time as they have not any tents to shelter in. We are remaining here all day today and expect to move on again either tomorrow night or early the following morning.

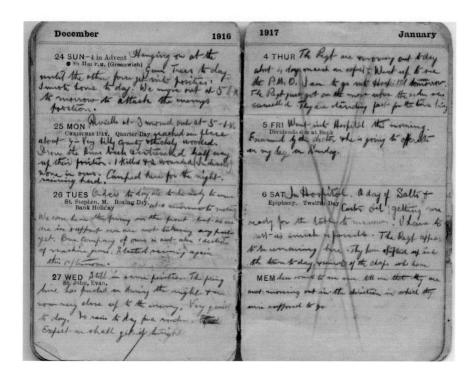

Sunday 24 December 1916

Hanging on at the Gum Trees today until the other force get into positions. I wrote home today. We move out at 5 am tomorrow to attack the enemy's position.

Monday 25 December 1916

Reveille at 3 moved out at 5 am reached our place about 7 – very hilly country and thickly wooded. Drew the Huns back and entrenched half way up their position. 1 killed and 2 wounded (Indians) none in ours. Camped here for the night.

Tuesday 26 December 1916

Orders today are to be ready to move at a moment's notice. We can hear the firing in the front but as we are in support we are not taking any part yet. One Company of ours is out also 1 section of machine guns. Started raining again this afternoon.

Wednesday 27 December 1916

Still in same position. The firing line has pushed on during the night and are now very close up to the enemy. Very quiet today. No rain today for a wonder. Expect we shall get it tonight.

Thursday 28 December 1916 to Wednesday 3 January 1917

The page for this period is missing from the diary.

Thursday 4 January 1917

The Regiment are moving out today about 4 days march are expected. Went up to see the RMD. I am to go into hospital tomorrow. The regiment just got on the move when the order was cancelled. They are standing fast for the time being.

Friday 5 January 1917

Went into hospital this morning. Examined by the doctor and he is going to operate on my leg on Sunday.

Saturday 6 January 1917

In hospital. A day of salts and castor oil; getting me ready for the table tomorrow. I have to rest as much as possible. The regiment appear to be remaining here and they have shifted up into the town today. Several of the chaps who have been around to see me tell me that they are not moving out in the direction in which they were supposed to go.

Sunday 7 January 1917

Been examined again this morning and I am for it at 2.30 this afternoon. Came too about 5 pm – feel pretty worthless.

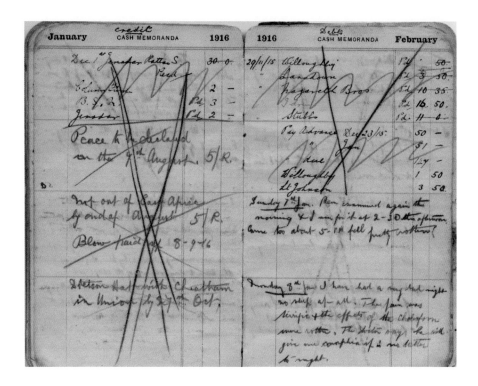

Monday 8 January 1917

I have had a very bad night – no sleep at all. The pain was terrific and the effects of the chloroform were rotten. The doctor says he will give me morphine if it is no better tonight.

Tuesday 9 January 1917

Did not wake up until about 5 am. The Dr gave me an injection of morphine last night that took all the pain away.

Wednesday 10 January 1917

Had a decent nights sleep – not so painful. Had Sam Adair And Wallie Heathy, Johnson and heaps of the chaps in to visit me.

Thursday 11 January 1917

In Hospital. Feel quite fit today had a lot of the chaps down to see me. Also Major Hazeldene came round to see how I was doing.

Friday 12 January 1917

In hospital getting along fine. Doctor says operation very successful but I shall have to rest a long time before I try any hard marching.

Saturday 13 January 1917

A good night last night. Doctor had to break open one of the wounds today. The others are doing fine.

Sunday 14 January 1917

Had a decent night. Quite a lot of our chaps came into see me today. I am much better today. Sam Adair came in. He is leaving Iringa tomorrow to join his regiment. He is with Marthys Force. (Mutton broth, roast duck and blanc mange.)

Monday 15 January 1917

Pretty good night. Had Johnson down today. And Duthie and a lot of the boys. Getting very fed up with being in here and unable to get off my back.

Tuesday 16 January 1917

Good nights sleep last night. Major Thompson came in to see me today. Says regiment is going back to the Union. I hope I shall be able to go with them. Hope to be about in a few more days.

Wednesday 17 January 1917

Had a good night. Got a letter today from you dated 4 Dec and also one from Mother dated 14 Nov. Had a lot of the chaps down today and they brought all kinds of gifts for me from them ....pipe, ...of tobacco, a jar of preserved ginger, soap,..............lozenges and all kinds of things which I thought jolly decent of them to remember me at all.

Thursday 18 January 1917

Decent night. Had the stitches taken out this morning. The doctor says I shall be able to travel in three or four day's time. Had Major Hazeldene and a lot of the chaps down to bid me goodbye.

Friday 19 January 1917

Good nights sleep. The regiment marched out this morning at 8.30 from Dodoma I hope to be after them in a few more days. The doctors let me get up for a few hours today. I was surprised how weak I was when I got on my feet. However, I managed to limp around with the aid of a stick.

Saturday 20 January 1917

Did not have a very good night. Had a different dressing on this morning. The doctor is sending me back to Dodoma tomorrow so I ought to be home shortly now. I got a nice Cheetah Skin today.

Sunday 21 January 1917

Had a good night. The cars came in this morning. Went to Iringa on stretcher in ambulance cars at 12.30 just before we left the doctor gave me a bottle of champagne to buck me up a bit. We reached the Ruaha river at 5.30 and halted for the night. We passed the regiment on the way at .....miles.

Monday 22 January 1917

Slept in the cars last night. Off this morning at 8.15 and reached Kua River at 11.30. Had to get out of cars and be carried across the river on stretchers on the pontoon and rest in the hospital tents with the cars came through the river. Left Kuruhi at 5 and halted at the escarpment at 6 o'clock.

Tuesday 23 January 1917

Left this morning at 8.30 after a good night with cars climbed the escarpment in good style. Our car cast a wheel during the afternoon and we had to be carried to another car. We arrived at Dodoma Hospital at 7 pm. Had a good meal and turn down to it about 8.30.

Wednesday 24 January 1917

Went up to see the doctor this morning and had the leg dressed and was put in 8 Division The food here is very good and plenty of it.

Thursday 25 January 1917

.... mate here is a Hull boy. He left Hull about 6 months ago when he was telling all about the Zep raids etc.

Friday 26 January 1917

Had a decent night. There are heaps of parcels here for our fellows. I suppose there will be one or two for me that I should have had months ago. Another heavy shower of rain today.. It will keep the regiment back as the roads are bad to begin with.

Saturday 27 January 1917

Got two parcels today with oxo, ...ph..........and ...., socks etc. Also a letter dated 20 Jan. I must try to get a letter away tomorrow.

Sunday 28 January 1917

Went over to see the chaps of the regiment in camp here. The regiment is expected in tomorrow or Tuesday. I feel pretty fit now and shall try to get over to them tomorrow. Got a tin of tobacco today from you. Arthur Rishton came to see me today. They expect to go away on Friday.

Monday 29 January 1917

In Hospital but expect to go out .... show .... 8 regiment.

Tuesday 30 January 1917

The regiment will be in tomorrow afternoon so Capt Ormond tells me as I am going out tomorrow. The chaps in camp here are busy getting ready for the regiment.

Wednesday 31 January 1917

I was discharged from hospital today. The leg is still weak but I want to be out when the regiment gets in. The regiment came in about 5 o'clock. I got 5 letters today, 4 from you and 1 from Fred Callow. The dates are Nov and Dec.

Thursday 1 February 1917
I took over duty this morning. There are heaps of parcels and comforts here. The chaps are loaded with tobacco, cigarettes, socks and all sorts of things that we should have received 9 months ago.

Friday 2 February 1917
Concert last night but as all the seats were reserved for officers we could not stay so came back to camp. The 8 Regiment left here for Dar es Salaam this morning.

Saturday 3 February 1917
More comforts given out today. I got a........parcel. I think it was from ....but the address was nearly off. Cigarettes, sweets, socks etc. Went to a Bioscope at the hospital but the rain came on ....

Sunday 4 February 1917

Church parade this morning. We have got orders to entrain for Dar es Salam tomorrow so that looks like going home. We leave in two trains. The first at 11 and the second after 5.

Monday 5 February 1917

Did not get away until 1 o'clock. Of course we are in trucks but these are covered so we don't mind.

Tuesday 6 February 1917

Had a rotten nights sleep. We got to Dar es Saleem about 11.30 and marched to the camping site. Very wet here and a nasty heat.

Wednesday 7 February 1917

Had a fine swim in the sea this morning. I am still very deaf. It is in both ears now so you can guess what I am like. Busy getting our kitbags etc. from Store. Mine was quite alright but some have been tampered with.

Thursday 8 February 1917

Rained heavy during night also this morning. Had a bit of a sing song last night at the YMCA tent. Kit inspection this morning for shortages and renewing. Got 2 letters today dated 17th and 24th Jan.

Friday 9 February 1917

The C.O. turned up today. Had a parade this morning and heard the damndest set of lies that it was possible to listen to from the C.O. Issuing kit today. Went to Dar es Salaam this afternoon. Got a few things to take back home.

Saturday 10 February 1917

The regiment parade this morning. Had a photo taken of the regiment this morning. Recruits parade at 4.30 Ben Johnson left us today to join the Pay Corps. Got my hearing back tonight. Hope it will remain.

Sunday 11 February 1917

Had a fine swim this morning. Hennie joined the mess in Ord. Room Sergent ... Johnson to the pay corp. Parades are still on in and the heat is absolutely unbearable but that does not seem to matter to our rotten C.O.

Monday 12 February 1917

Parade as usual. Busy getting kit made up today. Concert tonight. Freeth in the chair. The audience hooted him so you see he is popular. Very good concert indeed.

Tuesday 13 February 1917

Parade as usual. Johnson came down to visit me today. He has struck a jolly fine job.

Wednesday 14 February 1917

Parade this morning as usual in Batt. Formation for inspection by the C.O. Down town tonight with Ben Johnson and had a decent night.

Thursday 15 February 1917

Went down town today and bought a beautiful carving. Had parade today as usual in the boiling sun. The 8th regiment go aboard tomorrow. We sent our Heavy Kit today.

Friday 16 February 1917

Parade as usual today. We leave at 8 tomorrow. Went down town this morning for a final beer drink in the beer garden. Saw Ben and got some letters to post.

Saturday 17 February 1917

Reveille at 5.30 marched off 8 o'clock. Got Ben Johnson to send a cable away just before we left aboard the Kinfauns Castle about noon. Left for Durban at 3 o'clock. I am ship Sgt. Major for the voyage.

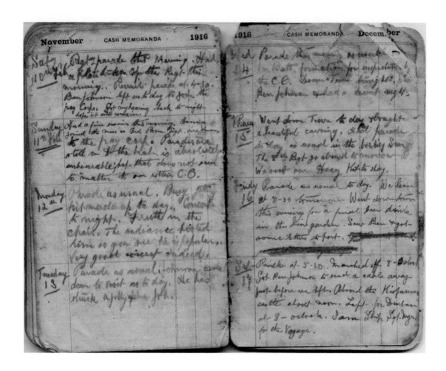

Sunday 18 February 1917
On Kinfauns Castle at sea. A very fine passage and enjoying it immensely.

Monday 19 February 1917
Physical drill this morning on the boat deck. Nothing doing in that line for me.

Tuesday 20 February 1917
Physical drill and nothing else much. Travelling very slow.

Wednesday 21 February 1917
Physical drill. We could have got into port today easily if we had kept going but we are only just moving. I don't know what the idea is.

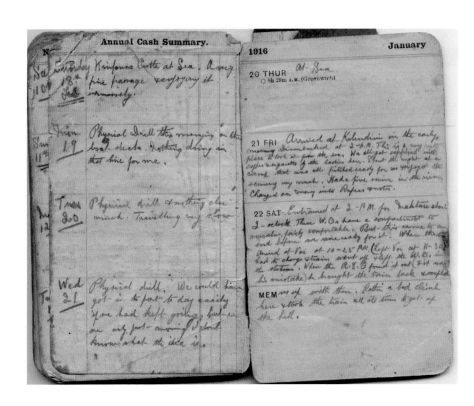

Saturday Kinfauns Castle at Sea. A very fine passage enjoying it immensely.

Mon 19 — Physical Drill this morning on the boat decks. Nothing doing in that line for me.

Tues 20 — Physical drill & nothing else much. Travelling very slow

Wed 21 — Physical drill. We could have got in to port to day easily if we had kept going, but we are only just moving I don't know what the idea is.

20 THUR — At Sea
Oh 29m A.M. (Greenwich)

21 FRI — Arrived at Kilindini in the early morning Disembarked at 2 P.M. This is a very pretty place to look at from the sea. We all got supplied with coffee & cigarettes by the ladies here. Spent the night at a camp that was all fitted ready for us enjoyed the scenery very much. Had a fine swim in the river. Changed our money into Rupees & notes.

22 SAT — Entrained at 2 P.M. for Mahtare about 3 o'clock. Three W. O.s have a compartment to ourselves, fairly comfortable. But this came to an end before we were ready for it. When that arrived at Voi at 10.25 P.M. (Left Voi at 11.30) had to change train went off left the W.O.s in the station. When the R.T.O found it out & it was his mistake he brought the train back & coupled

MEM — us up with them. Rather a bad climb here & took the train all its time to get up the hill.

7. Aftermath

William died suddenly in June 1917 after going into hospital for an operation on his leg. He had been weakened by fever. His funeral was held in Benoni with full military honours. The following is an extract from the history of the Witwatersrand Rifles – "A Bugle Calls" :-

"When one studies the history of the Witwatersrand Rifles in World War 1 one encounters the two dominant themes of complexity and paradox. The aspect of complexity is due to the disappearance of the group identity of the Regiment following the re-attestation of its former members in the European and East African contingents. This has involved a study of the movements of those units (principally 3 and 7 South African Infantry Regiments on the Western Front and East Africa respectively) in which former members of the Regiment served; and the corresponding endeavour to isolate these individuals and their contribution to these formations. In the process the roles of Capt R.F.C. Medlicott, Maj L.F. Sprenger, Maj B. Young, RSM W.R. Watson, L.Cpt R. Unwin and several others have clearly emerged. In order to carefully reconstruct the service of these personalities, it has been necessary to closely scrutinize the histories of the formations in which they were involved.

"To cite but one example, the achievement of W.R. Watson as Regimental Sergeant Major of 7 South African Infantry Regiment can only be fully appreciated (being but hinted at in the motivation for his Distinguished Conduct Medal) if one has an awareness of the trials and tribulations experienced by the unit during the period February – December 1916."

The War of 1914-1918.

South African Forces

No. 4421 R.S.M. W.R. Watson, 7th S.A. Inf.

was mentioned in a Despatch from

Lieutenant General The Honourable J.C. Smuts

dated 22nd November 1916

for gallant and distinguished services in the Field.

I have it in command from the King to record His Majesty's

high appreciation of the services rendered.

Winston Churchill

War Office
Whitehall. S.W.
1st March 1919.

Secretary of State for War

Coronation Medal
Volunteer Long Service medal
British War Medal 1914-1918
Victory medal
1914 Star
King's South African Medal with clasps
Queen's South African Medal with clasps Wittebergen,
Transvaal and Cape Colony
Distinguished Conduct Medal

~~~~~~~~~~~~

Witwatersrand Rifles Badge

2003—1/5/17—10,000

D.D. 240.

C.R.S/23144.

UNION OF SOUTH AFRICA.
UNIE VAN ZUID-AFRIKA.

IMPERIAL SERVICE CONTINGENTS.
IMPERIALE DIENST KONTINGENTEN.

DEFENCE HEADQUARTERS,
VERDEDIGINGSHOOFDKWARTIER,

PRETORIA, 19th AUGUST, 191 7 .

CERTIFICATE.
CERTIFIKAAT.

THIS IS TO CERTIFY that it has been officially reported that
HIERMEDE WORDT GECERTIFICEERD dat er ambtelik bericht is

ontvangen dat

No.......................(Rank)........ 2nd LIEUTENANT
No. (Rang)

(Name)........WILLIAM ROBERT WATSON, D.C.M.
(Naam)

of the........ 7th SOUTH AFRICAN INFANTRY :
van het

DIED

on (or about) the.. TWENTY-EIGHTH..day of........JUNE 191 7 .
op (of omtrent) de dag van

Next-of-kin... (WIFE) JANE SUSAN WATSON :
Naaste Bloedverwant

Address of Next-of-kin..... 204 HOWARD AVENUE ; BENONI ; TRANSVAAL .
Adres van Naaste Bloedverwant

MINISTER OF DEFENCE

LIEUT-COLONEL.

Officer in Charge of Records, Imperial Service Contingents;
Officier belast met Registers, Imperiale Dienst Kontingenten.

IB.

146

When William died, Jane was pregnant and she named her second daughter Olive May "for peace." The army assisted the family by arranging for the education at boarding school of her two sons, William (known as Bill) and Charles.

Bill seems to have been the one most influenced by his father. He was 9 years old when, dressed in his cub uniform, he accepted his father's war medals posthumously from Lord Buxton, Governor-General of South Africa.

Bill became a soldier like his father by joining the same regiment - Witwatersrand Rifles -

"in 1928 as a Company Sergeant Major... transferred to 1 South African Armoured Brigade Group in June 1943 ... saw service in the Western Desert in the Second World War ending his military career as Brigade Sergeant Major.

Capt Du Toit remembers RSM Watson as the finest Regimental Sergeant Major that he knew. Offered a commission on several occasions, he was plainly interested in being a Regimental Sergeant Major in the tradition of his father."

William Senior had attested as a private each time he enrolled and took commission only when it was offered and his son likewise "did not aspire to higher rank ".

Jane received an army pension of £9 per month. To augment this income, Jane, who was a good cook, took in 'table boarders' - people who came regularly and paid for a meal - and she did what she could to be self-sufficient by keeping chickens for the eggs and meat and growing vegetables.

She had a large grape vine, several yellow cling-stone peach trees and a hedge of quince trees. On occasions, she had taken in washing and ironing from the nearby boarding house to make ends meet.

Later on, Jane took in live-in boarders. One of these was David McCurdy who worked with her son, Charles, at Gray Smith the Grocers and became homeless after "his stepfather threw him out". Jane also took in twin girls, Betty and Carol Turner. They were friends of Toody and, on turning 16, they had to leave the orphanage where they had lived since they were foundlings left outside the Methodist Church. They worked in the same department store where Toody, who not only was the seamstress doing alterations to garments bought in the fashion department but also modelled clothes on occasions.

Toody recalls this as a happy time and her mother to be a sensible and stable influence with a quick wit and a saying for any problem or situation. Jane had a Phoenix treadle sewing machine where her daughters learnt to sew and her hobby was knitting jerseys for all the family. For help and advice, she consulted her copy of *Enquire Within upon Everything* published in 1906 and provided guidance to anyone:

> "Whether you wish to model a flower in wax; to study the rules of etiquette; to serve a relish for breakfast or supper; to plan a dinner for a large party or a small one; to cure a headache; to make a will; to get married; to bury a relative; whatever you may wish to do, make, or to enjoy, provided your desire has relation to the necessities of domestic life."

One of Jane's treasured possessions was the jewellery box which her husband had made for her from pieces of fine timber which he came across when working on the mines.

Jane remained a Londoner and a staunch Royalist all her life and always had sufficient money saved for a sea voyage home which she managed to do several times.

She was a hard-working member of the East Rand branch of the SOEWA (Sons of England Women's Association) and took pride in obtaining the most donations for this cause for she was not afraid to rattle her tin at anyone including the Mayor of Benoni.

But Jane had no time at all for the gold miners who went on strike in 1922 when the Chamber of Mines wanted to reduce costs and replace white miners with black ones. They caused mayhem all along the Reef, including Benoni where Jane lived, by rioting, setting the police station on fire and beating people with bicycle chains. Toody remembers when there was gunfire in the street that resulted in several stray bullets landing on the front wall of their house. The armed strikers were well-organised and it was a matter of time before they came knocking on the door of 204 Howard Avenue demanding weapons and donations.

However, Jane had no intention of meeting such demands. She had, Toody said, "had enough of killing" and it was many years later that Toody found out what her mother had done to thwart the militant miners.

One night when the moon was bright and everyone was asleep, Jane had taken the garden spade and gone quietly into the chicken run in the garden where she kept White Leghorn and Rhode Island Red chickens.

There she had set about digging a trench in the hard soil while trying not to startle the chickens into making a noise and disturbing the neighbours.

Then, she went and fetched William's gun case with its two rifles and ammunition and wrapped it in a blanket before going out to the chicken run and placing it in the trench she had dug. She filled the trench with the dry red soil, scattered the excess around and trampled the ground flat again.

There was no way that she was going to let marauding bands of disgruntled, vicious gold miners who were rioting over money get their hands on her husband's rifles. William would not want that. Better that his rifles also rest in peace.

8. References

Benoni History. Benoni Chamber of Commerce and Industries. Available from: http://www.benonicci.co.za/benonihistory.htm. [Accessed 8/03/2012]

Brown, J.A. (1991) *They Fought for King and Kaiser,* Johannesburg: Ashanti Publishing (Pty) Ltd.

Collyer, J.J. (1937) *The Campaign in German South West Africa 1914 - 1915,* The Imperial War Museum, London and The Battery Press, Inc.

Humphriss, Deryck and Thomas, David G. (1968) *BENONI Son of my Sorrow-The Social, Political and Economic History of a South African Gold Mining Town.* Cape and Transvaal Printers Limited, Cape Town.

Kipling, Richard. (1937) *Something of Myself - for my friends known and unknown.* Chapter VI - South Africa. Penguin Books.

Magwick, Houlston and Co. Ltd. (late Houston and Sons) (1906) *Enquire Within upon Everything* Paternoster Square.

Monick, S. (1989) *A Bugle Calls. The Story of the Witwatersrand Rifles and its Predecessors 1899 - 1987,* Germiston: Witwatersrand Rifles Regimental Council.

Struben, Charles. (1957) *Vein of Gold,* Cape Town: A.A. Balkema

Printed in Great Britain
by Amazon

Running
Marathons
for Charity

A practical guidebook for would-be charity runners

By
Gerry Hogg

MAPLE
PUBLISHERS

Running Marathons for Charity

Author: Gerry Hogg

Copyright © Gerry Hogg (2023)

The right of Gerry Hogg to be identified as author of this work has been asserted by the author in accordance with section 77 and 78 of the Copyright, Designs and Patents Act 1988.

First Published in 2023

ISBN 978-1-915796-13-4 (Paperback)
      978-1-915796-14-1 (E-Book)

Book Cover Design and Layout by:
     White Magic Studios
     www.whitemagicstudios.co.uk

Published by:
     Maple Publishers
     Fairbourne Drive, Atterbury,
     Milton Keynes,
     MK10 9RG, UK
     www.maplepublishers.com

About the Book

Can you run a marathon? Is there a charity close to your heart?

If you feel this venture is for you, there is certainly a pathway from the start of your training to the finish line. There is a mystique to running marathons, and this is often heightened if you are an amateur runner or a first timer because you are delving into the realms of the unknown. It is also given an extra edge if you decide to run a marathon for charity.

This book will help you successfully negotiate and sidestep many of the hidden hazards in marathon running. It will give you a training schedule that is easy to follow without any of the extra pressures associated with more competitive and regimented training plans. The book covers diet, injury prevention and your own training plan. It provides brief and inspiring stories from people like you who have successfully completed a marathon and raised funds for charity.

This book will instil in you a positive attitude towards your goal. Millions of people have run for charity, and you are no different. You will be guided all the way to the finish line – where you'll have a well-earned medal hung around your neck and you'll experience a feeling of elation and triumph.

About the Author

Gerry Hogg is a multiple-marathon runner who has competed in races all around the world. He has run 42 competitive marathons, including London 11 times and Berlin 3 times. He hails from Whanganui in New Zealand and now lives in Taunton, England, with his wife, Julia. He has one daughter, Lucy.

Gerry ran competitively in New Zealand for Whanganui Collegiate School, where he achieved the office of captain of cross country. He ran the qualifying standard as a schoolboy to represent New Zealand at cross country. He regards winning regional races in New Zealand in front of royalty – in the form of Prince Edward – as one of his more surreal cross-country-running highlights.

Gerry has been a fully qualified coach for over 10 years. He coaches at the Taunton Athletic club, as well as keeping his hand in with other local clubs.

Other interests include playing the guitar, heavy rock music and travelling the world.

Gerry moved to the UK in 1987. He previously worked at Queens College, Taunton, for over 35 years.

Dedication

For Don,

Who loved London,

Who never spoke, judged, or even advised. He didn't have to. He just watched with pride.

You watched me run as a little boy and teenager, but not as an adult. I guess you could say we ran out of time.

One of life's big regrets is not saying what should have been said at the time and saying things that shouldn't have been.

If only we'd had a little longer.

CONTENTS

Foreword

If completing a marathon is one of those bucket list things you would like to proudly say you have achieved, but can never really imagine yourself doing, the good news is that you are already closer to achieving your goal than you think. By the simple act of picking up this book, you have already taken your first step to completing your 26.2-mile challenge in the good company of a man who knows what he's talking about.

I met the author of this book for the first time over 15 years ago, through a shared passion for coaching and helping runners to achieve their goals. We've spent many a wintery evening in the build-up to the spring marathon season, standing roadside, watching runners train and chewing the cud over all things running related.

This wise and laid-back New Zealander manages to convey an unfaltering passion for completing marathons without the bug-eyed, adrenalin-fuelled, driven obsessiveness of some sports-mad enthusiasts. Gerry Hogg has a unique approach to marathon running – having competed some 42 marathons himself since giving up smoking in his twenties. He rarely seems to get injured; in fact, he takes so much recovery time between marathons that it seems at odds with his passion for running. And yet he is the most consistent marathon runner I know. I've come to value his sage-like approach to running marathons greatly over the years. It's straightforward, gently progressive and will prepare you for all that your marathon adventure may throw at you.

I can think of no better person for you to share your marathon journey with. Good luck and see you at the end!

Charlotte Fisher, Level 4 Coach

Acknowledgements

It's important for me to say that there are many people who have been instrumental in the writing of this book. I put pen to paper, but there is a group of you who made the eventual outcome possible. There are quite a few of you who have given me permission to use your name, a number of you who have been there and done it, so enabling me to use your stories and experiences to help inspire other future marathon runners. There are also those who have worked hard behind the scenes to help me produce this project. To all of you I am eternally grateful.

I feel I must mention a few of you specifically. I'll start by going all the way back to Texas to say thank you and a big 'howdy' to Steve and Paula Boone. When we were there for their race, the Texas Marathon, Steve and Paula looked after us and made us feel very welcome. I have so many fond memories: running in and winning their race, the massive medal that all the runners received, the copious amounts of pizza and soft drinks after the race, Steve and Paula giving us a lift home after the race and taking us out for lunch the following day. Yes, Steve, I agree: everything is bigger in Texas. Including the food portions! We have kept in touch to this day. Their history, as well as the story behind the Texas Marathon, is very poignant and an important part of this book in terms of what others have done in their marathons. Thanks, Steve and Paula, for your help and support and for taking care of us.

There are a number of people who work at Queens College, Taunton, here in the UK who have been extremely important, not just in helping me with my book but also by embracing my own marathon running and charity work over the years. We have raised thousands of pounds for both the NSPCC and Cancer Research. Thanks must go to Dave Cook and Laura Schofield who got the Queens College sixth form students to become involved with many of my London Marathon races. Own clothes days, quizzes, barbecues and pool tables all helped provide funds for the causes. It was Dave who, many years ago, got the ball rolling by speaking to the school's Chief Executive and getting the support for me. I can't thank Laura and Dave enough for their help.

I would also like to thank the school's art department. I happened to mention my book to Laura Burgoyne, one of the art teachers at Queens College. I asked her if the art students could design a picture for my book.

They used this project as part of their curriculum. So thanks must go to Bex and her team of Laura, Alison and Sandra.

One of the school's teachers, Mike Wager, looked at my book and did some early proofreading and restructuring. He gave me some good advice. Mike's incredible literary knowledge was worth its weight in gold. I owe Mike my thanks for his sound advice.

One of the former deputy head teachers at Queens College, Marcus Paul, also looked at a couple of chapters of my book a few years ago. As an English teacher he also gave me some sound advice. Having just written a book himself he told me to 'never give up' and being the quietly confident person that I am these words have always resonated. Thanks, Marcus, for your support at the time and encouragement.

Finally, from Queens I just want to say thanks to Matt, my sometime running buddy and something of a guinea pig running wise. I mentioned this book to him quite some time ago and many of the training runs for London we did were very similar to the structure of the training I have given you here. An awful lot of the training you will be undertaking in this book is partly down to experimentation in the training we did and getting things right, plus correcting things that needed tweaking. As an experienced marathon runner, I still learn from my own training, but by training with people like Matt and many others, I have been able to develop, trial and further improve the training schedules in this book. When Matt and I hit the road, we continuously talked while en route, we dissected things, looked for any early signs of niggles or injuries, noticed the feedback we got from the body while running – the lot! This is vital in terms of injury prevention and many other things. We do this with all our marathon runners, both seasoned and less experienced. The training runs we undertake with other runners and the feedback we get from them are an integral part of this book. Matt's successful London Marathon effort a few years ago is testament to this.

Away from the school there are more names I feel I must mention. One of these is a lady called Jo. I was given Jo's name through a friend called Fiona, who did our pre-marathon massages, knew. Jo also read through my work and corrected things that needed correcting at that time. For quite some time this book had not been the finished article and Jo certainly paved the way for me to carry on writing. Jo, your help has been invaluable – thank you!

I have mentioned the Taunton Athletic Club in this book. I must mention Charlotte Fisher. Charlotte is a level 4 coach and someone I have coached alongside for years at the TAC. Her knowledge, training sessions and overall mindset when it comes to all things running have been a fountain of knowledge for me. Charlotte has been one of the reasons that I continuously renew my coaching licence every three years. She has been very encouraging and taken an interest in this project and I have always felt welcomed by the Taunton Athletic Club. The club also helped put me through my coaching qualification process and have supported me all the way. This is down to Charlotte showing faith in me and thinking I was worth spending the money on. Without her I would not be here writing this book. Thanks, Charlotte, for your support, the sessions, the banter with our TAC runners and the evening chats about all things running-related. Let's hope we'll continue this for many years.

The very first running club of any description that I hooked up with was the Trull Troggers. Many years ago, I came across Brian and Sandra North. This was a rather difficult time for me as a few years earlier I had lost my dad to inoperable oesophageal cancer. Being so far away and getting a phone call to say your dad has passed away was not an easy thing to go through. Not being at his funeral to say the last goodbyes made it even harder. So I immersed myself in my running. This had not been planned. It just kind of happened because a guy I knew at the time, called Neil, who ran alongside me with another friend of mine called Derek, asked us if we would be interested in doing a couple of races. I entered them and did OK, getting a couple of podium finishes. This was the catalyst I needed – I stopped stagnating, spending too much money drinking at the pub and smoking cigars. I resurrected what could have been a rather promising running future after leaving school, and at the age of around 42 (after a 28-year hiatus) I joined up with the Trull Troggers of Taunton. I got to know Brian and Sandra very well, and the rest is history. Here I am at the age of 58 still going strong. The Troggers are still meeting up, and I still see Brian and Sandra. All I can say to both of them, as founders and main stays of this very popular and highly thought of club, is a massive thanks. This club got me back on the running trail, and I have a real affection for it. Brian and Sandra and the Trull Troggers paved the way for me to go on to much bigger and better things. Thanks guys – I owe you a lot.

While we are talking of the local Taunton running clubs, I have to mention Running Forever. I have not been down on the usual Wednesday night for quite some time to go running with them. They are the affiliated running club that I compete for. I must thank them for, years ago, welcoming me into the fold. I still run and compete for them, and although my coaching is done down at the TAC, Running Forever is the club whose colours I wear competitively. I know one or two of the committee members and know they do a sterling job keeping it going. I'd also like to include somebody we lost a while back, in 2019. I had known Mike Nicholls for quite some time from a running perspective and had always got on well with him. Mike was the Chairman of the club. We were liaising with each other before he passed away as he had said he could point me in the direction of his daughter who might have been able to help me with this project at the time. Like many at the club, I will miss him. RIP, Mike, and thanks, mate.

Lastly but certainly not least, while we are still on running clubs, I want to thank a lady called Jane Brown. Both of her children, Holly and Blair, were outstanding runners and were being coached down at the TAC. I had already gained my assistants coaching licence and they were looking for another coach just to help out. I was working in the school one day (both Holly and Blair were pupils at Queens College) and Jane, who was involved in the club, approached me to ask if I would be interested, and I was. She pointed me in the direction of Graham Fisher, Charlotte's father, who was also coaching down at the club. I contacted Graham, met Charlotte, and I am still there to this very day. As already mentioned, TAC helped put me through the process of gaining my full coaching licence. Wherever you are, Jane, thanks again. If you hadn't approached me back then, the last 15 years would not have happened.

One more running-based 'thank you' I must make is to my old Whanganui Collegiate School coach, Alec McNab. He not only taught me PE at school but also oversaw several outstanding athletes within the school remit. During the six years I spent at Collegiate, he took me from being a middle-of-the-pack runner, in what was a very strong team, to a 4th place at the national schools' cross-country champs and a 5th place in the road racing equivalent. The cross-country race was a performance that would have qualified me to run for New Zealand as a schoolboy. However, I did this in the wrong year. Had it been 1978 or 1980, I would have gone on to be an international runner. We didn't send a national team abroad in 1979. Those are the breaks! Alec also led the school's 4x400 m team to the national title, as well as various other notable performances. Am I showing off here? Yes, absolutely. Take me out of the equation for a moment. I want to explain just what he did for running at school. He set the bar very high, and we rose to this high standard. A fiery Scotsman who got the best out of us. He is another example of someone who has shown faith in me. Had it not been for him all of those years ago, I would not be here writing this book. Thanks for your help, Alec, and for showing an interest in this project when we last spoke. Now the borders have reopened in New Zealand, and that I can get back home, we will catch up again.

I'd also like to say thanks to a lady called Barbara Wilson, who did a thorough editing and proofreading job on my book. Mike Wager, the teacher at Queens I mentioned earlier, pointed me in Barbara's direction, and for the last few months she worked tirelessly on this project. She is a runner herself, so we have some common ground here. Her expertise is just what this project needed, and she keeps in touch with me regularly with advice and help when needed. Another reason the book took shape is down to Barbara's invaluable help. I needed someone to guide me here, and her knowledge and hard work has done just that.

Finally, I want to thank my wife, Julia, my daughter, Lucy, and my mum, Bev. Their support, especially at races and marathons, is a tremendous tonic. For 11 years in a row, Julia and Lucy were there at The Mall in London cheering me on. The Sunday mornings after I have done my 20-mile training runs, meaning for the rest of the day I am not much good for anything else, are totally accommodated. My hours of marathon training are never a problem. We have travelled the world with this passion and interest of mine and many times they have been there by my side. Julia and Lucy, thank you. I could not wish for a better and more understanding wife and daughter. As for my mum, she has never seen me run here in England. But she was a constant support to me in my running days at school in New Zealand. I owe these three ladies an awful lot. RIP mum.

To sign off, if there is anyone I have missed, I apologise. There have been many, many people with whom I have trained, coached, raced with and against and crossed paths. We all run for the love of the sport. Many of us put our running to good use. If you have been lucky enough to have the help and support of the many people I have, then you will find the whole running and charity thing an extremely rewarding experience. The best of luck to all of you and thank you all again. Happy running!

Introduction: the road to the finish line

'I have signed up to run a marathon for
charity, and I am full of self-doubt and fear.'

This is something that is heard often. Well, there is news for you: you needn't be! Running marathons for charity has become very popular. There is a certain mystique attached to running a marathon. This might be off-putting as you might be thinking that only an elite group of runners can achieve this. I'm hoping that this book will persuade you otherwise – and get you from your front door to the finishing line.

In late December 2009, in a hotel room in Humble (an area just outside Houston, Texas), I was lying wide awake in the early hours of the morning, just thinking. I wasn't suffering from insomnia or nervous thoughts about the impending Texas Marathon that I was due to run on New Year's Day. It was quite simply jet lag. However, it is said that the best thoughts come to you in the early hours, and that was certainly true in my case!

I began to wonder how many books there were out there aimed at helping people to run for a chosen charity. These events take place on numerous occasions and involve hundreds of thousands of first-time runners and experienced athletes alike – me being just one of them.

It may be just a short run for charity around the local track, a 5k, a 10k, half marathon or even the biggest beast of them all: the marathon! I wouldn't be at all surprised if the number of participants in these events runs into millions. After all, more than 36,000 people take part in the London Marathon – and most of them run for charity.

Anyway, this was the catalyst I needed to gather my thoughts and ideas and to begin to write a book aimed at helping both runners and non-runners in their quest to run a marathon for charity. I felt that first-timers in particular – those who may never have ventured onto the road before or whose running has been at a minimum – could benefit from a little advice. It surprised me to find out how little information there was (apart from the usual press reports, online information and articles in running magazines) to help and guide charity runners through the steps needed to successfully run 26.2 miles. Therefore, with such a large number of people running for charity, or wanting to, I thought it was time to put my thoughts and ideas into a book.

Many people have come to me saying 'I would love to run a marathon for charity, but I don't think I am capable'. 'Of course you can' is my usual response. Barring injury or illness, it is well within the body's capabilities to run 26.2 miles. While lying there at 2 am with these thoughts in my mind, I started to come up with ideas that would help other charity runners achieve their goal of successfully completing a first-time marathon, especially for a good cause.

I am a multiple marathoner myself, and there have been many highs and lows along my journey. More than once, 'the asphalt beast' has reared its ugly head with me at its mercy, so mistakes have been made. But it has also been possible to rectify them. Through trial and error (and a lot of reading and research), I have managed to acquire a practical know-how about marathoning, and I'd like to share this with you in my book.

Let me tell you about my first attempt. It was a disaster. I completely hit the wall. Luckily, my wife, Julia (who was a hospital matron at the time), was there to make me drink the proper fluids to stabilise my sugar levels. Otherwise, I could have gone under through hypoglycaemia. However, two years later, after a lot of tweaking and fine tuning, I ran the London Marathon (at the age of 47) in 2 hours and 37 minutes, coming 118th overall.

Through my long distance and endurance running, it has been possible to pass on my experiences to others and successfully help people – especially first-timers – run their marathons not just for themselves but also for charities. This includes people whose running has been minimal or perhaps non-existent. People have so many questions when they are considering running a marathon. How long should my training runs be? How fast should I run my training runs? How many miles should I run each week? What should I eat before running a marathon? What should I drink, and how much? The list goes on. I hope to answer all of these questions for you throughout the course of this book, and this will enable you to run with confidence, not just on your training runs but also on the day of the marathon itself.

I have just mentioned the word 'confidence'. This is an important word in the marathon-running vocabulary. It will be my aim to instil this confidence in you as you progress through your journey over the weeks and months of your training regimen so that you are ready for the big day. It is so very easy for someone like me, who has run 42 marathons, to say to you 'You'll be fine'. This is perhaps a little patronising for some people, and I quite understand if you feel this way. I know what a massive step this will be for some of you to take. There is an element of anxiety, even fear, involved, especially if you are not used to running. As you embark on this venture, and start to read this book, I hope that I can provide you with all the facts and information to guide you through everything you need to know and do to get through the 26.2 miles.

I will aim to quell any negative thoughts, anxieties or fears you may have about the big day, and even about the training itself. For example, let me say to you now that when you stand at the start line, having had a good, injury-free training schedule over the previous few weeks and months, there is a 99% chance you will finish – FACT! For more than 100 years, a huge number of people have successfully run marathons. Why should you be any different? There is no reason why you cannot have the utmost confidence in your efforts. Even if you are only half-thinking about taking on something like this, why not just have a go?

This book will help guide you around your first marathon and at the same time help you run it for charity. There are many worthwhile charities to run for, some well-known and some less so, but whichever charity you choose to run for, your efforts will most certainly be appreciated by those involved in the cause you are helping. Running a marathon for charity gives you a huge sense of achievement, both from the personal satisfaction and reward that comes from completing the physical and mental challenge and from the knowledge that you are helping those less fortunate through your fundraising.

It is important to mention at this early stage in the book that, if you do not have an athletic or social running background of any kind, it is vitally important for you to spend time preparing yourself for this. Aiming to run a marathon that is a year or more away is a great idea. It may seem a long way off, but it soon comes around once you decide to start your training. It will give you a good basic fitness and strong aerobic foundation. You will have time on your side and feel less pressure. When I have helped non-runners and more experienced marathoners in the past, it would be fair to say we have aimed at a goal which is months, if not a year, in advance. This is sensible thinking! 'Walk before you run' is good advice. In this book I will cover all of this and more.

You will not find pages and pages of training schedules in this book. Instead, I'll look at schedules on a more relaxed basis, building in plenty of flexibility, and complement this by discussing the types of training runs involved and how to carry them out.

Training schedules certainly have their place and are extremely helpful but, more often than not, these are just templates. These can be beneficial for many runners, including competitive runners who want to run personal best times, but you do not have to stick to any particular schedule. Having said that, if you find that a beginner's training schedule is for you, then that is fine. It is not always easy to stick to a regimented training schedule. We all have different things going on in our lives, and this often makes it difficult to keep strictly to a regular schedule.

As a coach and marathoner, I have found, through both my own training and that of others, that if a certain training run has not been carried out on a certain day, or the schedule has not been adhered to, it can cause unnecessary worry. So, as I say, just use a training schedule as a guide.

As a new marathoner you should only be concerned about incrementally increasing your mileage over a period of time. The main aim here is to successfully negotiate the 26 miles and 385 yards – and get there injury-free! This means forgetting how fast you run it; it is more about getting around and finishing. It is as simple as that. You will take a great deal of pressure off yourself by not worrying about target times for both your training and the marathon itself. So forget about speedy times and just focus your aims on consistency and simply hitting the road at a leisurely pace. I'll explain this in greater detail in Chapter 3.

If you are a person who enjoys helping a good cause, especially with the way the economic climate can be, you will find that your efforts will be appreciated. My running has raised funds for the NSPCC and Cancer Research UK, and it has been really encouraging to hear from their people just how welcome this fundraising has been.

You, the marathoner, are the important person here. You have the choice to run for any charity you choose. You may have one that is important to you. In Chapter 1, I will look at one or two stories of people who have raised funds for their chosen charities. Although the stories can be a little sad, they are certainly inspirational. You, the prospective marathoner, may just relate to these.

We all have to start somewhere. My first marathon was the Taunton Marathon in 2007 and, yes, it was for charity. But I ran it and prepared for it in the wrong way in every respect! I wished I knew then what I know now. I learned some invaluable lessons that day, and these have become the foundation on which I've built improvements in my own marathon running and in my fundraising efforts.

It would be fair to say, after that first experience, it could have gone either way. It was not a good experience for me. However, I was determined to learn from the experience. The need I felt to try again, to improve and to continue raising funds in the process was stronger in me than the urge to give up. My aim here is certainly not to put you off, but to bolster your attempt at your first marathon through my experiences. My first mistakes will be your strengths. You can learn not just from my 42 previous efforts but from everything I did wrong all those marathons ago – and when I say everything, I mean everything! If you feel the same way I do about marathon running and fundraising, then this book is for you. So read on – and good luck!

1 First steps

What I wish I'd known

Running your first marathon is easy – or so I thought until I attempted negotiating 26 miles and 385 yards for the very first time, lining up alongside 200 other hopefuls in the 2007 Taunton Marathon here in Somerset, England.

Now, before we continue, you may think I am trying to put you off when you read of my first marathon experience. Not so. It is just to emphasise that, without the correct preparation and groundwork, there are pitfalls that can booby-trap us along the way. I want to make sure that you understand what could happen if you go into this ill-prepared. This should in no way seem scary to you. All of the hurdles I am going to describe can be overcome. So, please, do not look on these challenges pessimistically – just the opposite. This chapter should most certainly encourage you and hopefully fill you with a positive feeling!

The aim of this chapter is to build a foundation and pave the way for the road ahead. This includes minimising all the risks that can hinder your marathon training. I will start by looking at why people have chosen certain marathons and charities for their fundraising. I will then explain how to choose your marathon and your charity. Finally, I will consider all the basic marathon-running preparation involved to set you on your way. There is some important work for us to do before you even hit the road in your training runs. But, without sounding condescending, it is not rocket science. It's just a case of getting the right structure and, as I say, building firm foundations. You can absolutely do this, believe me. With all of this on board, you can look forward to a successful training regimen, albeit a very relaxed one, with no added pressure.

So let's head back to Taunton to continue my story about my first-ever marathon ... three hours and two minutes later I staggered home over the finish line. I was finished, and for me it was a disaster. Since the age of six, I had been running competitively at every distance – from the 100 metres as a schoolboy through to the half marathon as a veteran adult athlete – so, with all my running experience, I thought I knew what marathoning was all about. How wrong was I! I hit the wall, walked, jogged when I could, staggered a bit – and just found the whole thing a huge wake-up call. But also a massive learning curve.

This wasn't the finish of it, either. Had it not been for my wife, Julia, I would have been really struggling after the race. Fortunately, because she is a nurse, she saved me from going into a dangerous post-marathon sleep due to hypoglycaemia. It was just a case of stabilising my sugar levels. But you can avoid all of this by eating, drinking and running sensibly, unlike me that day. In this, my very first marathon, I did everything wrong, and I mean everything! I did not train for it properly, and I ran badly on the day because I went off too fast.

From a training perspective, I had done nowhere near the right amount of mileage, both in my long runs and over the weekly training, to get me around in one piece. I was very capable over shorter distances, but this was a marathon, and this was different. I was arrogant and naive enough to think this would be just another race.

For you (and for me in this case), it is the long run that is the most important run of your training regimen. This is critical in terms of building what is considered to be a good, strong aerobic base. It is the most basic part of your training. Start learning now from what I did wrong here. I learned from this, and very quickly. Let my past mistakes be your strengths.

When I crossed the finish line, I had no feelings of absolute elation, the emotions which first-time marathoners normally feel after completing such a challenge. This is one of my biggest regrets in my marathon-running career – not having felt that natural high and feeling of achievement, knowing you have conquered the runner's equivalent of Mount Everest. I was quite pleased to finish my first marathon, but that was about it. I had lost my sense of enjoyment completely. Sure, I had finished, but it had not been a pleasant experience.

The one thing I do not regret, though, is having put my marathon running towards raising funds for a good cause. The marathon is an ideal fundraiser! Just look at the vast amounts of money that are raised every year by the London Marathon. Over half a billion pounds have been raised since it began in 1981. There is a lot of support for those of you who want to put your efforts towards running for a good cause.

Inspiration: everyone has a story

I will tell you why I have chosen to run for charity. With one exception, all my 11 London Marathon efforts have been for charity. Ten of these have been for the NSPCC, the National Society for the Prevention of Cruelty to Children. Quite simply, I don't like to see vulnerable children hurt or abused (or anybody for that matter), especially those who cannot fight back – hence my reason for helping the NSPCC.

My own daughter, Lucy, prompted me here. An advert for the NSPCC came on TV, and it must have been written all over my face. She quite simply said 'Dad, you want to do something about that, don't you?' She was right. I did!

The only time I raised funds for a cause other than the NSPCC was when I ran the London Marathon in 2012. I must take you back to 2008, when I had just run in the 10,000 metres during the South West Veterans' Championships at the Exeter Arena in Devon. After the race, I was sitting in front of Julia and her father, Arthur, watching some of the other events. 'Gerry,' he said, 'do you realise on the back of your ear you have what looks to be some kind of lesion?' Not being able to see it, I was totally unaware it was there. He then urged me to get it looked at as soon as possible. Both Arthur and Julia have a medical background, so they are pretty vigilant when it comes to health matters.

I went to my local surgery and was told immediately it was cancer. It was not benign, either, but was at the premalignant stage, fortunately. Trying to take all this on board, I felt a little numb – both concerned and relieved at the same time. The doctor blasted it then and there with cryotherapy, basically freezing it in its tracks. Luckily, I had got down to the surgery in time before any real harm was done and it had taken hold. Still, it was a strange feeling to have had something of a cancer scare.

Many Aussies and Kiwis (me being the latter) have skin cancer problems because of the very intense ultraviolet rays and the cleaner air over our part of the globe. We are very close to the hole in the ozone layer, so we have less protection. I think this is where my problem started.

Cancer is rife in my family. My father died young of cancer, and so did my grandfather on my mother's side. My mother has had skin removed for the same reason as me. So too has Arthur, probably from being under the sun too long when doing his national service in Iraq. Julia's mother has also recovered from two major operations to remove cancerous growths. Happily, everyone, apart from my father, has gone on to recover. This book is focused on helping you, the marathoners, in your quest. But I thought it was important to give you some background on why many of us want to raise money for good causes.

Ironically, as I am writing this section of the book, I have received the news that a very old schoolfriend of mine from New Zealand, someone called Richard, has recently passed away at an age that is too young after battling terminal cancer. By supporting these good causes, we can provide money to help bring about revolutionary breakthroughs to combat this awful disease. Losing friends and people I have known since a child, like Richard, makes me even more determined to try to do something to help.

Being inspired by others

Let me tell you about some of the people I know who have decided to run a charity marathon for causes that are close to their hearts. Their stories may prime you into thinking about your own reasons for running and perhaps about which cause you want to support. The decision is yours, of course, but the following few examples of charity marathoning may just be the catalyst you need to get you started. I hope you find these brief stories thought-provoking and enriching. They are simply about normal people with an agenda. There are a multitude of other inspirational stories out there, but these certainly inspired me.

Derek's story

I had a very good friend and ex-work colleague called Derek. Within a timespan of two weeks, he received two pieces of devastating news: that his wife, Doreen, whom I also knew, had been diagnosed with motor neurone disease (MND) and that he had contracted cancer. Unfortunately, Doreen lost her battle with MND but, at the time, on top of his illness, he decided to run the London Marathon and, of course, raise funds for a charity fighting the illness that took his partner. He confounded everyone by achieving this, including all the training, just weeks after losing his wife. This was a real show of determination and strength, which I very much admired him for. I hasten to add, he had weeks, not months, to train for this.

After all he had been through, he nailed it, running a successful London Marathon. A good mindset, a clear agenda and a sense of purpose certainly helped. He had a reason to do it. I can still see him in the charity T-shirt with the picture of Doreen on the front. I regard this achievement as heroic.

Very sadly, we lost Derek, too. He passed away in 2016. I fondly remember the races we ran together and the training runs we did with friends here in Taunton. We had a lot of fun, and he is sadly missed as a mate, as a former colleague at Queen's College, Taunton, where I used to work, and as a fellow runner and fundraiser.

Alec's story

There is another young man I run with called Alec, a former pupil of Queen's College, whose sister, Fiona, is my sports masseuse. They also lost their father to motor neurone disease.

Alec's agenda was also the London Marathon, and for the same charity. He finished in 2 hours and 56 minutes. Importantly, he raised a substantial amount of money for the cause.

Will's story

Lastly, I must mention one more person I have run and trained with. He's called Will and is also a former pupil of Queen's College. Having climbed Mount Kilimanjaro, Will decided that this was not enough and that he was going to run the 2010 London Marathon as well. He raised £6,000 for cystic fibrosis, choosing this charity because a family member suffered from it.

He had actually run the London Marathon once before, but was unhappy with his finishing time and effort, so he had another crack at running it under 4 hours. He succeeded in doing this quite comfortably, finishing in 3 hours and 53 minutes.

These are just three examples of people with fundraising goals who were driven to achieve their aim. We all have our own reasons for raising money for charity. These were theirs.

Which marathon should I choose?

I believe that it is very important to make the correct choice for your first marathon. By doing so, not only will you help yourself to successfully negotiate the 26.2 miles, but also you will find it much less of a chore! I am not saying for one moment that you will struggle to finish whichever marathon you tackle. I believe that, if you are focused and determined, you will finish.

Anyone can run their local marathon if there is one, and having one right on your doorstep is, of course, very convenient. However, by choosing a more prestigious one, such as London or Berlin, you will make running your first marathon a far better experience.

Please don't get me wrong here; smaller marathons have just as much right to be held as big ones, and I certainly like to see them supported. However, I believe you will help yourself by choosing a better-known event for your first effort. If this is not possible, then choose one with an added attraction.

For example, I have run the Midnight Sun Marathon in Tromsø, Norway. This was really quite surreal. You run during the hours of night, although it is still daylight all of the time. I finished just before midnight. It might as well have been midday! It is way up in the Arctic Circle. I have also run the Königsschlösser-Romantik Marathon in Füssen, Germany, where you are running in the foothills of the Bavarian Alps with these fairy tale-type castles in front of you. The setting is stunning and it's a pleasure to run there.

I am sure you catch my drift. You do not have to travel abroad, of course, to do a marathon. I have just used these as examples to prove my point. This would help to motivate you and certainly make the day memorable. I was going to suggest the Great Wall of China Marathon, but this is unbelievably challenging and most people's times are a good hour slower than they normally would be. You would certainly run or walk this simply to get around and say you have done it. But what an experience it would be!

Having run in smaller marathons and spoken to other runners who have completed less well-known marathons, I have concluded that there are greater benefits to running larger events first if you can. In a small event, there may be only 100–300 runners, and you could be out in the sticks with little or no one around you. The next water stop may be a couple of miles away and you have been on your feet for over three hours and are really losing heart. I have seen, and talked to, men and women in this situation who have literally been in tears.

Alternatively, imagine running the London Marathon, where you cross over Tower Bridge and run along The Mall and into Horse Guards Parade, or the Amsterdam Marathon, where you start and finish in the Olympic Stadium, or even the Berlin Marathon, where you run under the Brandenburg Gates to the accompaniment of thousands of people yelling your name and spurring you on all the way to the finish. There is no comparison. And remember, these are also flat!

All this big-event atmosphere dramatically increases your enjoyment and, more importantly, galvanises the likelihood of you finishing. You will take away a great memory of a momentous day, with a finisher's medal to boot!

The six Marathon Majors

Let's look at the biggest of the worldwide marathons. This may help to inspire you. These are known as the Big Six, or the Marathon Majors.

London, UK

This is a good one to start with. From a charity fundraising point of view, it is massive, with 75–80% of participants running for charity. They raise in excess of £50 million each year (indeed, nearly £900 million has been raised since it first started in 1981). However, it is very difficult to get into.

You can enter through the ballot, which gives you about a one in five chance of being accepted. You can also enter through the 'Good for age' scheme or get a 'Championship' place when you're competing for your club in the UK Marathon Championship. There are also guaranteed entries for anyone who can raise a considerable sum for a given charity. The London Marathon is a magnificent event in every respect. Many people would give their right arm to run in London, so, if you ever get the chance to do so, take it!

Berlin, Germany

This event is as big as London, and possibly the biggest of all six. Like London, it is fast and flat (London has a few undulations, but Berlin does not). Berlin is known as one of the fastest and flattest marathons in the world. Just for the record, Boston gets the quickest times. However, as it does not meet the criteria set out by the International Association of Athletics Federation (IAAF), world-record times cannot be set here. For this reason, world records are broken in Berlin more often than not. The marathons in Hamburg, Rotterdam and Stockholm are also very quick, but not nearly as big as any of the Big Six.

To give you an idea of the speeds set in Berlin, Wilson Kipsang broke the world record in 2013 in a time of 2.03:28. I was lucky enough to be running this marathon the year it happened – although he was a good 41 minutes in front of me! The world record was broken again in Berlin in 2014 by Dennis Kimetto in a time of 2.02:57. It is now held by Eliud Kipchoge (2.01:39) – also achieved in Berlin.

Berlin is a fantastic city to visit. You feel safe there. Like London, it can be a little warm, with temperatures getting up into the twenties, but I would totally recommend it. As with London, there is a ballot system for entry.

Boston, USA

The Boston Marathon is the oldest marathon in the world, having been first run in 1897. There is a historical side to the city, too, since this is where the seeds of the American Revolution were sown.

To run in Boston, however, you need to have run a marathon already, and achieved a qualifying time in any other certified race. There are different qualifying times for different age groups, so, if you are able to qualify for this race and have run another within the qualifying time, then great.

It is highly regarded in the USA. When I was in Texas, I asked the organiser of the Texas Marathon, Steve Boone, which other marathons he would recommend running and, without hesitation, he said Boston. Steve knows his American marathons, having run one in each of the 50 states. So his answer was good enough for me, and it is the first of the American marathons I want to run. It is quite downhill, apparently, although it does have the infamous 'Heartbreak Hill', which can make or break you.

New York, USA

Now, whereas I would like to run Boston from a marathoning and historical point of view, my wife and daughter are hell-bent on persuading me to run New York! For most people, New York is probably the favourite of the American marathons to run – it certainly wins from a shopping and sightseeing point of view.

New York is perhaps the most challenging of the Six Majors. It still comes under the 'flat marathon' category but, having talked to runners who have run New York, I understand it is an undulating route with a few climbs, and perhaps this makes it a little tougher than the others.

The swirling wind conditions can make it challenging, too, and it can be cold there in November. I can still remember as a teenager watching Alison Roe of New Zealand (our own former world-record holder plus Boston and New York winner) lining up in New York in gloves! Paula Radcliffe, likewise. So, if you run New York, prepare for a colder temperature.

However, it must be fascinating to run through places such as the Bronx and Central Park. I have a running friend who has run New York twice, and raised a considerable sum of money for the UK Heart Foundation on both occasions. He could not recommend it highly enough.

Chicago, USA

Chicago is flat, like Berlin – and relatively fast, too. In fact, if you want to improve your time or work towards a personal best, this is possibly the best of the Six Majors to run. It's ideal for a first-timer, too. Boston can be quick, but you have to reckon with Heartbreak Hill. Chicago is known as the Windy City, and the windy conditions can cause havoc when not favourable. Like Berlin, Chicago has a lottery, or ballot system, along with qualifying-time criteria if you want to get in.

Tokyo, Japan

This is the most recent of all the marathons to be given Major Marathon status. The Tokyo Marathon has been running since 2007 and, unlike the five other Majors, it was pretty big from the outset. It has grown considerably and attracts around 36,000 runners.

The Tokyo Marathon is supposedly a little downhill, although fairly flat. But the weather can be the problem here – it can be very windy, especially in the last few miles near Tokyo Bay. It can also be cold, and there may be a few snow flurries. However, on the other hand, it can sometimes be sunny, too. So the weather is a bit of a lottery – but what a fascinating city to run a marathon in!

That was a brief summary of the six Marathon Majors. The following marathons may also interest you.

Other marathons

The Paris Marathon is also very big, and the registration fee is cheaper if you enter early. It is also unique in the way you need a doctor's certificate to confirm you are physically fit enough to run it. This, in a way, goes back to what I was saying about consulting your doctor. The marathon takes in such sites as the Louvre, the Eiffel Tower and Notre Dame. It is also pretty flat.

As for marathons in the UK, there are many to choose from, such as Luton, Edinburgh, Belfast, Loch Ness, Brighton, Liverpool and Manchester. The Royal Shakespeare in Stratford-upon-Avon is very popular.

The Brighton Marathon is very new and is becoming very popular with runners. A marathon-training partner and friend of mine, James Watson, of the Taunton Athletic Club, has run Brighton for the charity Kids Get Going. The Brighton Marathon is highly recommended by him and many others.

I feel that, once you have made your decision and chosen the right marathon for you, then you have an agenda. It will help encourage you to make the effort. If you have already entered a particular marathon, you will now have to go out and do the work. Good for you! This will be the start of a great adventure.

Whether you want to run something big or something a little out of the ordinary, the choice is yours, so choose wisely!

Which charity should I choose?

After looking at a few marathons, albeit briefly, now is the time to decide on your charity. Doing it now is not imperative, but if you do have a specific charity in mind – and especially if you sign up for a particular marathon – this will give you an agenda and an aim.

If you have not yet run for charity, let me quote Lucy MacAlistair, an elite marathoner who has represented Great Britain and who won the 2008 Austin Marathon in Texas. She told me about how her perspectives were changed after running in the London Marathon as a lead to a blind runner.

> Its effect on me has been long-lasting as, until then, from my first marathon to my last, I had only ever run marathons in the elite field, so I hadn't really experienced the atmosphere and camaraderie of running in the crowd with charity runners. The purpose they had was so different from chasing a qualifying time, which was always my goal. This new experience – with the added complexity, challenge and experience for someone running it without sight, but only with the sound and internal feedback of running the marathon – was incredible. It opened my mind to the bigger significance of the race and supercharged senses other than sight, which enabled me to share and enjoy the experience of my running partner. I would recommend that all elite marathon runners, at some point, should experience their sport from a different perspective, as it has since helped me to enjoy and experience running as more than just time on the watch.

Contacting your charity

I think it is important at this stage to think about which charity will benefit from your marathon – and to find out when that marathon is going to take place. I think it is a good idea to consider doing a marathon that is anything from six months to a year away, without worrying at this stage about the amount of training you will do in the future. A long-term goal is great as it gives you plenty of breathing space, and your training can be done one step at a time.

You would do well to contact your chosen charity at this point as they will (or should) be very keen to get you on board. Let them know what you are going to do. There may be associated training groups you can hook up with. Or you may just prefer to train independently of them. You will certainly be sent a sponsorship form and probably a vest and other potentially useful things. They may well send you training tips and offer to contact you if you need extra help.

A pre-training checklist

Firstly, how much experience of running do you have? You may never have run at all – or only run for enjoyment, perhaps to keep fit. On the other hand, you may be a club member, running competitively or just for the social side of it. Whatever your experience, if you have never run a marathon, you are still a novice marathoner, and must not try to take on too much too soon. Fortunately, though, even if you have never run before, you can still train for and run a marathon just as successfully as a more experienced and regular runner as long as you train correctly. So don't be afraid of giving this a go. I will give you advice to make sure you train correctly.

Secondly, what is your fitness level like? If you are happy with your fitness – or your GP, for example, has given you the all-clear to get started – then you are good to go. However, if you have any doubts about fitness, get some advice. If you are in work and would not be able to work if you picked up an injury when training, it could cost you dear.

Thirdly, do you have the correct footwear? Regardless of which shoes you may have bought, you need to try them out and see how they stand up to the training involved. If they are OK, they will mould into the shape of your feet and you will get used to them. However, if at any stage you are unhappy with them, then they might not be the right shoes for you.

Fourthly, do you have the correct clothing? Clothing should be comfortable enough so it doesn't rub or chafe. Avoid cotton as it is heavy and will rub when wet. You would do well to experiment, so on your training runs wear the clothes you will be wearing on the day of the marathon. If you have been sent a vest from your chosen charity, wear this and get used to it.

And lastly, what is your diet like? Sometimes people get a little concerned about this, when really it is something that is easy to get right. At this stage, if your mileage is going to be minimal, then diet will not be such a necessary concern. The importance of a good balanced diet (and enough fluid) will increase, however, as you progress into your training and as your mileage increases.

Questions to ask yourself

I am now going to take you back to the running side of this book. Perhaps reading about my first marathon experience, earlier in this chapter, was enough to make you run away from any marathon, not run in one! I certainly hope not. My aim is to help and guide those of you who have decided to run a charity marathon – from your first mile to the finish line.

You may think that running a marathon is just a case of clocking up your mileage in training runs, avoiding injury, turning up on the start line ready to go and, of course, finishing. That is partly true, but you will need to make sure that you do not make any basic errors and that you prepare yourself correctly. You won't go far wrong as long as you do as I suggest and run sensibly.

As the title of this chapter suggests, there is a place you have to start from – the beginning. I will look at some guidelines that will not only help you to start running but also take you to the start of your marathon training.

If you are new to running, it is a very good idea to get a little experience under your belt first. There are some very important areas here that will take you up to this starting point, and no further. I will go through them one by one in this section. Perhaps it will be a good idea to take a look at yourself first before even attempting to hit the road. There is a good, but obvious, saying when taking on a marathon. One step at a time!

So here is a suggested checklist of some things to consider before beginning your marathon-training schedule. These questions will help minimise any risks involved and ensure you start off on the right foot.

Am I too old to run a marathon?

This is a very good question. Your level of fitness, rather than your age, is the best indication of whether you can undertake the challenges of a marathon at this stage in your life. If you have any history of illness or injury, it is very important for you to consult your doctor. If your physical fitness is fairly good, but you still have doubts, please still consult your GP and tell them that you are preparing to take on this challenge! They may actually give you all the encouragement you need to begin your marathon journey. It is worth noting that, by taking on a marathon-training schedule, you will improve your quality of life by maintaining a high standard of physical fitness. You will feel better all round, both mentally and physically, and it will encourage you to lead a healthy lifestyle. So it really does tick many boxes.

As a first-time marathoner, you need to understand that it is not a boot-camp style of training regimen. However, there are some very long training runs you will have to carry out and you will need to be in a reasonably good standard of physical fitness, so, please, if you are unsure, ask your doctor! Be sensible and only take on what you are capable of handling.

To help encourage the older ones amongst you, let me tell you that there are marathon runners who are in their nineties. One is an incredible gentleman by the name of Fauja Singh, who ran his first marathon, the London Marathon, in 2000. He was 89 that year and went on to become the first-ever 100-year-old marathoner. He ran his last 10k a while ago and then retired from running competitively. He still jogs every day, though. He holds records for his age group in many races. He ran the 2012 London Marathon in 7 hours and 45 minutes – at the age of 101!

By the way, it took me 43 years to get round to running my first-ever marathon. I have now run 42. I hope this encourages you older ones to hit the road. Personally, I think Fauja Singh is a huge inspiration and an incredible human being who puts the question of age into perspective. You are never too old.

Am I too young to run a marathon?

Quite possibly. Most marathons have a minimum legal age requirement of 18. I believe there are some marathons that have a minimum 16-year-old age requirement. Mind you, I have heard of marathons in countries where there are runners as young as 10! Anyway, if you are aged 18 or over, and have a burning desire to run a marathon, then I suppose no one is going to stop you.

However, my personal opinion is that you should leave it until you are a little older. There are an awful lot of microscopic traumas that occur in the muscle fibres when running, especially in a marathon. The body takes a real hammering (we will go into the physiological side of what happens when you run a marathon later), but your body is capable of taking this punishment. Over the months of your training schedule, you will prepare your body and mind for this, and it will stand up to it. However, care needs to be taken with young bodies that are still growing and developing. This is especially true for female runners, who may encounter what is called the triad syndrome. The cells, cartilage and bones in the growing bodies of young adolescents are softer and far more susceptible to damage and injury. This could lead to potential problems when combined with the long training runs and issues related to diet, low immune systems, etc.

I think you can see where I am going here! The marathon is far more suited to the older body. By 'older', I mean anything upwards from the early twenties on, which is when you have stopped growing. I strongly urge you younger runners, or anyone at an adolescent age, to run shorter distances, such as 5ks, 10ks, 10-milers or half marathons. Run the quick stuff while you are younger. As you get older, the speed goes a little, but the endurance kicks in a little more.

Not too many sprinters would be running at their best beyond 35 or so. Look at Haile Gebrselassie or Martin Lel, for example, who were still racing marathons competitively in their mid-30s! Even at amateur level, you can run to a very high standard, and that would include running a marathon simply to get around and finish. So my advice is to finish growing and only then think about serious marathon running – ideally, beyond the age of around 25.

What should I wear?

Your trainers and clothing are vital in terms of being able to train comfortably and, of course, to avoid any injuries.

Running shoes

There are a few reasons why injuries occur, shoes being one of them – and perhaps not in the way you might think. Both too much cushioning and an elevated heel can cause injuries rather than minimise them. I will look at injury prevention later in the book and running shoes will be discussed then, too. But I want to look at trainers in a little more detail here because, without the right shoes, how can you expect to get through all the training and the marathon itself successfully? It is your shoes that will carry you through this long journey, so they are very important. After all, if you become badly injured, you will not be running anywhere. This section on shoes is quite long but, as I say, it is such an important topic, so I hope you will bear with me here. If you are already sorted in terms of trainers and this does not interest you, then please skip this section.

Along with normal, standard trainers, there are shoes you can buy that are called 'minimalist' running shoes. Minimalist shoes are designed to have you running in a more natural way, which is closer to barefoot running. There is less padding in these compared to normal trainers, and this has become big business in the world of trainers.

You may already have a pair of trainers that suit you and you are happy with, and that is fine. These may be minimalist training shoes, too. If you are used to minimalist trainers, then keep using them. However, if you do not currently wear minimalist shoes, then I would certainly not recommend you trying to adjust to them as you begin training for your marathon. Changing to these shoes can be effective over the long term, but they take some getting used to and your calf muscles will ache for a while. You are teaching yourself how to run in a whole new way in terms of your gait and running style.

Finding the right shoes is mainly down to trial and error. If, for example, you have been running for a while, you may have been going out and doing runs of up to 10k (6.2 miles), and you may be very happy with the trainers you use. Don't forget that you will be doing much longer runs than this, so some experimentation is a very good idea. I would certainly advise you to look online and research the best type of trainer for you. You'll need a pair that can withstand the miles in your training schedule – which will take you up to at least a single 20-mile training run – and those of the marathon itself. This means a total mileage of somewhere between 300 and 500 miles (depending on the level you start training at) and perhaps more – so your shoes need to be able to stand up to this.

Just briefly, as an aside, please do not be concerned or put off by this seemingly high amount of mileage that you will be running. It is quite deceiving. All the shorter runs of 3–4 miles quickly mount up and you soon build up the mileage. It is important not to become too focused on the bigger picture at the beginning. Just concentrate on your running target each day and week.

To help you find the right trainers for you, I would recommend having a gait analysis done. There are places that offer a gait analysis all over the country – usually good running/sports shops. The analysis involves running on a treadmill for about 20–30 seconds and having your style monitored – how you land, where you land and whether there are any misalignments within your ankles or knees. They will then recommend the type of shoe best suited to your running style in order to prevent injury.

If this doesn't appeal, you could just find out what shoe is best for you through trial and error, and by simply hitting the road to see which shoes suit your running style. However, using a trial-and-error method may seem a little hit-and-miss – and it may prove a little expensive if you have to try more than one shoe. So, if you can get a gait analysis done, it may save you getting a few blisters and be kinder on your pocket.

Be aware of the shape of your feet and of different 'pronations'. Underpronation means your feet roll outwards, and overpronation means your feet roll inwards. Pigeon-toed people and those with high arches, like me, are more likely to underpronate (or 'supinate'). But duck-footed people and those with flat foot arches are more likely to overpronate. These particular biomechanics tend to determine which type of shoe is most beneficial for each individual person. If you are neither, however, then a neutral shoe may be the one for you.

As I said earlier, research has shown that too much padding on the heel of a shoe can cause injuries rather than prevent them. This makes sense because a lot of padding and cushioning causes a heel strike rather than a midfoot or even a forefoot strike. Your heel striking the ground is a totally unnatural way of running. Just try running up the road unshod and landing on your heels. You won't get far. It hurts. You have to run with a mid- or fore-foot strike.

Minimalist shoes are another option, but they might not be the right shoe for a first-time marathoner of limited running experience. James, my running buddy, was full of praise for Newton Gravity minimalist shoes and has made this transition. But there was quite a long transition stage after running in normal trainers – and sore calf muscles to boot! There is a risk of injuring yourself here, too, if you try to do too much too early in minimalist shoes.

Just for interest, if you run barefoot on the road and land on your heels, the force generated is something like 2.5–3 times your body weight. One analogy that has been used is that it is like a hammer hitting you on the heel at three times your body weight. The impact force of running downhill is also multiplied by around 15 times. So you can imagine all of this stress travelling up through your legs and core. Therefore, you can see how important it is to get this right in terms of footwear. If you are unsure about whether you have high, neutral or low arches, you can do the wet towel test. By wetting your foot and putting it onto blank newsprint or a white towel, you can see the shape of the sole of your foot. This will show what type of foot arch you have.

I have used Mizuno Wave Riders and Brooks Adrenaline before, which I liked. I have also used New Balance 890 version 3 and version 5, both of which I found outstanding. They cost me around £40–50 at a reduced price. I found they can take nearly anything I throw at them, from short, sharp, fast training to long endurance runs of 20 miles and over, and up to a marathon itself. The New Balance 890 v3 is probably my favourite shoe to date. It is also very light. However, this is just my personal preference. Your shoes will also eventually mould into the shape of your feet, just as mine have.

A few years back, my daughter, Lucy, and I went into a sports shop to find a pair of trainers for some running, as she was quite keen on hitting the road for a couple of miles with the possibility of entering a road race at some stage in the future. The young sales assistant told us it was vitally important to have as much padding as possible for road running. There was no asking if she would prefer a neutral shoe, what gait she thought she had, how far she would be running, whether it was for 5k or 10k runs, half marathons, off-road running or the like. We politely said thanks for the advice and left.

Do not be talked into buying a very expensive pair of trainers with a lot of unnecessary padding. We are all built differently, so get what shoe suits you. Do some research. I am quite happy to spend somewhere in the region of £40–60 for a decent pair of shoes. When you do decide on a pair, and they suit, it is a good idea to have a second pair of the same shoes as a backup. Rotate them if necessary and don't start to wear the second pair new nearer the time or in the marathon itself. This could be a recipe for disaster.

Break them in, too. Your feet will mould the shape of the shoes and a brand-new pair that have not been worn will not have the same shape as the ones you have been wearing – even though they are the same! This is important.

Other clothing

This is perhaps not as crucial as getting the right footwear, but still important, especially in terms of rubbing and chafing. It is a good idea to avoid wearing any vests that are made of cotton or any heavy material, especially if it is raining or wet. This also includes shorts.

I have had chafing only once. This happened when I was running in the rain and the shorts I was wearing were rubbing on my inner thigh. This was most unpleasant, and it stopped me from running for 3–4 days until it cleared up. You may think a little rubbing isn't too bad. Wrong. Chafing can be very disruptive, and this was.

The best way to combat this is to apply Vaseline to any areas that are likely to be affected. Vests and T-shirts can rub and cause bleeding of the nipples. You should find clothes that suit. Try them out on your long Sunday runs. Once again, on your long runs, try to wear exactly what you intend to wear on the day of the marathon.

What stage am I at?

Obviously, the beginning is a very good place to start. I am not trying to be patronising here. It is true. A few times in the past, I have talked to people who got a little too keen about the training involved in their schedule and were doing too much too soon. Don't put yourself at risk of injuries, or overtraining syndrome, by being too eager. It is important that you start from the beginning and get a good foundation to your training.

The analogy of building a house is a good one to use. You don't build a house by putting down a flimsy foundation and walls, and then putting a heavy roof on top. Of course, it will collapse. It's perhaps an unusual analogy to use, but marathon training is similar to this. You need a strong foundation, which is the basic training you will do at the beginning of your schedule – that is, runs of short or minimal mileage just to get you underway. I suppose you could say this is at ground level.

You have to start somewhere, but this basic training paves the way for longer runs requiring greater endurance later on. These foundation runs will be no more than six miles and will be run at the slowest pace you feel comfortable with. Speed at this stage is unimportant. In fact, as you progress, you should not run any of your training runs at an intensive pace – unlike marathoners, who are training to run competitively. But I will discuss this later in the book.

In the analogy I used before, the walls of the house are the runs of medium mileage that you will do. These are distances of between six and nine miles. Why nine miles? Simply because it is not into double figures! I think it is psychologically easier to get your head around running mileage in single figures at this stage of your training. For some people, running 10 miles or more can seem a little daunting at this stage. As I said earlier, you need to take it one step at a time.

Lastly, to finish our analogy, there is the roof of the house, in other words your long runs. I regard anything over 10 miles as long-run territory. Anything over 14 miles I call very long-run territory. Again, you may ask, why 14 miles? Quite simply because half marathons are 13.1 miles long, so 14 miles or more takes you into the realm of the unknown. Many runners train for and run half marathons. But this is a step beyond! By this stage you will have built up a very good endurance base, which will enable you to run very long runs up to and including a marathon.

So, taking all this into consideration, we will start from the beginning and look closely at the training runs you should be doing over the coming weeks and put it into some sort of order. You will build up to a single 20-mile training run, which you'll do around three weeks before the marathon.

I think it is very important to assess your fitness levels before starting on your marathon-training schedule, especially if you are new to running. If you have any doubts at all about your fitness, consult your doctor. Explain to them that you are hoping to take on a marathon-training schedule over the coming weeks and months.

Before we look ahead to the training you will be doing, I think it is fair to say that we all have different abilities when we start our marathon training. There are some people out there who are already used to running. Some of you may already belong to a club and race regularly, perhaps anything from 5k up to marathon distance. You may even run to a very high standard. Therefore, your training will be somewhat different to the novice first-time runners.

I know quite a few first-time marathoners who have run stunning times. I mean well under 3 hours. But they run competitively. There are club runners, though, who are just happy to compete at their own level. If this is you, I recommend that you aim to finish and no more. Save the more intensive stuff for your second or third marathons, if you decide to do any more, and feel you want to improve on your first marathon effort.

As this book is really aimed at first-time marathon runners who just want to complete their task of raising money for charity, it is important that you don't get too concerned about going out and doing very long, intensive training runs of very fast speeds. Instead, just concentrate on miles on the road, and on building up this mileage at your own leisure.

As I said before, speed is not the essential thing – mileage is. It does not matter how long it takes you to build up your mileage over the weeks and months. Give yourself plenty of time and don't put yourself under any unnecessary pressure by giving yourself too little time – for example, by choosing a marathon that is perhaps less than 16–20 weeks away. I would really look at something that is a good six months to a year away. Some coaches recommend a year of just running before you even think about marathon training. You are perhaps the best judge of this, as you as an individual know your own fitness levels. Personally, I think if you give yourself 6–12 months, that will be enough time to get up to marathon-running standard. Don't forget that it is not about breaking any records; just aim to complete it. So this should give you enough time.

Thinking positively

One thing that will help you considerably is to go into this challenge with a positive mindset. Now, don't worry if you think this challenge is bigger than it actually is. I have drawn up a few guidelines that you can follow as you go through your training, which I will pass on to you as you progress through your training schedule. These guidelines are tried and tested – some of them are factual and others are pure common sense. In the training I have done preparing for my 42 marathons, I have used them many times, and I wish I'd had the knowledge when preparing for my very first marathon.

In the past, I have done either too much or too little training. I now have a far more relaxed attitude in terms of the amount of training I do. It is far better to be a little undertrained than overtrained. This may sound contradictory, but, when we look at it, it will make perfect sense. I will explain this further as the book progresses, but there is a real danger of doing too much!

A sensible attitude towards your training is important. If, on a particular training run one day, you are not feeling 100%, it does not matter if you reduce your mileage by around half the distance, or even more if necessary. Or if the going is getting tough, but you are able and determined to complete the run, it does not matter one bit if you stop and walk, just to complete your workout. Walking is allowed – contrary to the opinion of some!

It does not matter, either, if you forfeit a training run, perhaps because of an illness, or if you have a slight niggle that might get worse, or for any other reason. This will have very little impact on your overall fitness levels. The loss of fitness levels over the course of a few days is going to be minimal in this kind of situation. Easing off when necessary is actually the sensible thing to do.

By taking thoughts like this on board, you are making it easier for yourself because the challenge will not seem quite as daunting. It is, in fact, just common sense, too. I often used to feel guilty and a little concerned about missing a couple of days of training, but now I don't. I know that it can actually be quite beneficial. In my own training for running competitive marathons, I have now added a week off into my training schedule. This is just to recharge myself both mentally and physically.

Another sensible guideline comes from Hal Higdon, the world-famous marathon-training coach, who says in his book *Marathon: The Ultimate Training Guide*: 'It is better to walk because you want to, not because you have to.' This is very good advice both for your training and for the marathon itself. Think of yourself as being in control here. Think 'I am calling the shots', not the other way round. 'I am the boss in this situation.' Notice the positivity kicking in here! This should help you to produce and maintain thoughts of a positive nature.

When I look at people who are training, I remember the experience of a good friend of mine. He is called Matt, and he was a non-runner. Our challenge was to get him up to standard for the 2011 London Marathon. He was also raising money for a mental disabilities charity, the Orchard Vale Trust. His is an encouraging marathon-training story for any of you who have self-doubt. Matt's story is an ideal case of what can be achieved by having the right mindset and through positive thinking. He was absolutely focused on the challenge and had an iron will. Please don't think I am dismissing any of you who have self-doubts – I will try to alleviate those. I am just using Matt as an example of what can be done if you are in the frame of mind that he was.

Basically, Matt had nothing to be afraid of when looking at the situation and weighing up the reasons as to why he should succeed against why he shouldn't. Everything was overwhelmingly in his favour. It should be the same for you, too. He simply did not entertain any ideas of failure within his brain, even though sometimes it meant not quite hitting our targets or forfeiting the occasional run for whatever reason. However, it would be foolish to think you are invincible. This is why, when we were running together, Matt and I often discussed how he was feeling, both mentally and physically at that moment, and how we could combat the challenges ahead. Your body, in a way, speaks to you. If it isn't happy with the way it is feeling, it will soon tell you!

Our mid-run discussions helped in terms of fighting against injury and overtraining syndrome. So going out for runs was not just about getting fit. It ticked more than one box. The feedback your body gives you is very important. Take notice of every little thing you may not be too happy about. By nipping things in the bud early, you can avoid bigger problems later. In Chapter 2, I will be looking at injuries and how to avoid them.

Leaving Matt for a moment, let's concentrate on you, the prospective marathoner, and look at the reasons why you can approach this training, and the marathon itself, with some degree of confidence. I would be lying if I said it was going to be easy. However, you can make it as easy as you can by adhering to some fairly simple tasks. This quest is not impossible. It is important that you get this into your train of thought.

The following would actually make a good mantra to say over and over to yourself as you are running: 'It is well within the body's capabilities to train for and run a marathon.' Sure, things can go wrong. But by training and running sensibly you can certainly minimise the risks considerably. I work on this all the time with other marathoners that I help coach. I am always watching to see if they are doing too much or if there are things we may need to tweak. It will work for you, too.

Obviously, accidents or pure bad luck could scupper your training, or keep you out of the marathon. But as far as training goes, sensible training and running will get you to the start line. I really mean this. It cannot go any other way. You can't become less fit by training for your marathon, as long as you do it properly. You will improve your fitness and general overall wellbeing both physically and mentally. You will maintain a balanced and healthy lifestyle by taking this on.

Let me tell you that every challenge and fear you may have about this venture can be surmounted. Keep telling yourself 'This is achievable'. Use it as another little mantra and you will start believing it. And, as you progress, I will give you little snippets of information and reasons along the way as to why you can do this, and that will help put you in a relaxed frame of mind. Meanwhile, if you're already feeling confident about running a marathon, that's great. Good for you!

My parting shot at the end of this chapter is this: There are millions of people of your ability who have completed a marathon. You are no different, so why shouldn't you succeed?

2 Pre-training considerations: diet, hydration and injury prevention

Diet

As with rehydration (which we'll cover later in this chapter), eating the right things does not really become important until you pick up the mileage later on in your training runs. However, it does not mean to say it is unimportant either, as there are certain foods you still need.

Carbohydrates are the marathoner's fuel. I just want to give you a basic grounding on what carbohydrates do. There are carbohydrates in many things you eat. You get carbohydrates in food such as bread, potatoes, rice, pasta, and also in fruit and vegetables. When you eat carbohydrates, your body converts them into what is known as glycogen, which is then stored in the liver and muscles. Glycogen is the readily available fuel in the body. This means that your body has no problem accessing this to fuel the muscles to run. Although fat is another fuel in the body, it is harder for the body to access and burn, so glycogen is the fuel that is tapped into first. You will not start to use up the accessible glycogen in your body until you start to hit a mileage of around 16 miles (or 2–3 hours of running). So, if you are running a mileage of 10k or less, then you will always have glycogen readily available in your body.

Glycogen is a sugar in the form of glucose, and is known as a 'slow-release' fuel for longer mileage. However, refined sugar is what you would have for much faster races such as 5k and 10k – and even up to half marathon distance. It is known as a 'quick-release' fuel. It has always been believed that refined sugar gives you what is known as a 'sugar rush' or 'spike' and is burned extremely quickly to give you your speed over quicker, shorter distances. There are different types of sugar, but the sugar I am talking about here is what is known as 'simple sugar' or sucrose. The sort you put in tea and coffee.

I had always believed that refined sugar was something to be avoided at all costs when running longer runs and marathons. I thought there was a risk of 'crash and burn'. Now there seems to be research suggesting this may not be the case. Basically, if you take sugar in your tea or coffee, or on your cereals, keep doing so. It will not negatively impact your training. This is unless you are on a diet-conscious training regimen; then you will be trying to avoid it most of the time.

The other part of the diet question here is about taking on board protein. Protein is vital for repairing the muscle damage that happens when you run, especially over longer distances. But it is also important for you to take this on board at the outset of your training runs.

When you run, you actually damage the fibres within your skeletal muscles. Skeletal muscles are the muscles that are connected to your skeleton and, when you run, the muscles in your legs are obviously the ones that take the brunt and impact of the forces produced. Do not be concerned by the term 'damage', as this is a totally normal physiological part of your running. The soreness you feel after a run of any intensity is muscle fibre damage. The pain you feel walking up and down the stairs, for example, is the soreness derived from this fibre damage. It is known as delayed onset muscle soreness (DOMS) and is quite normal. You will probably feel it more around 48 hours after exercise.

There is also a common misconception that this soreness is caused by lactic acid. In fact, lactic acid (or lactate, as it should be called) goes back to its original levels after one hour of even the most intensive exercises. Your fitness levels increase when the muscle fibres start to repair themselves. Once they repair themselves, they become stronger, meaning your fitness levels rise and you can run faster and longer than before.

By eating food with protein in it, you are helping to speed up the repair and recovery process of your muscles. Protein helps rebuild muscle fibres. Therefore, this makes what you eat in order to help this recovery process quite important. Protein foods are things like milk, eggs, cheese, meat and fish. The idea is to get protein on board after exercising as a way to help you rebuild your muscles and be up to speed for your next training session.

I used to believe firmly that, after exercising, there was a window of opportunity to get protein on board as a way to help rebuild your muscles, and be up to speed, for your next training session. However, a while ago, here in Taunton, I attended a workshop on nutrition run by Renee McGregor, who is a registered dietician and sports nutritionist working with many elite marathoners and ultra-runners. She said this:

> If you have another training session scheduled within 12 hours, then recovery within 30 minutes of finishing your session is essential. Carbs and protein milk are an obvious choice (certainly chocolate milk). If, however, your next training session is well over 12 hours away, then recovery with your next meal (within 2 hours) will be sufficient.

I was very grateful for Renee's workshop as it put me right and taught me something I was unaware of. She also told us there is no need to be obsessed about carbohydrate loading during our training regimen and reinforced the fact that a balanced diet ticks most boxes.

Therefore, the bottom line here is to refuel, take protein on board and rehydrate, without being too obsessed about it. As first-time marathoners, your sessions will not be too intensive yet and probably not within the 12-hour window. So simply go with the flow, eat a balanced diet and perhaps get some protein on board within two hours of your training run.

Regarding recovery drinks, let me mention chocolate milk. I have been using this for post-run and race recovery for years now. Despite all the different types of electrolyte and recovery drinks out there on the market, I feel none of them really are quite as effective as the chocolate milk drink. I am not dismissing them completely, as they are all good at aiding recovery and replacing electrolytes. I just do not feel they have that extra edge that chocolate milk drinks have. They have protein, the essential electrolytes you need, plus carbohydrates and sugars. Recognised sports drinks brands have also put protein shakes on the market, and they are fine and tick all the boxes. But chocolate, to me, beats the lot; it is cheaper, too.

In case you are not aware, electrolytes are the salts (such as calcium, sodium, potassium and magnesium) that you lose through sweat when running. However, with any runs of less than an hour or so, the need for this sort of recovery is not as great. By the time you are running 10k distances, your muscles will also be more toned and less prone to fatigue and soreness.

For those of you who are lactose intolerant and who cannot have chocolate milk, there are protein shakes containing whey or soya on the market. However, if possible, milk in your diet is ideal for recovery after a training session. The combination of protein and calcium is great for muscle repair and bone strengthening.

Finally, if you're concerned about your hydration, the next time you go out for a run of limited mileage, take note of how thirsty you are. Take your bottle with you if that is what you do. But you will probably find you are drinking water just because this is what you feel you should do. I used to take a bottle with me on my long runs, but I found it just hindered my running style and I could not run as freely, so I stopped taking one. However, do what you are most comfortable with. We are going to look at hydration a little more closely now.

Hydration

Before reading this section on hydration it is very important for me to say that regarding hydration you must do what suits you and keep it safe. I must again reinforce the fact that I am not a medical person. I have spent years working on hydration strategies that work for me, but remember that the way I run, train and hydrate may be different to what you should do. If you feel you need to hydrate in your training runs, and this is what you always do, then carry on doing so. I have written this section from the perspective that the body can deal with a certain amount of dehydration, and it is actually better and safer to be a little under hydrated than over hydrated. This is all explained in this section. But please do what works for you, keep it safe and listen to your body.

People feel a great need to take on water when it is not actually quite so imperative. You may think this is a slightly risky opinion, but I say this with the utmost respect for the human body in this situation. When undertaking long training runs and in the actual marathon, the human body will soon tell us when it needs a little top-up in fluid. Unfortunately, many new runners think it is necessary to increase their water intake even over shorter distances.

The body can put up with a lot of dehydration and, in fact, it is better to be slightly dehydrated than over-hydrated. This may seem a little strange to you. But think about it – it is easy enough to take fluid on board if you need it, but it is not so easy to expel it once you have drunk too much. Yes, you will sweat some of it out and may be able to go to the loo, but this will make for an uncomfortable training run or marathon if you have to keep making pitstops! Too much water can also sit in your stomach, sloshing around and causing gastrointestinal problems. However, you should be aiming to avoid being both dehydrated and over-hydrated when running your marathon and long training runs.

So how much water do you need to drink? When starting out with training runs of minimal mileage, then very little, if any. If you are eating a balanced diet, you will be taking on more fluid than you actually think you are. By eating fruit and vegetables, and by having the normal amounts of (non-alcoholic) liquids that you drink through the course of the day, you are continuously rehydrating.

There is a common misconception that tea and coffee will dehydrate you. This is not so. They are diuretics, so you visit the loo more often, but they are not a cause of dehydration. Alcohol is, though, and should be avoided at certain times. So, if you are a big drinker of tea or coffee, the diuretic effect in terms of fluid loss is minimal. The only side effect of this is, of course, more loo stops.

A word about carrying water with you. I often see local joggers going for an easy jog around the block once or twice. They are running probably no more than a mile or two. I notice they often carry a water bottle with them – even in cooler temperatures. It could be that they simply feel comfortable doing this, which is fine. However, the body will not really become that dehydrated over such a short distance.

Perhaps they feel they have to take on fluid, rather than waiting for the feelings of thirst over such short distances. But the bottom line is this: if you are thirsty before a run, possibly dried out after an evening at the pub, then rehydrate with a glass of water first – or, even better, save your run until the following day.

When I have been out with my wife and daughter for low-mileage training runs, my daughter has run between two and four miles on her jogs and my wife around a mile to two and they have never needed to take a water bottle. But if this is your security, keep doing it! It is very important to be comfortable with what you do. Just remember that you should already have enough fluid in your system to see you through any low-mileage training runs. It will only be on your longer training runs, and especially on warmer days, when temperatures might go up into the high teens or twenties, when there will be a need to rehydrate properly.

I would suggest that, over short distances of 1–3 miles (2–5k), you experiment to get to know your own body's limitations. Start by taking a bottle with you for reassurance. If you find after a short run you don't need it, and you don't run too far from your home, then next time try without it. Above all, do not be afraid to try again if your first effort does not go according to plan. Over time, your whole physiological system will get used to and will adapt to the stresses you subject it to.

Even when you begin running distances of over a mile or so, not much will change as far as rehydration goes. Many coaches and nutritionists will tell you that your body's normal levels of hydration can sustain a run of anything up to 10k (about 40 minutes' running). Even over this distance, the body will not need much rehydration. If the temperatures are up in the mid to high twenties, then by all means take your water bottle with you – or make sure you are rehydrated pre-run. And if it is a race, there will be water stops if you need them, so you won't need to carry water with you.

Heat exhaustion

It may surprise many of you that recent research suggests that heat exhaustion may not be quite so connected to your levels of hydration as you may think; it comes from simply running too fast in high temperatures. On hotter days, the core temperature of the body rises, and the heat given off by the body does not disappear into the air as efficiently as on cooler days. This is exacerbated if the hotter temperatures rise while you are running. When you exercise or run, there is friction in the muscles which generates heat. The faster you run, the more heat you generate – in fact, too much water will do more harm than good. The only way to bring your core temperature down is to run more slowly – and generate less heat. But rehydrating before is still vitally important too.

In Finland, a few years ago, I ran the marathon for New Zealand in the World Masters Track and Field Championships. The temperature that morning was in the twenties, and it peaked at about 33 degrees Celsius. As

Finland is full of water, having something like 180,000 lakes, the humidity was very high, too. It was extremely uncomfortable, and most people's times were at least 5–10 minutes slower than normal. I had run 2 hours and 38 minutes in London only five months previously, but in Finland I had to settle for 2 hours and 49 minutes. Even with the fine-spray sprinklers en route (which are far more effective at helping lower core temperatures than drinking copious amounts of water while running), I simply had to run more slowly.

That experience had me taking a little more fluid on board at the water stops. Drink when you feel a little thirsty; this is far safer than guzzling large amounts. You lose a lot of fluid when sweating and this fluid needs to be replaced, but keep it minimal because drinking too much can lead to hyponatremia (which we will look at later on).

Much will depend on the timing of your marathon. If you decide to run a spring marathon, say in London, Paris, Brighton, Manchester or (locally to me) Taunton, much of your training will be done in the cooler autumn and winter months. However, if you decide to run an autumn marathon, such as Amsterdam or Berlin, you will be training through the summer months, so just take care to train and run sensibly according to the conditions.

If you train for over a year, then you will encounter all conditions – snow, ice, heat, rain, the lot! You may also need to use a treadmill if conditions become too treacherous – or even forfeit a run or two. Do not worry; you will soon pick it up again.

Here are a couple of tips for you if the temperatures start to rise when you are running. Firstly, try to run in the shade if it is safe enough to do so, avoiding traffic, of course. Secondly, it is a good idea to wear a hat – perhaps also pouring some water into it from your bottle or at water stops before putting it on. I suppose, it would be fair to say that, if your brain is overheating and not operating correctly, then the rest of your body will struggle to function efficiently.

A foolproof way of knowing how hydrated you are is by observing the colour of your urine. If it is the colour of pale straw or practically colourless, you are very nicely hydrated. If it is a darker yellow colour, then you will need to look at rehydrating more. However, the bottom line here is that your levels of hydration will be perfectly adequate for low-mileage training runs providing your diet is balanced and you regularly take on fluid during the day.

Injuries and how to avoid them

Frustration and pain are two things that runners just want to avoid when training or competing. By adhering to some simple rules, you can certainly help minimise the risks of becoming injured or suffering from overtraining syndrome. Without wanting to worry you unnecessarily, there are some fairly common runners' injuries that I think we should look at. I am no doctor and would not pretend to be an expert on the human body, but I have been around runners for long enough to know something about the more common injuries runners can succumb to.

It is important to know the difference between acute and chronic injuries. Acute injuries, such as sprains and breaks, happen immediately and are more traumatic, whereas chronic injuries are those that happen over a period of time. They are more degenerative, and you will get dull aches and pains that gradually get worse. The injuries we are looking at in this section are mainly examples of chronic injuries.

Plantar fasciitis

One of the most common causes of pain in your heel or ankle is plantar fasciitis. The plantar fascia is a fibrous tendon that runs from the bottom of your heel along the foot bone to the toes underneath. It basically acts as a support and shock absorber to your foot, and it can get inflamed if you are not careful.

Just for the record, unlike a ligament (which attaches bone to bone), a tendon such as the plantar fascia attaches muscle to bone. It is predominantly collagen, which, unlike muscle, does not bring much blood flow to the injured area. This means it takes longer to heal.

There are many causes of plantar fasciitis. These can include overdoing hill work, overtraining, overdoing speed work, not stretching properly and not strengthening your calf muscles and Achilles tendon. There are also biomechanical reasons, such as high or collapsed arches in the feet.

Your footwear can contribute to this – for example, wearing high heels and then immediately putting your feet into flatter trainers or shoes.

Wearing old and worn trainers is another possible cause. You may find you can wear yours for a lot longer than the recommended 500 miles. That is fine and will save you some money. But just be careful, particularly if (no disrespect) you are of a heavier build.

I would also avoid running on grass. Only those who are used to it and have the strength and flexibility of the foot and ankle tendons and ligaments should try this. I have certainly heard of people with feet issues running on grass and it has helped them. But I do know that the foot will be stressed by grass running, so my recommendation would be to keep right off it.

One of the main symptoms of plantar fasciitis is a sharp stabbing pain under the heel. It is usually more painful in the morning when you get up. It basically feels like a hot needle being stabbed into your foot just under the heel. It is more noticeable when the plantar fasciitis has started to heal itself after long periods of inactivity. When you take your first few steps in the morning, the injury tears again after having started to mend itself.

Recovery from this sort of injury is not quick, but one thing I would recommend is putting your feet straight into footwear first thing in the morning to take some of the strain off the unstretched ligament. This happens because, after inactive periods with this injury, the plantar fascia shortens and so, when stretched, it will cause some pain.

If you can, wear footwear with orthotics all the time, from first thing in the morning until you go to bed, and do as many of the following stretches as possible.

Sit down on a chair with a belt, towel or something similar wrapped round the ball of your injured foot. Hold each end of the belt and gently pull the ball of your foot towards you and then relax it. Do this about 15–20 times, holding for about 20 seconds before relaxing it.

Similar to the above, stand on a step with the ball of your foot on the step and the rest of your foot over the edge of the step. Gently drop your heel so that it is below the surface of the step, then raise it back up so that it is level again. This exercise works on the same principle as the exercise above. Do this 15–20 times, holding it for 20 seconds, 2–3 times a day. You can use this stretch as an alternative to the first one, or do both. Do not be aggressive with it. It is a gentle stretch. Try to do the first set of stretches first thing in the morning.

Get a tennis ball. Put it on the floor and roll your foot over the ball backwards and forwards and around and around for about 5 minutes. This should help relieve the pain and gently massage the plantar fascia and surrounding area.

Try the iced-bottle massage. This is a stretch or massage that you can use to reduce inflammation on your injury, while gently stretching the plantar fascia at the same time. It should help to soothe some of the pain of the injury, too. You get a soft drink bottle, or water bottle, fill it with water and freeze it. You then roll your foot over the frozen bottle for up to 10 minutes to stretch the plantar fascia.

Another couple of options worth trying are night splints and Strassburg socks. The splints are rather like a boot you can wear at night that will stretch the plantar fascia while you are sleeping. The Strassburg socks do the same thing as splints and are probably more practical than splints as they are less bulky. Both of these keep your foot pointing up – known as dorsiflexed. The splint or sock keeps your foot continuously stretched overnight, which means you do not have the re-tearing, or re-stretching, of the already healing and contracted plantar fascia.

Since prevention is better than cure, you would do well to strengthen your calf muscles. There are two muscles to target: the gastrocnemius and the soleus. The gastrocnemius is the big muscle just below the back of the knee. The soleus muscle is another big muscle that fuses into the gastrocnemius and is just below it. Stretches and strengthening exercises are a good idea to help prevent injuries.

Heel raises are particularly useful for preventing plantar fasciitis. From a normal standing position, raise your heels off the ground so you are standing on tiptoes. Hold this for around five seconds, then lower your heels again. Do this about ten times, three times a day. This will also help strengthen the tendons in your feet – but do not try these if you already have a plantar fasciitis problem.

You can also stretch the two calf muscle groups. To exercise the gastrocnemius muscle, stand about an arm's length from a wall, place one foot behind you and keep it straight. With the other leg, lean into the wall, bending at the knee. You will feel the calf muscle stretching at the back of the leg. Hold for 20–30 seconds. Do not overdo it by stretching it too far, though. Repeat with the other leg. For the soleus muscle, as with the gastrocnemius muscles, stand facing a wall, placing your hands on it. Then put one foot about 12 inches behind the other. This time, slightly bend both knees and lean into the wall until you feel it stretch and no more. Again, hold this pose for 20–30 seconds. Repeat with the other leg. For all static stretches, do not bounce. Bouncing can produce a pulled muscle. Just feel your way into the stretch and hold it there for the allotted time.

My experience of plantar fasciitis

Back in 2010, I was in the middle of my training for the London Marathon when, a few weeks out, I noticed this uncomfortable feeling around my ankle area. It was not too bad for a week or two, so, naively, I did not take too much notice. First mistake! One evening I was off doing a training session with a running group I was meeting up with and it actually seemed a little worse; however, I carried on out the door and met up with the group for a more intensive session. Second mistake!

As we ploughed our way through the session, the ache around the ankle became more pronounced. The best way I could sum up how it felt was an achy tightness. By the time the session finished, I jogged back home. Actually, I didn't really jog; I limped. Now, common sense would say, if I had to limp home after a session, I should not have gone out the door in the first place. Or, at least, I should have cut my session short and gone home earlier. Big lesson learned.

It wasn't too long before the pain got worse, especially first thing in the morning. By now the uncomfortable feeling around my ankle had become a sharp isolated pain underneath my ankle bone. Everything pointed towards me having a plantar fasciitis injury. However, my doctor told me it was mild and that, as far as running the London Marathon was concerned, I would probably be OK. This was a big relief because, as usual, I was raising money for the NSPCC, and not running would have meant a deferral until the following year. I was lucky enough as I would still be able to run if I managed it properly.

Armed with some advice from my doctor and by doing some research myself, I began managing my plantar fasciitis injury. The first thing I did, though, was to keep off it. I did not run on it for eight days. I had a very intense period of concentrating all my efforts into doing everything I could to help the injury. I bought myself some orthotics to put in my trainers and all the shoes I would be wearing. That even included my work boots! I also began a stretching programme, which had me doing stretches in the morning, during my lunch hour and in the evening. I also made sure from the moment I got up until the moment I went to bed that I was wearing shoes (or boots at work). I got myself a tennis ball and a small coke bottle full of iced water, and I rolled my foot over them. After eight days, the fasciitis was still there; however, it was feeling slightly better.

Fortunately, my injury was mild. A full-blown plantar fasciitis injury will have you off for months, if not years. I was lucky enough to be able to finish off my London Marathon training and I ran London successfully, raising a tidy sum for the NSPCC. I hasten to add that, although I ran London successfully, I did not finish the Riga (Latvia) Marathon, which I was due to run a few weeks after London. I had signed up to run Riga through Running Crazy Ltd. Running Crazy is the brainchild and a running company owned and organised by Malcolm Hargraves. I have used Malcolm and his company many times for races abroad. This was one of those running tours I signed up to.

In Riga, just before the halfway mark, we ran over cobbles, and this felt very uncomfortable on the injury. I decided to run on to halfway to see how it felt then, but finally decided to pull out. This was a very tough decision to make as I had travelled all that way. But it was a wise one, as it could perhaps have got worse and, who knows, I might have been off for months. Fortunately, I went back to Riga the following year with Running Crazy and successfully completed the marathon injury-free. But after coming home from Latvia, I decided to take over a month off from running. This break combined with all the stretching and injury management tactics worked. My plantar fasciitis disappeared, and I have never had a problem with it since.

Patellofemoral pain syndrome

This injury is more commonly known as 'runner's knee' and it affects the area where the kneecap (the patella) meets the thigh bone (the femur). It is basically a misalignment of the kneecap, which does not move properly within the thigh bone, and the pain can occur around the kneecap or just behind it.

Poor biomechanics can be a cause of this injury, but so can overuse and an increased training load. Ramping up the mileage and the intensity too soon can cause problems. You need to give yourself time to recover between increases in training loads. So increase your training gradually and give yourself recovery time.

Overpronation or underpronation can cause this injury too, and muscle imbalances such as stronger hamstrings and weaker quadriceps can pull the kneecap out of alignment. Sitting down for long periods with the knee bent can cause discomfort. It also might be that your trainers do not suit your particular running gait.

The symptom of the injury – pain around the kneecap or behind it – will be most noticeable when running up and (especially) down hills. Stairs may be a problem, too. You may also feel a grinding sensation in the knee (known as crepitus) that may be observed by your GP or, in my case, when having a sports massage. Your knee may become uncomfortable with a dull ache after sitting down for long periods of time. If you find that the pain disappears as you run, this may be nothing to worry about. However, if your pain levels increase as you run, then keep off it immediately!

I have what I call my 'painometer' for injuries. Out of a score of 10, if it gets around 2.5/3 out of 10, do not run. This is the case with any injury – things hurt for a reason, so it is important that you do not exacerbate and worsen any injury (or niggle) by continuing to run.

There are a few things you can do to help ease patellofemoral pain syndrome. They are associated with strengthening the muscle groups in your legs, especially the quadricep muscles because the quads play a big role in kneecap movement.

Firstly, try doing some straight leg raises. Sit on the ground or floor and straighten your left or right leg, with your foot and toes facing up, so it is locked at the knee. Lift your leg about six inches from the ground and hold it for five seconds. Then relax it. Do this exercise 10 times, then switch to the other foot. Do this 2–3 times a day. This has the advantage of not stressing the knee by bending it.

Then you might try doing some clams. This is where you lie on your side and bend your knees to 90 degrees. Slowly lift your upper leg and knee and then drop it back down again while keeping your feet together. This will help strengthen your gluteus muscle (the strongest muscle in the leg) and your hip muscles, helping your stability while avoiding muscle imbalances. Do 15–20 of these. You should feel fatigue on the side of your backside and hip. Alternate this by doing the exercise on the other side.

Finally, check your footwear. Make sure you have trainers that suit you. Consider using orthotics, as these can help if you have biomechanical issues such as pronation problems associated with flat or raised arches. They can help stabilise your gait by helping to redress biomechanical imbalances that can go all the way to the hip. This could all contribute to helping to realign the knee. If there is a swelling, you can also ice the knee. Above all, if it hurts, keep off it. Do not run again until you are pain-free.

My experience of patellofemoral pain syndrome

Personally, I have had a fleeting experience with an uncomfortable knee. Around four years ago, I was having my usual pre-marathon massage with Fiona, when she noticed what she called a 'grinding' feeling in my right knee. As I knew what runners' knee was, I was a little surprised as, until then, I had not noticed anything untoward with my knees, nor felt any discomfort. But the word 'grinding' was a little concerning, as this was one of the symptoms of patellofemoral syndrome, and it is how it can feel. I was also intrigued, as I had no previous knee problems caused through running at all. Yet Fiona was spot-on.

She confirmed that one of the benefits of a sports massage is helping identify problems before they happen. It would not be a diagnosis, but early detection helps the treatment of chronic injuries – this is less so with acute injuries.

Fiona did diagnose my knee correctly, though. About a week later, my knee really was quite sore, so I took a couple of days off. But bizarrely I found that if I walked up and down the stairs backwards, I did not feel it at all. So this is what I carried on doing, and it disappeared in a couple of days – just as quickly as it had appeared in the first place.

I am not saying for one moment that this was the magic cure. However, because it was not hurting, I was certainly not doing it any harm. Finding out all the little things that seem to ease the pain can be a great help when it comes to injury prevention. Often a combination of things can help ease injuries. It is a case of considering any small things that seem to benefit, taking these on board and doing them. For me, curing injuries is a bit like doing a jigsaw puzzle: fill in all the missing pieces and eventually you will get there.

There is a very good section on injuries in Matt Fitzgerald's book *Brain Training for Runners*. It discusses injury prevention and is very informative if you are interested. Having time off and doing anything that seems to help can work wonders. My tender knee has come back on the odd occasion but has never become a full-blown injury. If it happens again, I will be keeping right off it as I am a real believer in time being a great healer where injuries are concerned. Remember: never dismiss any niggles – keep a close eye on them.

Iliotibial band syndrome (ITBS)

The iliotibial band (ITB) is a ligament that runs down the side of the leg from the hip to the shin (the tibia) and is also connected to the knee. Because of this, it is possible to mistake this for a knee injury, as pain is usually felt along the side of the knee – although pain can occur right down the whole ligament and around the entire knee area.

Iliotibial band syndrome (ITBS) occurs when there is rubbing and friction of the ligament on the area on the outside of the knee. The ligament becomes inflamed and swollen, especially when the foot hits the ground and, as with runner's knee, if the knee is bent during long periods of inactivity.

ITBS is caused by a number of factors. Overuse and poor biomechanics cause stress on tissues, tendons, ligaments, etc. Weak glutes and quads along with weak hip muscles can also play a role. Unsuitable trainers will contribute to a poor gait. Finally, the training regimen can be a factor – for example, excessive downhill running or a sudden increase in training mileage.

You should consider the possibility of ITBS if you notice any of the following: a stinging sensation around the knee area (and maybe down the side of the leg); any increasing pain over time when running or any other activity (the pain may be OK at first or even subside for a while when running, but it will be only temporary); any swelling around the outside of the knee; and any pain when running downhill, sitting down for long periods of time, bending the knee, or when running (notably when the heel strikes the ground).

For recovery and prevention, there is a range of solutions. Firstly, consider doing some stretching. For example, while standing up, cross your injured leg behind your front leg and lean over to the side that is not injured. Hold this for around 30 seconds. Alternatively, while sitting down, cross the injured leg over the uninjured one and pull it towards your chest. Again, hold for 30 seconds. Do these two stretches 2–3 times a day.

Icing the injury will also help reduce inflammation. Similarly, a sports massage will help. If you cannot get someone to do this, then try using a foam roller. Also, consider running on the opposite side of the road during some of your runs. If you train on a track, run the opposite way sometimes – this can act as a preventative measure as well as a way to help ease the pain. However, you should not be running on it at all if it is still tender. Last but not least, rest until the injury site is pain-free.

Achilles tendonitis and tendinosis

The Achilles tendon is found at the back of the leg and connects the heel bone to the calf muscle. It is the strongest connective tissue in the human body. This tendon has a surrounding sheath containing synovial fluid which lubricates it. But even this tendon, as tough as it is, has its stress limits.

Firstly, I think it is a good idea to distinguish between -*Itis* and -*osis* in injuries. *Itis* is an acute injury. It happens fairly quickly and becomes inflamed. An -*osis* is a chronic injury and happens over a longer period of time – that is, it is degenerative. I cannot help feeling that whenever someone has an Achilles injury, they refer to it as Achilles tendonitis, where tendinosis may be the correct term. An acute Achilles tendonitis can lead to degeneration and degradation of the tendon if not treated properly. But it can also work the other way too, where a chronic tendinosis leads to Achilles tendonitis.

Because the collagen that forms the tendon cannot heal itself very quickly, it becomes damaged, and eventually scarred, leading to a possible rupture or tearing of the tendon's collagen fibres. Unlike muscles, which have a constant blood flow to the affected area, which helps them to recover more quickly, collagen takes much longer to repair and recover as there is very little blood flow to the damaged area. A tear or rupture will keep you off the road for weeks to months, and you may possibly need an operation. So, again, I must emphasise that if you feel anything untoward in the Achilles area of the foot, stop running immediately!

The causes of Achilles injuries are multiple. They can stem simply from overtraining, of course, doing too much hill work, speed work, or long distances too soon. Biomechanical issues such as overpronation can also play a role. Injuries can be caused by having weak calf muscles; this has a knock-on effect and puts a strain on your tendon. And again, not warming up properly before races and training can do harm to this area. Then there is footwear. Girls need to beware of high heels; they may look nice, but these cause the tendon to shorten and can cause all sorts of problems when reverting to flatter shoes or bare feet. More generally, be sure not to wear shoes with little or no arch support, such as flat-soled shoes, flip-flops, etc.

There are several symptoms for tendonitis. You may have pain or swelling at the back of the heel, which may have come on quite quickly. It may feel warm to touch. Also, it may feel most tender first thing in the morning, and you may have a limited range of motion in your foot or ankle area. Bear in mind that an acute Achilles injury is possibly more painful than a chronic one.

As for the symptoms of chronic tendinosis, the main difference here is that the pain is more gradual than sudden. This is degeneration that happens over time as the Achilles tendon becomes more damaged. And damage in this area can work both ways: a degenerating chronic Achilles injury can lead to an eventual rupture or tear; and a sudden injury to the Achilles can lead to degeneration of the tendon as well.

As to recovery from Achilles injuries, the first and main thing to do is keep off it. Go for total rest, as with other injuries, and run again when pain-free. Do calf muscle stretches such as heel drops. Consider icing it to help reduce inflammation. And (as with plantar fasciitis) wear a night splint or Strassburg sock to stop the tendon from contracting while sleeping. Don't forget to look at your shoes – both running trainers and other footwear – to be sure you are using shoes with good arch support. Also, consider using orthotics.

Calf muscle injuries and strains

The calf muscle is made up of three main muscles. The plantaris, the gastrocnemius and the soleus muscles. All three can be subject to injury. There are varying degrees of severity, so medics categorise the symptoms from grade 1 to grade 3. The most common calf strains appear in the gastrocnemius muscles. Plantaris and soleus muscle strains are less common.

The causes of calf strains are similar to the causes of the other injuries we've looked at – sudden increases in hill running and speed work, overstretching, not warming up properly and overtraining in general. Biomechanical problems (overpronation) can stress the muscles, as can increasing your running mileage too quickly. The more specific cause is explosive exercises, such as full-on sprinting, hill sprints, etc., along with other sudden movements, or lunges from a stationary position, in sports such as tennis or squash.

A grade 1 injury will perhaps be sore for just a few days. You may notice slight bruising and a little swelling. There may be some tenderness during and after running, and it may feel tender when stretched. However, you should be able to walk normally on it and the tenderness after rest should go within a week or so. A grade 1 injury is a slight or partial tear at most. Some TLC and rest should see you running again soon.

Most calf strain injuries tend to be grade 2, which are acute. You will generally notice it straight away, and you will have trouble walking. You will feel a strange pull or twinge, and it might be uncomfortable to touch. It may show some bruising and there will be some inflammation. When the foot is plantar flexed (pointing the toes down like a ballet dancer) or dorsiflexed (lifting the foot at the ankle so the toes point upwards) it will be uncomfortable.

A grade 3 injury is a complete rupture, so the pain is immediate and acute. You will immediately be unable to walk or exercise. After a while you will notice bruising and swelling, and you will probably feel a gap in the muscle where it is torn. You will find you will not be able to contract your calf muscle.

Recovery from a calf muscle injury will depend on the grade of the injury. For a grade 1 strain, rest and keep off it. Ice it for about 15 minutes, twice a day or so, and try to keep it elevated. Do not stretch it. Wearing a compression sock might help. Ice, compressions and elevation help with inflammation and swelling. After a couple of weeks, you should notice an improvement. Run again when pain-free.

For a grade 2 strain, you must take a complete break from running and any other exercises that could damage it further. Ice it for 15–20 minutes at a time at least three times a day – or whenever possible – and elevate it. Consider wearing a compression sock, too. After a few days, get a sports massage, if you can, possibly combining it with physiotherapy, and even electrotherapy. If you want to keep your fitness levels up, cycle for an hour each day – but only if you do not feel the injury when doing so. This will help keep your aerobic or cardiovascular fitness levels up – although not so much your running fitness levels. You could also try aqua pool running. But only if it does not hurt. Run only when pain-free.

For a grade 3 strain, you will be out of action completely. A total rupture means getting to your doctor and perhaps hospital. It will mean an operation to repair the injury. This will keep you off for months, so it is fortunate that grade 3 injuries are very rare. Grade 1 and 2 injuries are more common. If you are preparing for a marathon, you will not be doing any explosive exercises, so you should avoid these injuries as long as you train sensibly and take it step by step.

My experience of calf injuries

Preventing this sort of injury is also similar to the advice above for other injuries. But let me add a couple of anecdotes that may help you if, like me, you get painful calf strains.

Once, after I injured my calf, my coach's advice was to get on my bike after school and cycle for an hour. I had a route that I could take home which was over 10 miles, so I did this. He also told me to get some physiotherapy on the injury, so I did this, too. Finally, he insisted I was not to run on it until I was pain-free. All of this worked. I had six painful weeks away from all running and sport before I was ready to hit the road again. As expected, though, I made a full recovery.

On another occasion, I had some tenderness in my calf, and I was finding that the jarring of running on the road was quite uncomfortable. So I turned to grass and also did some off-road running where possible to help lessen the impact. As I mentioned before, if you find any activity or form of training that helps any injury (remember me walking up and down the stairs backwards), you should keep doing it and make a note of what seems to be helping.

So, if for some reason you do pick up a calf injury and want to try grass running, go for it – just be careful and tread carefully. Try a lap or two to see if it helps. Grass running is more energy-sapping than running on the road, as your muscles have to work harder on a softer, spongier surface. It is a great muscle-strengthening exercise, but it can also be a strain on your niggle.

Hamstring injuries

I have to say that, along with ITBS, shin splints and Achilles injuries, I have never had a hamstring injury. I believe that one of the reasons I have never succumbed to a hamstring injury is because I run endurance and not regular explosive sprinting. In fairness, I do very quick hill sprints, but this is only for a few seconds and when I am warmed up properly. The fastest distances I run for my marathon training are 400–800 metres on the track. I do run a pretty brisk 200 metres within the 400-metre sessions I do, but it is not quite at full speed. So it does not get much faster than this, which greatly reduces the risk of pulling a hamstring. But hamstring injuries are still something we should look at anyway, even if you will not be doing any sprint training, since they are well-known problems.

There is a range of causes of these injuries. The first is from not warming up properly before exercising – especially if you are doing sharp, short, sudden movements or sprinting, including hills. Hamstring muscles are less pliable and elastic when cold, so be careful in cold weather.

Poor running form or technique can also lead to hamstring injuries, as can weak glute muscles. The latter are connected to the hamstrings and can overload the hamstring muscles. Another imbalance is when your hamstrings are weaker than your quadricep muscles. This can overload your hamstrings, and the muscle imbalance has a knock-on effect.

Hamstring injuries are also graded from 1–3 in terms of severity. For example, if you have a grade 1 hamstring injury, you will be able to walk properly, but you may have tightness at the back of your thigh. There will be minimal swelling, but ascending and descending hills may be uncomfortable. You may not feel the tenderness until after exercising, but there will be slight pain when extending or contracting the muscle.

Grade 2 injuries are more acute, however, so there will be immediate pain, and touching it will hurt. You will limp and find it difficult to walk properly, there will be more prominent swelling, and bending at the knee will hurt the muscle.

Grade 3 is the worst type of hamstring problem and, being an acute injury, there will be immediate and extremely sharp, stabbing pain. Internal bleeding will mean it will bruise, which will be visible after a few days, and walking will be extremely painful. You will feel a gap where the muscle has torn and a lump of muscle just above the gap. It will probably need surgery. Moreover, if it is an acute and aggressive tear, you (and others) may hear a very audible 'pop' sound.

Recovery from hamstring injuries is similar to other 'graded' injuries, in that it may take just a few days to recover from a grade 1 injury, but weeks or even months for grade 2–3 injuries. The advice is not to run and to keep off your hamstrings. Even if it is a grade 1 tear or strain, let them recover and run only when pain-free. Follow the RICE protocol – Rest, Ice, Compression and Elevation.

Beyond this, elastic bandages for compression can be bought from a chemist, and a gentle sports massage can be helpful. Also, try stretching the hamstring, but do not stretch it immediately after injuring it. Only start light stretches when you can walk on it and carry out other activities when pain free.

At worst, a total and severe grade 3 tear may need surgery, so always aim for prevention. Think about doing the stretches I mentioned. Also, strengthening glute muscles, hip flexors and quadriceps will help to stop muscle imbalances, thus avoiding stressing or overloading the hamstring muscles.

Shin splints

Shin splints (or medial tibial stress syndrome) is an injury that can be felt on either the inside or the outside muscles of the shin. It can be mistaken for a stress fracture or vice versa. A stress fracture is more localised, whereas shin splints are felt over a more general area of the shin. However, an untreated shin splint problem can lead to an eventual fracture. It's important to know the difference between the two. Shin splints are a tearing in the muscles and tendons (or any other damage) where they attach to the tibia (shin bone). A stress fracture, on the other hand, is a fracture of the actual bone.

One other thing that can be mistaken for shin splints is 'compartment syndrome'. This is when swelling and inflammation of a muscle, or bundle of muscles, within an enclosed muscle space after an injury causes discomfort. Compartment syndrome is felt on the outside of the lower leg and tends to have more of a nerve feel to it – like the sensation of pins and needles.

Shin splints can be caused by biomechanical factors, such as overpronation, or imbalances in muscles in the lower leg, hips and glutes. Over-striding can play a part, as can overstressing the bone and muscles by doing too much too soon and not having enough recovery time. Another factor can be taking part in sports where you stop and start regularly with explosive movements, such as racket games, football, netball, basketball, etc.

The symptoms of shin splints are shared by other conditions – for example, inflammation and heat coming from the shin, or an initial dull ache that becomes more intense or sharper when exercising. If severe, the shin will be painful when at rest, or it might hurt when touched or prodded. It might be most tender first thing in the morning (overnight, the tissues shorten and tighten). But a good guide is to consider how comfortable it is when dorsiflexing the foot (lifting your foot at the ankle pointing your toes up); if this hurts, it is very likely to be shin splints.

Advice for recovery from shin splints is also familiar. You should cease all running. If need be, swim and cycle to keep fit. Shin splints can last for months if severe. Run again when pain-free. You may find that icing will help with inflammation.

Prevention is better than cure, so to help avoid shin splints, ensure you warm up properly before exercise, be sure to do strengthening exercises for all the muscle groups, recover properly between training sessions, and do not ramp up the mileage and intensity of your training too quickly.

Consider your diet, too. Calcium in your diet is good for the bones, and looking after your bone health is beneficial. When you exercise, your bones get rid of the old material and produce new bone tissue. You may have problems if your body cannot keep up with this process. Strong bones will help keep injuries at bay. Milk – especially a chocolate milk drink – is a winner, notably after exercising. By drinking this, you will do yourself a massive favour, not only in recovery but in bone health, too.

Give thought to doing minimalist and barefoot running. This is said to help prevent shin splints. It takes the stress away from the tibia (shin bone). However, it takes time to adapt to barefoot and minimalist running – and it can also cause injuries if not done gradually. If you like the thought of barefoot running, then be very careful. I have touched on this earlier in the book. It can be a very good way of preventing all manner of injuries. But please tread carefully! Remember what I said about plantar fasciitis. It can also put a strain on the calf muscles and the Achilles tendon. If barefoot running interests you, I can thoroughly recommend the book *Born to Run* by Chris McDougall – it's a fascinating read.

Finally, think about the direction you run around a track. At the Taunton Athletics Club, where I coach and help Level 4 endurance coach Charlotte Fisher with the Academy group, it is not uncommon to see athletes running in the opposite direction when doing a warm-up or a longer session. It is worth considering this when doing track sessions, so you are not favouring one side all the time.

Additional information for injury recovery

Sleep is a great aid to recovery. Getting at least eight hours' sleep a night is what is recommended, not just in running, but in general. It has been said that you should sleep until you cannot sleep any more. Eight hours should be the minimum. In fact, in terms of recovery from injuries, and to help you run well, adequate sleep is very important. It is a known fact that your brain is as active while you are asleep as it is when awake. Sleep re-energises you and allows the body to clear wastes and toxins (and from the brain too). As far as recovery is concerned, damaged tissue (bone and muscle) is regenerated. So getting enough sleep is as important as diet.

Incidentally, if you are wearing a compression sock for an injury, then remove it before going to bed, as the swelling is less of a problem when lying down. The compression should be comfortable and not constrictive.

Be aware that your brain also needs carbohydrates. When you are asleep, your brain taps into your carbohydrate stores, contradicting some people's thoughts that, when resting or sleeping, you are saving your stores of glycogen. This is one of the reasons why bananas are my breakfast on marathon day. They refuel the body and brain pre-race!

A lack of sleep will raise the levels of the hormone cortisol. This is the same hormone that is produced when you become agitated. It follows, then, that sleep will help in the recovery from and prevention of injuries. When you are asleep, your body produces more growth hormones and sends more blood and nutrients to any areas affected by injury. So, if you want to get the best out of your running and injury recovery, get plenty of sleep.

By the way, if you have a lousy night's sleep the night before your marathon, don't panic! It doesn't mean you will struggle to run your marathon. One or two nights' sleep deprivation pre-marathon will not have much of an impact. It is the sleep you get in the previous week or two that counts. I know of several people who have had a bad night's sleep before their marathon and have gone on to run very well – and that was in competitive marathons, not just where they were aiming to finish. So the odds of you finishing are still very much stacked in your favour.

A good policy on pre-marathon night is to go to bed when you are tired. Do not go to bed early when you are not tired, thinking this will help you. Chances are, you will lie there wide awake, thinking of the day ahead. In the past, before a race, I have gone to bed at midnight just as tiredness is taking over, and I have slept like a baby. Getting to bed slightly later than normal on the night before your marathon will have no impact on your marathon whatsoever.

Lastly, in this section on injuries, along with sleep, I still maintain that the most potent force in recovering from injuries is time off. Obviously, if you are that badly injured, then you will not be running anywhere anyway. However, I regard the day that I stop running because of an injury (or niggle) as the day that I start to recover. Patience is a virtue here. Things hurt for a reason, and time is a great healer. The human body is a fantastic piece of equipment and is very good at repairing itself, so let it do its work and do not be in a rush to get back to running. All my injuries or niggles have recovered because of the amount of time I have allowed myself to let them mend.

Let me put it this way. If you are injured and have used all the injury prevention methods I have discussed in this section, but you still keep running, then you may totally break down. However, if you stop running and carry out the same methods, you will be on the recovery road. When necessary, take time off and let your body do the work. Also, try to keep a good, strong, positive mindset. This is very important.

A note on stretching

It is good practice to stretch before any exercise, especially before any training sessions and anything of any real intensity. Before faster races such as 5k and 10k or any explosive training like hill repeats or sprints on the track, it is imperative. Admittedly, your training pace will not be explosive or quick, as speed is not your main priority – finishing is. But I still think it is a good policy to stretch before your sessions.

There are two different types of stretches: dynamic stretches and static stretches. I see many people doing static stretches before a training session or a race. By static stretching I mean touching your toes, lifting up your leg up behind your backside to stretch your quadricep muscles, putting your foot behind you and leaning against a fence or a tree to stretch your calf muscles, etc. Just for the record, you must never do this before races or training sessions. You are basically stretching out cold muscles and this will considerably increase the injury risk. You do your static stretches after a race or training session. This is when your muscles are warm and more elastic.

Instead, the type of stretching you do before your session or race is dynamic stretching. These are exercises like leg swings, arm rotations, lunges, trunk twists, strides, and so on. There are a multitude of dynamic stretches you can try. There are many online you can look up with good examples of how to carry them out. Before my track sessions, I normally do something like 15–20 leg swings, backwards and forwards, for each leg. Arm swings and rotations and trunk twists are the same. There is a good neurological benefit to doing dynamic stretches. They also help to lubricate your muscles, to raise the heart rate and to get the blood flowing around the body. After this, you should be nicely warmed up and ready to go for your run. I also think there is a psychological benefit to them, too. They focus the mind and mentally prepare you for what is ahead of you.

After your session, do your static stretches. Try to target all your muscle groups – that is your calf muscles, your quadriceps, Achilles tendons (which is not a muscle), your hamstrings and your iliotibial band (this runs from the side of your thigh down to your knee). There are even stretches for your arms. They are still a part of running. Do not overstretch; just stretch your muscles until you feel a minimal pull. It should not take you outside your comfort zone and should not hurt. Hold this for 20–30 seconds. If it does take you outside your comfort zone, then stop! You are overdoing it, and you risk being laid off for months – as I was once, when I totally overstretched my calf muscle.

Taking pain medication and anti-inflammatories

This is a rather controversial subject. I am not very keen on the idea of taking pills or medication to help recover from injuries. As I said, things hurt for a reason, and I am very much in favour of letting the human body do its work in terms of repairing itself. Medication masks this pain and probably gives you a feeling of confidence when things don't hurt so much. The one area where painkillers may be of benefit is in helping you to relax by easing discomfort. This means you will sleep better, thus aiding your recovery. But I still like the idea of letting the body do its thing naturally. Certainly, ask your doctor if you are unsure.

Inflammation is another reason people take medication. Inflammation is the first process on the road to recovery when injury strikes. It is the body's natural response to trauma or injury. Almost immediately the blood cells concentrate on the injured area. This warms it and provides all the good nutrients to the damaged tissue. So, rather than inflammation being a bad thing, it is just the opposite. Swelling, pain, redness, and the like are certainly uncomfortable, but they are very necessary in the healing process and are part of inflammation.

There is a very good article on Runners Connect online by Jeff Gaudette (a former US Olympic trialist in the marathon and 10k, and a coach) on taking anti-inflammatory medication. He claims that taking them within 2–3 days of becoming injured can be beneficial, but after that he suggests letting the body do its own healing. Let's face it, delayed onset muscle soreness (DOMS) is the result of microtrauma to the muscle fibres. These become sore and inflamed, then recover and become stronger, making you faster and fitter. This is also the healing process. The principle is the same with any injury. Why interrupt the healing process with tablets? If you find the inflammation too uncomfortable, use ice. At least it is natural!

Lastly, remember the 'painometer' inside your brain! If anything gets above 2.5–3 out of 10 on the pain scale, then keep off it and stop running. Think prevention rather than cure. You may just nip the injury in the bud before it becomes severe. Better to not run anywhere for a while than not run at all.

Your first month in training

So it's time to hit the road and start your marathon training. My advice to you is to keep it minimal and only attempt what you are capable of. This may mean just running up to the end of the road for starters if need be. It is best to start off by running one mile – just that.

For the first week, I advise just going out of the door and getting used to running. It is a good idea to get your hands on a watch with GPS if you can. Mine, for example, is a Garmin Forerunner 10. A GPS watch gives you accuracy in terms of the mileage you run, along with calories burned. It works off satellites and is accurate to around 100th of a mile – very handy for monitoring your exact mileage. If you do not have one, then gauge the distance by perhaps using a local running track (if the running track is 400 metres, then four circuits = 1 mile). On the other hand, you might use a treadmill to measure your run – or even gauge the distance by using your car!

What follows is advice for your first month of training – in stages, so that you can just take it step by step and tackle any issues that may occur along the way. And if you feel that your fitness levels are more advanced, then feel free to enter the training schedule at a stage that suits you. At this point, my comments are aimed more at those less-experienced runners.

One thing that may help you feel more at ease, as it will relieve some pressure, is if I tell you that you can walk if you feel you want to. This is allowed! A run/walk strategy is a good idea and will help you to cover the distance.

I recommend running on a Sunday. Later in the schedule, Sunday will probably be your long-run day, since most races are run on a Sunday and your marathon is highly likely to be run on this day, too. It is of course a day when most people have more time to run. So I suggest starting your training on a Sunday and ending the week on the following Saturday.

The training schedule that follows is intended to last one month, getting you started, basically, from scratch. Please don't feel that this is written in stone and you have to follow it religiously. Use it as a template or a guide to get you started and to build you up to slightly longer distances. If you find that you are able to build up the mileage at a quicker rate than the schedule here suggests, then that is great. On the other hand, if it takes you longer, then do not worry, either.

Let me give you an example. In the first week, you will be doing a very slow run of only a mile three times. You will then build up one of the runs to two miles the following week and so on. If you feel a particular week's training is a little too much for you, however, just repeat the previous week's sessions. Time is on your side, and it is important for you to take one step at a time, building gradually and going at your own pace.

And don't feel tied to the schedule. We all have other things going on in our lives such as work, our home and family lives, holidays, etc. This may mean you cannot do a certain run on a certain day. This happens to me regularly, so I just rearrange my schedule to suit my needs. I usually have a Monday as a rest day and I go to the track for a session on Tuesday. But if I am unable to go to the track on a Tuesday, I will go to the track on a Monday, providing my Sunday run has not been too taxing (as I try to avoid two harder sessions in a row). You can mix and match to suit you. Rearrange the schedule to suit your circumstances and fit in with your everyday life.

I have also included rest days after the days you run, just to make sure you are fully recovered before you go out again. Even over this shorter distance, a beginner may pick up some muscle soreness. Don't worry as this is perfectly normal muscle-fibre damage caused by exercise. Your muscles will repair themselves and come back stronger. This is how you get fitter. However, it is very important not to run on sore muscles – hence the two rest days in between your runs. You can also do recovery runs, but that will be for later.

You may be fortunate to find that, running only one mile, you may not be very sore afterwards. But when I helped my wife, Julia, do her Couch-to-5k training, we found she needed to run for just one minute at a time. She covered around one mile, but often felt a little muscle soreness, so we had days off in between. She found, and you will find, that the microscopic muscle-fibre damage that exercise causes needs to repair itself.

One other important thing to remember is that, from now on until the very last training run you do, you should not be aiming for any particular speed or intensity. It is just a case of hitting the road and getting around – and the same will apply when you run your marathon.

3 Time to hit the road

In this chapter, we are going to look at the first four months of training. I have put together a training schedule for you for these first four months. After each schedule I will explain what you will be doing that month and why.

Also, remember to wear the kit and shoes you will be wearing on marathon day when you do your long runs. You need to get used to wearing your shoes and clothing, and the long runs you do are a good test to see if anything rubs or chafes – consider them to be a dress rehearsal for the big day. Once you get used to running long distances in your long runs, and are happy with the way your vest, shorts and shoes feel, then you should wear the same kit in your marathon. Here is another very important point to consider. Your chosen charity may have sent you a T-shirt or vest for advertising purposes. You will need to wear this regularly in your training just to make sure you feel comfortable running in it.

Month 1

The schedule

	Sunday	Monday	Tuesday	Wednesday	Thursday	Friday	Saturday
Week 1	1 mile	Rest day	Rest day	1 mile	Rest day	1 mile	Rest day
Week 2	2 miles	Rest day	Rest day	1 mile	Rest day	1 mile	Rest day
Week 3	2 miles	Rest day	Rest day	1 mile	Rest day	2 miles	Rest day
Week 4	2 miles	Rest day	Rest day	1 mile	Rest day	2 miles	Rest day

That is your first month. You will notice there is an increase by 1 mile on Sunday of week 2, and on Friday of week 3. As you are an absolute beginner, it is important to increase mileage volume, per running day and over the week, very gradually.

There is a 10% rule that is popular with some runners in increasing your mileage from week to week. But at this early stage this is not so much of a concern as the mileage is minimal. The last two weeks are the same. If you have to rearrange this schedule to fit in with your everyday lives, please make sure you take the rest days as these are very important! This is the same throughout the whole training schedule from week to week and month to month. I know many runners who find it hard to take time off. Because of this they do not improve and normally become injured or have constant niggles – not to mention the risk of overtraining syndrome. A constant plateau of continuous hard work with no recovery is just a recipe for disaster. If you get used to taking rest days at this early stage, and are comfortable with it, then great. You will certainly help decrease the risks of injury and overtraining.

Thoughts on the 10% rule

I was recently discussing the 10% rule with Charlotte Fisher (a Level 4 endurance coach at the Taunton Athletic Club). We meet up on Tuesdays and put the Academy group through their paces. We obviously get an opportunity to talk about all things running. We both agreed we were not entirely comfortable with this rule. There are too many variables involved. So much depends on whether you have a twinge or are coming back from injury, or how much mileage per week you are doing (or per month). If the mileage is minimal, then over one week this rule would mean you would not increase your mileage that much, but over a 10-week period this would increase by quite a rate, especially if your mileage is already high.

As an aside, I recently told my wife I was starting the training schedule in this book at one mile. She then pointed out the fact that many people may not be able a run a mile. A fair comment, and this may be the case. I then pointed out that at the beginning of her Couch-to-5k training, in the first of her training runs, using a run/walk strategy, she had covered, yes, one mile, and she was definitely starting from scratch. But you must begin with what you are comfortable with.

Cross training in your schedule

Cross-training is any form of training other than running. If you enjoy cycling, swimming, lifting weights at the gym, or even walking, this will help. I have not included this in your monthly training. But it is something you can certainly do on one or two of your days off. This, too, will help in raising your overall fitness levels. As long as it is not too intensive, this should not impact on your running. However, I would recommend you do this on your rest days. When you cross train you are using different muscle fibres. The ones you use when running are actually being rested when you cross train. You will still get all the other fitness benefits through cross training. You are using different muscle groups from the ones you normally stress during running. Cross training strengthens non-running muscles, so it can help with muscles imbalances – and this also helps to reduce the risk of injury. A muscle imbalance means one muscle group is disproportionate in strength to another, and this can cause problems. For example, runners tend to have stronger quadriceps and calf muscles, whereas cyclists tend to have stronger hamstrings. So cycling will help strengthen your hamstrings, thus strengthening a muscle that is not normally strengthened during running. Swimming will also help with your cardiovascular endurance. So in running there is definitely a place for cross training. I will leave it to you to decide if and when you want to do this. It is not imperative, but if you can do some form of cross training it can certainly be beneficial. You need not cross train in all of your rest days as it is important to have days off completely. Perhaps cross train on one or two of your recovery days. It also takes away a little of the boredom factor of just continuous running.

Rest days and why they are important

You will notice that in all of the training schedules there are designated rest days. Believe me, these are vitally important. Every runner from a total beginner to an elite marathoner will have rest days in their training schedule. A rest day will give your muscles, and anything else that has been stressed during your training, a chance to recuperate. This is when your muscle fibres recover from the microscopic trauma and tearing that occurs when you run. They repair themselves and come back stronger. So basically, after a rest day, you actually get fitter. This is a bit of an antithesis, but your fitness levels go up when you take downtime. It also gives you a mental break too. Without rest days you are far more likely to become injured or suffer from overtraining. So, please, do not be afraid to take time off as it is really important.

Month 2

The schedule

	Sunday	Monday	Tuesday	Wednesday	Thursday	Friday	Saturday
Week 1	2 miles	Rest day	Rest day	2 miles	Rest day	2 miles	Rest day
Week 2	3 miles	Rest day	Rest day	2 miles	Rest day	2 miles	Rest day
Week 3	3 miles	Rest day	Rest day	2 miles	Rest day	3 miles	Rest day
Week 4	3 miles	Rest day	Rest day	2 miles	Rest day	3 miles	Rest day

Your second month's training, as you will see, has shown a slight increase in mileage from month 1. You will continue to progress in mileage through the weeks. Again, do not be afraid to use a run/walk strategy if you feel you cannot run all the way. You will also see that you are still only running three days a week. You will not progress up to four days running a week until month 4. You may feel after two months of training that you are capable, but I strongly encourage you not to yet (unless, of course, you have entered the schedule at a later stage). It is vital that you gradually build up the mileage first. I feel that only after three months will you be ready to add an extra day. This may seem a little precautionary. But you have time on your side – plus, injury prevention is the key to successful running.

In month 2 you have also reached your first milestone. That is 5k (3.1 miles). So for the sake of 0.1, miles you are up to a 5k distance. There is no reason why you cannot go down and run in your local parkrun. These take place every Saturday morning. They cover a 5k distance and are very sociable. You most certainly do not have to race it. You could use Friday as a rest day and run it on the Saturday. Just treat it as your normal 3-mile training run, and this will really help to build your confidence levels. No pressure here at all. It is your call. If you think it will help, have a go. It is race conditions without the pressure of treating it as an actual race. Some people do treat it as a race. But very many go down just to jog around and use it as a chance to get in a run to help their fitness, or whatever. I absolutely do not mean this to sound derogatory or condescending. Just the contrary. I think parkrun is a magnificent thing. Many people throughout the country benefit from them for a number of reasons. You could too! But, as I say, you do not have to.

Pacing yourself

If at any stage you feel uncomfortable with the pace you are trying to maintain, and you are feeling fatigued, as already mentioned, walk for a few moments, or slow your pace. Again, speed is not the important thing here. Finishing the session in one piece is. This is even more important as you increase the mileage. For competitive runners, and those who are running for fitness, the idea is to 'hurt' a little. This is not the case for you. It will be challenging enough at times just doing what you are doing. So leave the speedy stuff to other runners and consider walking or slowing your pace to accommodate finishing your training run. I have helped more than one runner who, at the end of the run, has turned to me and asked: 'How fast did we go?' It is human nature, I suppose, but telling them not to worry about the pace does not always seem to hit home. As you progress, I will look at pace for an entirely different reason – one that does not include speed for fitness gains. I think it is very important for you to get comfortable with a pace that allows you to finish your run. If you can get your head around this, you will take an awful lot of pressure off yourself. I, for one, have walked in more than one race and training run. I certainly do not look on walking as a sign of failure. Take comfort from this attitude. It will help you.

Month 3

The schedule

	Sunday	Monday	Tuesday	Wednesday	Thursday	Friday	Saturday
Week 1	3 miles	Rest day	Rest day	3 miles	Rest day	3 miles	Rest day
Week 2	4 miles	Rest day	Rest day	3 miles	Rest day	3 miles	Rest day
Week 3	4 miles	Rest day	Rest day	3 miles	Rest day	4 miles	Rest day
Week 4	4 miles	Rest day	Rest day	4 miles	Rest day	4 miles	Rest day

Along with a gradual increase in daily miles, you will notice that you are increasing your weekly mileage too. Your very first week's total mileage volume was 3 miles. At the end of month 3, you have increased it to 12 miles. As you progress you will be increasing your running mileage, which is obvious. The biggest increase will be your long run on Sundays. I will be explaining the importance of your long runs at the end of month 4. The more miles you do over the course of the week, the more you help to build your overall endurance. There are many things that happen to you physiologically when you increase your mileage. Many adaptations take place.

Month 4

The schedule

	Sunday	Monday	Tuesday	Wednesday	Thursday	Friday	Saturday
Week 1	5 miles	Rest day	2 miles	4 miles	Rest day	4 miles	Rest day
Week 2	5 miles	Rest day	2 miles	5 miles	Rest day	4 miles	Rest day
Week 3	5 miles	Rest day	3 miles	5 miles	Rest day	4 miles	Rest day
Week 4	6 miles	Rest day	3 miles	5 miles	Rest day	4 miles	Rest day

Congratulations! You have just completed your first block of training runs. You have also passed a couple of milestones along the way – that of 5k distance after month 2 and 10k distance after month 4. 10k = 6.2 miles. Forget about the extra 0.2 of a mile. You are there. You have been steadily building your weekly mileage, and this will provide you with a good aerobic base. Remember the analogy I used of building a house and having a good strong foundation. This is what you have done in your first four months and will continue to do.

Increasing the distance

I said in month 3's schedule that I would explain the importance of increasing your weekly mileage and that of your long Sunday runs. As you increase individual daily training runs, you automatically increase your total weekly mileage volume (or TWMV as I call it). I have already said this will help build your overall stamina and endurance. However, there is also a great amount of importance attached to the long weekend runs you do on a Sunday. I will split your longer runs into three simple categories: the average run, the long run and the very long run! Personally, I regard an average run to be anything up to 9 miles, a long run to be between 10 miles and 13.1 miles, and a very long run to be anything from 14 miles to 20 miles or more. I have briefly explained why in Chapter 1. Please don't stress at the thought of running up to 9 miles as an average. Of course, for many runners this may seem a long way, and that is understandable. I am just using these three categories for convenience. There is not too much to concern yourself about when you run distances up to 10 miles. You will be giving yourself plenty of time, and over time you will cover this distance before progressing. Trust me. Once you get beyond the 10-mile mark, you will have no problem running a 10k distance. But once you start running distances over the 10-mile mark (especially over 16 miles), it's important to let you know what is happening to you physiologically. But please don't panic. The progressive nature of your training will have you reaching all of these targets.

I will explain the long run now. I will look at very long runs when you do these later in the training schedule (see Chapter 4).

You have already laid the foundation and done the basic groundwork (the foundation of the house), and you will now start to build the walls around it. Your next block of training runs will take you from a 10k distance to 10 miles on your Sunday run. These will be your average runs in terms of distance.

What happens when you increase your mileage from a 10k distance to 10 miles?

To be honest, not an awful lot more than when you worked your way up to the 10k distance in your previous sessions. Sure, it is longer mileage and a bit of a grind. But a natural progression is taking place. You are continuing to improve your stamina, endurance and cardiovascular fitness. Your leg muscles are becoming more toned and stronger too. This was happening before when you progressed up to the 10k distance. You are stronger and fitter and can now start to handle a step-up in mileage. You are still incrementally building your mileage, and this is preparing you, both mentally and physically, for longer mileages to come. Your brain and body are starting to get used to this longer mileage. You have also done this gradually as a way of avoiding injuries. I have not made you stick to the 10% rule. If anything, it has been a little less, and more cautious! To me this makes perfect sense for anyone just starting out. It may also seem painfully slow, but you will be surprised because after a few weeks you will be running 20–30 miles per week and increasing this to a higher TWMV!

I firmly believe that missing the odd training run during the week does not matter too much. It is about long-term consistency. As long as you are sticking to getting out on a regular basis you should be fine. If you find you cannot get out on a Wednesday (or whatever day) please do not stress. It is still fine. As long as you keep some sort of consistency over a long period of time you will be OK. Take it from me. A while back, in my marathon training, preparing for the Barnstaple Marathon in North Devon, I went from a 40-mile week to a 13-mile week because of work and coaching, plus other commitments, limiting my training for that week. Did this mean I was any less fit? Did I struggle in future runs? Not one bit. I know over a month to six weeks I will be hitting my targets anyway. This will be the same for you. As I said, training schedules are flexible.

You will find over the next few weeks that there is not much of an emphasis on the amount of mileage you do in your mid-week runs. After a while this will not increase very much at all. The important aspect of your training will be in the long weekend runs you do.

The long run is the single most important run of your schedule! This is the backbone of your marathon training. As you increase your long Sunday runs, your mileage for the week also increases. Your long runs are the training runs where you get the most bang for your buck! There are physiological adaptations that take place, especially when you hit very long run territory. But even though you will be building up to a distance of 10 miles, with longer runs to come later, I think it is important to know what is happening to you as you ramp up the long run mileage to 10 miles.

As I have already said, adaptations do happen over time, but not too much is happening to you as you go from a 10k distance up to 10 miles in your training. There are psychological adaptations, and I will touch on those in a moment. Physiologically, though, the real changes happen later on. By now you will have built a good base and foundation to your training, and the adaptations your body is going through are improving your strength and endurance, making you a better runner overall. As you get closer to very-long-run territory, your stamina will also be improving.

You will be getting used to running longer. There is not a huge step from 6.2 miles (10k) to 7 miles and beyond. So in month 5 you will start off at 7 miles and will concentrate on reaching the 10-mile mark at the end of the month. This is another very good milestone – that is an increase in mileage of just 3 miles over the whole month in your long run, but it is an excellent step forward. There are big psychological boosts to be gained here. You can really feed off this. It feels great to tell someone you have run 10k. But to say you have run 10 miles puts you in another league. Be very encouraged! At 10 miles you will also be at the halfway stage in terms of the longest run you will do (20 miles). That will come later. Please do not worry about that now. Too many runners look too far ahead at the bigger picture and get despondent. Concentrate only on where you are and what you can do for the moment. This is important. The natural progression of your training will get you to the end eventually. Once you reach 10 miles at the end of month 5, you will have every reason to be pleased with your efforts. You can celebrate the fact you have hit the halfway mark in terms of your long-run mileage.

It may be an idea to keep an eye on your fluid intake. You are now running longer distances. If, for some reason, you felt you were OK and did not need too much in the way of rehydrating on your previous runs up to 10k, you should be OK up to mileage of 7–8 miles, and perhaps further at this stage. However, take your water bottle with you if you feel you need it, and keep within the safety guidelines. We are all different when it comes to this. I have touched on this before. I know people who run more than 20 miles and never take one as they do not need it. But I also know of people who run 2–3 miles who do take one. Do what is best for you. Of course, this also depends on the weather. If it is hot, rehydrate.

Hyponatraemia

I said earlier in the book I would have a look at hyponatraemia, what it is and how to avoid it. Hyponatraemia is a condition that is caused by drinking too much fluid. It is basically a water intoxication. I must underpin what I am saying here about not drinking too much fluid as I think it is important. I also have to say to you that there is really nothing at all that you need to be scared of or worry about. Hyponatraemia in runners is extremely rare. It is a case of not stressing too much about what it can do and being comfortable with the fact that it can be totally avoided, 100%.

The body can put up with a little dehydration, but it is also important to not overhydrate. Both of these can be avoided by eating a balanced diet and drinking sensibly. By drinking too much fluid you dilute the electrolytes in your body. This is what hyponatraemia is. When you run, of course, you sweat, and this means you do have to take on a certain amount of liquid. Just make sure you don't guzzle too much. If you take in too much fluid, sure, you replace what is lost, but you also dilute the electrolytes in your body, especially sodium. But, to put this into perspective, you would have to drink something like 5–6 litres of water. A huge amount.

My advice to you is to drink to your thirst in your training runs and marathon. Rely on your body's natural thirst mechanism to tell you when you need to top up your fluid. Too much fluid sitting in your stomach jostling around can also cause gastrointestinal problems. So, if you drink sensibly and stick to a balanced diet, you will be fine. I will repeat it again: hyponatraemia is incredibly rare, so just be aware of it, but don't let it worry you.

If it helps, I'll explain what I do for hydration. On the day before my marathon, I have around a litre and half of water (not all in one go; over the whole day). Then on the morning of the marathon, I have a couple of glasses of water (also a couple of cups of coffee as this also counts towards fluid uptake), and then I am ready to roll. Of course, if the conditions are much warmer then you may need just a little more.

4 Building towards longer mileage

In this phase of your training you will start to build the walls of the house (going back to the earlier analogy). This is the training you will do that establishes your aerobic capacity to run for longer and points you towards your final long run of 20 miles. It is still very important not to worry about speed; it is just about getting the mileage under your belt. As I have said, there are few changes when you go from a 10k distance to 10 miles, and this is what I will cover in this segment of your training. The real psychological and physiological changes start to take place when you reach around 16 miles – but I will discuss that later. First, here is your training schedule for month 5.

Month 5

The schedule

	Sunday	Monday	Tuesday	Wednesday	Thursday	Friday	Saturday
Week 1	7 miles	Rest day	3 miles	5 miles	Rest day	4 miles	Rest day
Week 2	7 miles	Rest day	3 miles	4 miles	Rest day	5 miles	Rest day
Week 3	9 miles	Rest day	3 miles	4 miles	Rest day	5 miles	Rest day
Week 4	5 miles	Rest day	3 miles	4 miles	Rest day	5 miles	Rest day

You will notice that there is a slight change in your mileage over the four weeks. In week 2, there has been a reduction in mileage on the Wednesday from 5 miles to 4. This mile has been added on to your Friday run, increasing it from 4 miles to 5. The reason for this is quite simply to avoid you doing too much in the middle of the week when you are running on consecutive days. This may seem minimal to you, but you are now getting into longer Sunday runs (especially in the next few weeks). It makes sense to increase your runs (at the moment), marginally, on the Friday when you can have a rest before your long Sunday run. Think about it. By week 4 of month 5, over Tuesday and Wednesday, you will be running 7 miles over 2 days. On Friday, you will be running 5 miles, with a day off the day before and the day after to recover before your Sunday long run. So during week 4 you will be running 4 miles less than you did in week 3, but if you can keep injuries and overtraining syndrome at bay, even at this early stage, then all the better.

Also, like me, you may have a physical job. I must admit, sometimes I really have to motivate myself to get out the door to train and hit my targets in the middle of the week. After a hard day's graft, the thought of going to the track to churn out 8x 800 metres, 6x one mile or 10 hills is a little daunting when you are already a little physically tired. I do it anyway, but it is also flexible (remember me saying training schedules can be tweaked to your advantage). However, I find that by Friday, Saturday and Sunday I have a renewed sense of vigour. It may be psychological, but with the approaching weekend I feel far more ready to hit the road. I usually have Friday as my rest day. Because of this I find I am more than ready to tackle my long run on Sunday. I run on Saturdays, but I have not pencilled this in for you. For you, a day off on Saturday will leave you ready to do your long run on Sundays. My own training is for a competitive, multiple marathoner with thousands of miles under the belt. Yours is not.

Try to stick to what the schedule suggests. Sure, you may have to tweak it to suit your own circumstances and needs, but keep the overall structure the same. As your overall mileage increases weekly, it makes perfect sense to up the mileage a little on the Friday, rather than Saturday, keeping you as recovered as possible before running long on Sundays. As well as this, you will not be running such a long way on the Friday that it will jeopardise your Sunday run. But too much mileage in the middle of the week may have a knock-on effect, and I am also thinking of this from an injury point of view. So a rest day before and after your Friday run is the way to go. Continuously increasing your mileage in the middle of the week gradually, when you are running on consecutive days, would more than likely be OK, but I feel it is not a bad idea at the moment to just be a little cautious.

There is also an increase from 7 miles to 9 miles in your long run. You should be able to handle this increase now. Your runs in the middle of the week will hardly increase at all from now for the time being – only a little.

I will tweak this a little later in the schedule when you are perhaps a little more conditioned to handling an increase in midweek mileage. However, later, as you near the end of the schedule when your Sunday mileage starts to climb up to around 16 miles, I will be changing the schedule to suit. At the moment, however, concentrate on what you are doing month by month. Do not look too far ahead. This will look after itself as you progress.

I have now also included what is called a step-back week. From now on, every three weeks, your mileage will be cut in the fourth week as a form of recovery. You will see that you are going from 9 miles in week 3 to 5 miles in week 4 in your Sunday run. This is a step back in weekly mileage from the week before. This will help your muscles and whole physiological system to recover from the miles you are running. This will also help mentally, too. It is nice to have a rest and break from constant long runs. Up until now you have been increasing your mileage at a very gradual rate. If necessary, repeat this fourth week if you feel you are not ready to carry on into next week's/month's schedule. But now, as you are progressing towards 10 miles, step-back weeks are very important indeed. You need to give your whole system a break every now and then. Remember what we said about getting fitter when you ease off. However, if your fitness levels are high and you are a little more experienced than some of the people starting from scratch, enter the training at whatever stage suits your fitness levels and ability.

Month 6

The schedule

	Sunday	Monday	Tuesday	Wednesday	Thursday	Friday	Saturday
Week 1	7 miles	Rest day	3 miles	5 miles	Rest day	5 miles	Rest day
Week 2	9 miles	Rest day	3 miles	5 miles	Rest day	5 miles	Rest day
Week 3	10 miles	Rest day	3 miles	5 miles	Rest day	5 miles	Rest day
Week 4	6 miles	Rest day	3 miles	5 miles	Rest day	4 miles	Rest day

Congratulations, you have reached another milestone: 10 miles! You have also got another step-back week in your training schedule. That is in the fourth week. You have peaked at week 3 with a weekly mileage volume of 23 miles, then cut it back to 18 miles in week 4, with a reduction of 4 miles in your long Sunday run. As I said above, this step back in mileage is very important in terms of recovery. You will have a step-back week every three weeks from now on.

I have also said already if you feel that any week's training is a little too much, repeat that week until you are ready to carry on with the schedule. It is a good idea, too, if you are feeling a little jaded or under the weather to cut any of your runs a little short. It would not be the first time that I have gone out with the aim of completing a 10-mile run and cut it short to around 5 or 6 miles if I am not happy with the way I am feeling. This is the same if you feel a niggle or potential injury coming on. Be vigilant and listen to your body. You can always repeat the week if necessary. Time is on your side, and this will help you to prevent injuries. Remember, training schedules are templates. Use them as a guide to help you along the way. Tweak them in whatever way to suit you.

As far as missing the odd run here or there is concerned, do not stress over this. I firmly believe that when it comes to marathon running, less is more. It will not make any difference to ease off every now and then if you are not feeling up to it, or for any other reason. Better to miss a session or two than not be able to run at all for weeks or months. If you are not well or have a niggle, you can also cut your long Sunday run short, or forfeit it completely. There is always next Sunday! However, if you are feeling capable, and can handle your training, try to finish your sessions and meet your targets. This is absolutely the case with your long weekend runs. Try not to cheat on the long weekend runs as they are very important.

As an aside, there are many articles and sites on the internet and in magazines about the amount of fitness you lose if you have to stop running for a few days, a week, or however long. I do not think it is a case of one size fits all. We all have different rates of recovery. Some people can handle a higher volume of training than others (another reason why I am not so keen on the 10% rule). So, basically, even though the principles are the same, in our training and running we are all different. There are many different ideas on how much you cut your step-back weeks by. But I never adhere to any particular rule. Most coaches seem to think that around 20% of your overall mileage is a good guide. However, I feel it is not written in stone. I go by how I am feeling at the time. I have no problem cutting my 20-mile training runs to around 10–13 miles if I feel I need it. This isn't a cop out. Just sensible thinking. I will still get the required number of long runs on board. For you, if you do not feel right, then either forfeit it or cut it back in mileage. Keep it safe. You will still need to get that long run done. But perhaps not on this particular day if you are really not up to it. The step-back weeks I have given you in the schedule are around 20% to keep in with the general idea of how much to cut back, so you should be fine with this. But do not be afraid to cut back as much as you feel you need to.

I am sure the following two stories will interest you. One concerns myself, and the other concerns fellow runner and coach Adrian Marriott, an elite GB marathoner whom I've got to know over the years as a fellow athlete and coach. These are classic examples of less being more (in Adrian's case) and perhaps not being stressed to the eyeballs about having to take an amount of time off (in my case).

A few years ago, Adrian was injured when running the Bristol Half Marathon, so, during the three-week taper before running the Toronto Waterfront Marathon, he hardly ran a step. He then ran his marathon in Canada in 2 hours and 18 minutes, a personal best. In his words, he said he felt 'as fresh as a daisy'. A few years before, he had been due to run the Amsterdam Marathon, but had become ill six weeks out from this race. He missed a couple of weeks of training, so had a pre-taper. This time off meant he was well recovered. He also had a great run here too. As part of my research for this book, we emailed each other to discuss the effects of missing training for a set amount of time, and he quite correctly said to me, 'The caveat around missing time for illness and injury is that the more training that you have in your body over months/years, the better you cope with a break.' And he is absolutely right. So, if you have been training for a good year or so, a few training runs missed here or there are not going to be a problem for you. No one wants to become injured or ill, and this can be frustrating if it is long term. My advice to you is, if for whatever reason you have to miss a few days to a week or so, do not stress! Even if you have not been training long, the odd day or days off here or there will not matter too much. Don't forget you are not running competitively, nor are you racing – you are just aiming to finish. If for whatever reason you have a longer lay off, but you have months of training under your belt and a good aerobic base, you will be in a much better position to meet your eventual target. Adrian's performances are proof of this.

My own story, which also has a connection to the Amsterdam Marathon, involves an injury that kept me off running for a period of time (I did not mention this in the injury section of this book). Back in 2010, I was running the Battle of Sedgemoor 10k road race here in Somerset when my foot went. I did notice a little discomfort in it pre-race, but as I was running it just seemed to blow up, and I hobbled around the rest of the route. After the race it became very sore indeed, so I had to make some decisions. I was due to run the Alderney Half Marathon in the Channel Islands the following weekend, and I had the Amsterdam Marathon to run five weeks after this. There was no way I was going to be able to run in Alderney. I went to Alderney anyway to support two friends, Debbie Marsden of the South West Vets and her husband John Terry of Exeter, who were also running the Alderney event. They both won their respective races, Debbie the 10k and JT the half marathon. As I watched them win their races, I was still in quite a bit of pain. However, as frustrating as it was, I had decided to have a month off. No matter how much I wanted to run in Alderney, it was just not going to happen. Since I've been living in England, this is the only race I have had to miss through injury – this covers 15 years or so of competitive racing. When the injury kicked in, I had x-rays done, but these showed no fractures or breaks. The doctor I saw did tell me that hair line fractures do not always show up in x-rays, so it was still possible that I'd had one. It felt sore enough. I rested up, but two weeks before the Amsterdam Marathon the pain stopped, so I did what little I could in the remaining time. This included a 12-mile long run followed by 9 miles the week before the race, plus some shorter faster runs. I have to say that I did have a 20-mile training run on board early in the training schedule before the injury, so this helped. I then ran Amsterdam in a chip time of 2 hours and 47 minutes dead. I do not want this to sound conceited or arrogant, just to show that having a good training base or months of training on board, even with time off, can get you to the start line.

Month 7

The schedule

	Sunday	Monday	Tuesday	Wednesday	Thursday	Friday	Saturday
Week 1	10 miles	Rest day	3 miles	5 miles	Rest day	6 miles	Rest day
Week 2	11 miles	Rest day	3 miles	5 miles	Rest day	6 miles	Rest day
Week 3	13 miles	Rest day	3 miles	5 miles	Rest day	7 miles	Rest day
Week 4	8 miles	Rest day	3 miles	5 miles	Rest day	7 miles	Rest day

In week 3 your training is almost at the half-marathon distance – a half marathon is exactly 13.1 miles. This month your step back is a five-mile reduction – from a weekly mileage volume of 28 miles in week 3 to 23 miles in week 4. You will have noticed a pattern emerging: three weeks of gradual build-up, then a step back of 4–5 miles in the fourth week of the month. This is enough to keep you in good shape and also to give you a good recovery between each monthly training cycle. This pattern will continue until your taper. The taper is the last 3 weeks of your training, where you drastically cut your mileage as part of your recovery and final build-up to the marathon. This is a very important part of your training at the end of your schedule. I will go through this in greater detail in Chapter 5.

By now you will be starting to build something of an aerobic base. You should be able to kick on to longer mileage. The next few months' training will take you on to very-long-run territory, so it is a good idea to practise refuelling for your very long runs. From now on, make sure you have some carbohydrates on board. Experiment and try out different foods until you find something that suits you. I am not trying to say that this will happen to you, but quite often runners find certain things do not always agree with them. The normal pre-run refuelling foods such as bananas or porridge are excellent. Try to top up the night before your long run, too. Potatoes, rice, pasta are good things to eat the night before to top up your glycogen stores. I have previously touched on refuelling in Chapter 2. I have also said that a balanced diet will have you taking on board most of what you need. But it is a great idea to try things out and see what does or does not work. I guess you could call it a 'refuelling' dress rehearsal in your long runs for the main event.

Some people find certain foods may give them stomach and gastrointestinal problems, so, as I have said, experiment, and find out what works best. Personally, I find bananas the best thing to have. They are a magnificent pre-run, or pre-marathon, superfood. Here is why.

Bananas are a very good source of electrolytes (salts). Electrolytes carry electrical impulses around the body and play a vital role in things like muscle contractions and maintaining optimum PH levels in the body as well as carrying out other tasks. I will look at all of this again in Chapter 6 as a final run down of what to do on the morning before your marathon. However, it may help you to get used to putting this into practice now as your long runs are getting longer.

Electrolytes and what they do

Again, if the slightly technical side of this is of no interest to you, then feel free to skip this part of the text, but, if like me, you like to know what is happening to your body, read on. I will use bananas as my example as I think they are so good.

The main electrolytes found in bananas are:

1. Potassium
1. Magnesium
2. Phosphorous
3. Calcium

Let's look at these in more detail.

Potassium: Bananas are a very good source of potassium and contain far more of this electrolyte than many other fruits and food. Potassium is very good for muscle contractions. When you sweat while running, you lose more potassium and sodium than any other electrolyte. Potassium helps regulate fluid in the cells. It also helps transmits nerve impulses, hence helping with muscle contractions and to keep blood pressure normal.

Magnesium: This is another important electrolyte found in large amounts in bananas, although not nearly as much as potassium. It is the fourth most common mineral in our bodies. Magnesium is very important for your bones – it is said to be just as important as calcium for bone health. Magnesium is vital for heart, kidney and muscle health. Many sports scientists, doctors and nutritionists believe it is the most important of the minerals in sports nutrition. There are a multitude of other important functions carried out by magnesium. One that caught my attention was that it helps to convert glycogen to energy, and it helps mitochondria (the powerhouse, or battery, of the body) to function properly. Mitochondria provide energy to the body's cells. The more mitochondria we have, the further and faster we run. Magnesium also helps muscles to contract and relax.

Phosphorous: This helps repair muscles and acts as a buffer to acidic and alkaline levels in the body, neutralising the body's PH levels. It is second on the list of the most abundant in the human body.

Calcium: Bananas have only a small amount of calcium, but there is a little there, all the same. Calcium is important for building strong bones, regulating muscle contractions and helping with blood clotting.

To be honest, there are a large number of activities that the above electrolytes carry out – for example, electrolytes also help prevent cramping. I have listed only a few. I think the important thing here is just to let you know that bananas are a good source of electrolytes and are very beneficial. There are other electrolytes in the body, such as sodium, which are important; however, bananas only contain a small amount of sodium. Common salt is a good source of sodium, but not in large doses. Sodium works with potassium to regulate water levels within the body. It is actually said to be the most important electrolyte in the body – just not very abundant in bananas. You lose roughly 500 milligrams of sodium for every pound of sweat lost during exercise, so it is still important to have a certain amount of salt in your diet. The body still needs it.

Other nutrients

Pectin

Pectin is not an electrolyte but a soluble dietary fibre which is high in carbohydrates. Pectin helps to sustain sugar levels and is useful for runners who have gastrointestinal issues.

Bananas are a very good source of carbohydrates and contain fibre. However, do not be concerned about the fibre in bananas. We often think of high-fibre foods as foods that make us go to the loo – not good when running a marathon! However, the fibre in bananas is known as soluble fibre and has just the opposite effect, so you are safe here.

As I have said, bananas are a very good source of carbohydrates. They contain slow-release carbohydrates, which means that they do not give you the sugar spike associated with fast-release carbohydrate food. You do not want a sugar spike or sugar rush when running a marathon. I will cover this in more detail in Chapter 6 when we'll be looking at what to eat in the morning before the marathon. You will have more of an understanding of this then.

Vitamin B6

This is important for the transportation of oxygen to the cells and for keeping a healthy immune system. It helps in the formation of red blood cells and to regulate blood sugar levels. Bananas are a rich source of this vitamin.

Vitamin C

Bananas are full of vitamin C as well. This helps fight against colds by boosting your immunity and reducing inflammation. You can be susceptible to colds after running a marathon, when your resistance is low and your immune system is at rock bottom. Vitamin C is a powerful antioxidant that protects us against free radical damage, which is a side effect of exercising and running. It can also help in post-marathon recovery.

There are other nutrients in bananas, but these ones I have listed are the most abundant. This should give you an idea of what an excellent food it is as fuel for marathon running.

You may ask what is wrong with other types of fruit. During the week and after a run, nothing. All fruit is full of nutrients and water, fibre and carbohydrates and good for recovery. However, other fruits are generally more acidic, especially citrus fruits. This can cause reflux and will probably make you feel sick, especially when churning out long miles. Bananas have only a small amount of acid, and this is folic acid. So you are safe to eat bananas before a long run and a marathon. Experiment with them before your long run and see how you go. This will be very important as you get into distances of around 16 miles or more – that is, where you will really need to replace your carbs.

If you don't want to eat bananas, try porridge or toast/bread and peanut butter. Bagels, pancakes or waffles with syrup are all good. This reminds me of being in the USA where these foods are very common for breakfast. They are also a good way to start your marathon running day. I have mentioned bananas, rather than these other foodstuffs, as an example here because I use bananas to fuel my running all the time – and it works!

I will leave this subject here and come back to it in Chapter 6 when I look at pre-marathon preparations on the morning of the event.

Refuelling and rehydrating on the run

As your mileage increases beyond the 10-mile mark (with possibly up to 1.5 hours or more of running), now is a good time to start thinking about rehydration and taking on fuel, not just before your run or marathon but during it too.

As I have already said, over a lesser mileage, rehydrating and refuelling is not such as issue. But over longer distances it is. If you are already comfortable with taking your water with you, then fine. But if you don't, then there are one or two things you can do. They may not be entirely practical, but at least it will keep you safe. One is to hide a water bottle on your route. Seriously, if you are running in the country, there may be one or two strategic points where you can hide a water bottle. It's not ideal, but I have heard of people doing just this. Another is to have a partner, or friend, accompany you on a bike and hand you water as you need it. It is also a good idea to have your training run route close to your home base. You are within striking distance of home if anything goes a little wrong. You can also use your home as a base to replenish yourself mid-run if you go past it too – although there may be a temptation to stop if you run past your home. Do what is best for you, but keep it safe.

As for refuelling, have something before you head out on your long run. But make sure it is a good couple of hours before and not too much in terms of quantity. As I have mentioned, bananas or porridge are a great idea. Take a gel about 15 minutes before you head out the door. You can experiment with different types of gels (we'll look at these again at the end of Chapter 4). I find Science in Sport (SiS) gels are perfect. Gels may take a little getting used to. SiS gels are less viscous than some others and I find them easier to swallow – more so if you wash them down with a mouthful of water. They are my 'go to' gels for my marathons. A good idea if you are carrying a water bottle and don't have enough hands to carry gels (or if like me you really do not get on with gel belts) is to put half a dozen jelly babies in the pockets of your shorts. They are real power packs and full of carbohydrates. They are probably easier to eat and really should not give you gastrointestinal problems. To be contradictory here, some people seem to think that certain gels will do. So experiment with everything you are going to eat and digest on your long runs. That means breakfast, gels, fluid, the lot. As I have already said, use your long runs as a refuelling and rehydrating dress rehearsal for the real thing. Find out what works for you and what doesn't. Now is the time to do it, so experiment. You can then go into your marathon with peace of mind, knowing what will work for you. Also, do not forget to wear the same gear you will be wearing on the day of the marathon. Cover every base and tick every box. The less you have to worry about, the more stress-free it will become.

Month 8

The schedule

	Sunday	Monday	Tuesday	Wednesday	Thursday	Friday	Saturday
Week 1	13 miles	Rest day	3 miles	8 miles	Rest day	5 miles	Rest day
Week 2	15 miles	Rest day	3 miles	8 miles	Rest day	5 miles	Rest day
Week 3	16 miles	Rest day	3 miles	8 miles	Rest day	5 miles	Rest day
Week 4	10 miles	Rest day	3 miles	8 miles	Rest day	5 miles	Rest day

You are now into what I call very-long-run territory. That is 14 miles or more, although 16 miles is around the distance where the physiological and psychological changes start to happen. The physiological changes are things such as an increase in mitochondria and the recruitment of muscle fibres. The psychological benefit you get from long runs of 16–20 miles is an increase in confidence, knowing that you can run for longer distances and can spend two hours or more on your feet. Your glycogen stores should last for 16–20 miles of running, or around two hours. I find when I run my marathons, if I get to 16–20 miles and I feel OK, then I will finish. If anything is to go wrong, it is usually at this stage. But do not worry about this. It only goes wrong if you have not prepared yourself correctly and have not done everything you should. By ticking all the right boxes in your training and preparation, you should be absolutely fine.

In month 8, there is a slightly bigger step back in mileage after week 3. In running 16 miles you will have run the highest number of miles, both in your long run and your weekly mileage. So step-back weeks are paramount for recovery purposes and for being able to carry on with the following week's training without being too fatigued. You are getting closer now to your eventual very-long-run target of 20 miles. I still regard this eighth month as the 'build' phase of your training. The walls of the house analogy again!

Month 9

The schedule

	Sunday	Monday	Tuesday	Wednesday	Thursday	Friday	Saturday
Week 1	14 miles	Rest day	5 miles	6 miles	Rest day	5 miles	Rest day
Week 2	18 miles	Rest day	5 miles	8 miles	Rest day	5 miles	Rest day
Week 3	12 miles	Rest day	5 miles	10 miles	Rest day	5 miles	Rest day
Week 4	20 miles	Rest day	5 miles	8 miles	Rest day	5 miles	Rest day

This is now the furthest you will run, and the mileage is as high as it gets in both your long runs and your weekly mileage – so well done! You have hit the magical 20-mile mark in terms of your training runs. You are nearly at the end of the road as far as your training is concerned – not quite there, but nearly.

After the 20-mile run on Sunday, week 4, you will start your taper period. The taper is the period of training where you drastically cut your mileage after your last long run leading up to your marathon. I have dedicated a whole chapter to the last 3 weeks of training (see Chapter 5: The taper). This is because it is very important that I concentrate on your cut in mileage, not just from week 4 of month 9, but also for your final few weeks.

You will notice that in your long runs on Sundays I have alternated longer mileage with shorter mileage each week. Again, this is for recovery purposes. I would not recommend you follow an 18-mile Sunday run with a 20-mile run the following week. Experienced marathon runners would be able to handle this. And, of course, it is possible that you may be able to as well, but I feel that at this stage, so near the end of your training, a shorter mileage week following a longer one can only be beneficial from an injury-prevention and recovery point of view. Again, by keeping it safe and sensible, you dramatically increase your chances of success.

In week 3 there is a slight increase in mileage on Wednesday. As you are cutting mileage on your long Sunday run for the week, I think it is a good idea to give you two runs of averagely long mileage within three days to keep your aerobic base and endurance ticking over. Not too stressful but enough to give you some sort of benefit.

It is also very important at this stage to make sure you take rest days. I have mentioned the importance of this before, but it is even more imperative now with this long mileage. If you have to juggle your training schedule about, make sure your rest days are after the most intensive training days – that is, after your long Sunday run, or days when you are training for two consecutive days, etc. Because you are first-time marathon runners, I advise you not to train for any more than two consecutive days. If, for any reason, you feel you have to tweak or juggle your weekly training schedule, and if you find there is a time where circumstantially you have to run on three consecutive days, then take two to three rest days after this. Again, this is very important.

By now you will have such a good aerobic base and standard of fitness, that you will not lose anything in terms of fitness levels over a couple of days of not training and taking rest days. I know of runners who almost panic if they miss a day or two of training runs. It will not matter one bit. I say this as a competitive marathon runner who has had this happen many, many times. I have regularly missed days here and there because of things happening in my everyday life. I have not always been able to get out when I want to. Has it made a difference? Not at all! Please do not panic; a couple of days training missed will not matter. You are still getting the work on board regardless. But, if possible, make sure you do not miss your long run! This is the backbone of your whole training schedule.

If you train hard every day, that is seven days a week, you will pick up an injury, guaranteed. This is probably more applicable to those of us who train to some sort of intensity as our training regimen is more full-on. But all the same, running every day of the week is, to me, not a good idea. I don't it and never have done (unless I include a recovery run, which is the same as having a rest day). For one, you do not really need to. If you have a continuous plateau of hard work, day after day, only one thing can happen: injuries and overtraining syndrome. Hence, the importance of rest days and days off.

Overtraining syndrome

Basically, overtraining syndrome is a condition that can strike any runner. As a rule, any runner who ups the intensity and mileage to such an extent that their bodies do not get adequate rest and recuperation is at risk of becoming overtrained. It is basically an imbalance between stress and rest. I personally think this subject is extremely important. It is something we must get right, so I want to look at it here in more detail.

You may think because your mileage peaks at just short of 40 miles (in month 9, week 4) you will not be at risk of becoming overtrained. Certainly, compared to someone who runs 120–140 miles weekly, it would be fair to say that the chances of you succumbing to this are far less likely. However, there is still a chance it could happen. True, your running mileage over the whole training cycle is far, far less than someone who is aiming to run a competitive marathon to a high standard, so are you at risk? Possibly! I would say that if you are training sensibly, you are minimising the risks considerably. However, upping your mileage and training too hard are not the only reasons overtraining can set in. In some ways the term is something of a misnomer as there could be a combination of things causing this. There are other things to consider. Before we consider these other factors, here is a list of some typical symptoms of overtraining syndrome:

1. Constant fatigue
1. Moodiness, short temper, irritability
2. Becoming depressed
3. Interrupted sleep patterns
4. Loss of appetite and weight
5. Total loss of enthusiasm
6. Muscle soreness that is constant
7. Susceptibility to injury (plus niggles/injuries that do not clear up)
8. Susceptibility to illness (let's face it, your immune system will be low)

Even after taking a few weeks off, if you are suffering from overtraining syndrome the time off may not help things improve. It could take months to sort it. But don't worry – I am not going to let this happen. Hence the importance of this section where we are going to look at it in a little detail.

Overtraining syndrome (also known as underperforming syndrome) can be defined as the time where adequate rest and recovery is not sufficient to allow for all the stresses of the training schedule. Whether training for a competitive marathon or just aiming to finish, you still need downtime. I have incorporated rest days into the training schedule, and these will have you recovering adequately from the sessions you do. I have also told you what to do if you have to tweak or rearrange your weekly schedule. That is all fine, but there are other things to consider. It is worth knowing that, along with the stress of training, other stresses will hinder recovery. I will list them and explain their importance.

Sleep

I have looked at sleep already, but I will include it here too from an overtraining point of view. One way of raising stress levels is by lack of sleep, and this will have an impact on your recovery. Lack of sleep raises the levels of cortisol (a stress hormone) in your body. This is the same hormone that is produced when we are stressed, angry or irritated. Elevated cortisol levels can affect your immune system, and in the long-term continuously high levels can be harmful to your health. It can result in lower bone density and can cause stress fractures. It also hinders muscle damage recovery because high cortisol levels actually break muscle down. When we are sleeping this is when the repairing and regeneration of our muscles is happening from our previous workouts. The combination of a lack of sleep and high cortisol levels makes this a bit of a vicious circle. However, the body does produce some levels of cortisol. These normal levels are produced naturally and are of benefit to our liver (for removing toxins) and help regulate sugar levels. So it is not all bad. It is just elevated levels that are detrimental.

When we sleep our bodies release growth hormones. This stimulates muscle repair and helps build bones. Even though we are 'out for the count', the body and brain are at their busiest repairing everything from the stresses and activities from the previous day. Runners need eight hours or more of sleep in order to let the body do its recovering. So try to get plenty of sleep – it's good for illness and injury prevention too!

Illness

Any illnesses or infections can put extra stresses and strains on the body. I would advise you to cease any training runs if you succumb to any sickness. You will not be doing yourself any favours by training when you are under the weather. If you are not well, get yourself right first. Then carry on with your training when you feel well enough, restarting at a stage in your training cycle where you are able to handle it. Do not be too ambitious and try to take on too much if you have had time out. Remember, you have been unwell, and your body needs a little TLC. Do not try to play catch up. You will get back to your original fitness levels. Obviously, this depends on the amount of time you have been off for. The longer the time off, the more time you take in trying to get back to your original levels of fitness. Take your time!

Diet

While you are training and ramping up the mileage, you need to take on board enough calories to avoid a calorie deficit. However, because you are not training at a very high intensity – churning out hill reps, doing speedy training sessions on the track and the road, etc. – you will probably not have too much of a problem here. This just goes back to what we have already said about having a balanced diet. As you approach the longer mileage, it will be a good idea to make sure you get enough of the right food on board to cover you for these extra miles. In my research, I recently looked at how certain levels of carbohydrates can lead to underperformance and the overtraining syndrome problem. A low carbohydrate diet leads your body to utilise protein and amino acids to produce glycogen. Since both of these are the building blocks of muscle, you will get a muscle breakdown. The body is using amino acid and protein to fuel the body. This will lead to muscle damage. The experts claim that muscle damage interferes with glycogen storage and metabolism. By now, if overtrained, even a high carbohydrate diet will not help keep up glycogen stores. This is a real vicious circle.

This is all a little deep and technical. But I am sure you will agree that it is worth knowing what can help cause overtraining syndrome. I am totally convinced that a balanced diet (in addition to carbohydrates, remember that protein and fat are also important) will have you pounding the roads with no real problems. I have already said that your training is not all that intense. It is the mileage that you do on the road that will get you round. But just be aware of the diet question and try to keep it balanced. I do, and my training is far more intensive. Without trying to sound arrogant, I have never had a problem with overtraining. To be fair, one size does not fit all as each person's body reacts to different things. But I do feel that not overdoing things helps considerably. By having a good attitude towards recovery and taking rest days when scheduled, I have probably been slightly more undertrained than overtrained, which is fine. But eating a healthy diet, getting plenty of rest and having the right attitude will go a long way to making sure you hit the road in a fit state.

Stress: lifestyle and work-related

Any stressful situations in your private life or at work can have an impact on your training, resulting in underperformance. These are common causes of overtraining syndrome. Both lifestyle and work-related stress can certainly lead to a lack of sleep – and then a whole vicious circle could kick in, especially when combined with the other factors listed above.

If you follow this training regimen, eat a proper diet and get enough sleep, you will be fine. But if you do feel a little stale, fatigued or lethargic, and your enthusiasm levels are low, it's very important that you take time out.

I said earlier in the book that I want to take away any fears and concerns you may have when it comes to taking on the training and marathon itself – that is, to make it as stress-free for you as possible. So you may be thinking that overtraining syndrome is another thing to worry about in your quest (along with hyponatremia, injuries and any other issues I am looking at through the course of this book). Not so! Just be aware of these issues, but do not stress over them. I am covering these topics as they are very important to your wellbeing. The training and advice in this book are designed to get you through this schedule (and the marathon) in one piece. Look on this with a positive attitude, not a negative one. None of this is unsurmountable. I am covering all of this to make you aware of some of the pitfalls along the way and to make sure you steer clear of them. As a competitive marathoner, my way of training has kept me, by and large, injury-free. As I have said, I had the foot issue and the plantar fasciitis to deal with. But in all the competitive marathons and the thousands of miles I have logged, I've done so almost entirely injury-free. I have also not suffered from any of the other conditions I have mentioned. Not least overtraining syndrome. It has worked for me throughout my 42 competitive marathons. It will work for you too – **keep going!**

The magical 20-mile training run!

I regard the 20-mile training run as the holy grail in terms of your training. This is as far as you go! The pinnacle of your training regimen. To be honest, I never have the intention of running any more than 22 miles in my longest training runs. If my longest runs are no more than 20 miles, then that is absolutely fine. And I run competitively. I actually aim for 20 miles. Now and then circumstances may have me running a little further. For racing competitively this may be beneficial, but, as I say, this is often circumstantial and not imperative. So, as a first-time marathoner, there is absolutely no reason for you to run any further than 20 miles. In American running coach Hal Higdon's book *Marathon: The Ultimate Training Guide* (it's an excellent book to read and not too technical), he regards the last 6.2 miles of the marathon as sacred territory. In his training schedules for novices to advanced runners, he has no training runs of more than 20 miles for the longest run for anyone. As far as you are concerned, if you can run 20 miles, you will cover 26.2. The aim for first-time marathoners is just to finish – even by using a run/walk strategy if you need or want to. Remember what I said – walking is fine and, if it helps you to finish, do not be afraid to do just that. I would bet my last dollar that, if you walk towards the end of your marathon, you will find the strength to run the last few yards to the finish line.

There is something really quite rewarding in completing your last very long run of 20 miles. It is a massive confidence booster for a start. It gives you the mental and physical edge to complete your marathon on the day of the event. It is also vital in terms of getting you used to being on your feet for a long time. Another thing it does for you is it says 'I can do this'. You look back on all the training you have done with a sense of achievement. More positive thinking here. Maybe even a slight feeling of superiority. These positive thoughts are a great weapon to take with you into the taper period (more about this coming up in the next chapter) and into the marathon itself. However, keep these feelings in check. In the past, I have gone into marathons almost with a sense of arrogance – and have come unstuck. There is a difference between arrogance and confidence here. Keep it grounded.

Once you have completed your 20-mile run (even if you have to walk some of it, that is fine), you are nearly there, not quite, but nearly. However, reward yourself. Have that pint or glass of wine. It will do you no harm, and you have earned it.

My work colleague, Matt, whom I have mentioned before, did his last run of 20 miles three weeks before he ran London in 2011. He walked some of this, but we (I joined him for it) covered it in 3 hours and 5 minutes. He ran London in a time of 4 hours and 34 minutes and raised a tidy sum for the Orchard Vale Trust, a charity that helps people with learning disabilities. So a run/walk strategy was very beneficial and did not impact on his marathon on the day. The important thing here is covering the distance as comfortably as possible, both in your training runs and in the marathon itself.

Is there any benefit in running 26.2 miles in your training?

This is perhaps debatable. I have talked to runners who say, yes, you do. But as a coach and runner I disagree with this. Each person, of course, is entitled to their opinion on this subject. However, mine is certainly to take the cautious side here. Let me look at each side of the argument: yes (run the full distance) vs no (run 20 miles max).

Why some people say you need to cover the whole marathon distance in your training runs

The recurring theme on the 'yes' side of the argument is that it gives you the confidence to run the whole distance come marathon day. To be honest, with everyone I have asked and the research I have done, it seems to come down mainly to this one thing: it is a confidence booster. There are also one or two arguments on the 'yes' side that claim there will perhaps be a 'running on fatigued legs' benefit from the 20-mile mark for the last 6.2 miles of your training run, which will also prepare you for the big day. But the main reason seems to be being mentally able to handle the distance.

As far as I can see, these are perhaps the only two credible reasons for people to cover the whole distance in their training. I will throw this in here too: ultra-marathon runners will more than likely run these distances, or further, in their training. But they are training for races that can be up to 100 miles or more, so this changes the dynamics of the long training run completely. This is totally different to what is required of a first-time marathoner.

So the bottom line here is that by running the full marathon distance in your training runs, you will build confidence and be able to practise running on fatigued legs for those final few miles.

Why I say you should not run the full distance in your training run

Well, as far as I am concerned, based on the people I have helped, I am overwhelmingly in favour of first-time marathon runners *not* running the full distance during their training runs. There are exceptions, of course, as a number of these runners are competitive marathoners – but actually I feel it should be the same for them too.

One question for you here: why on earth would you need, or want, to run a full marathon three weeks before you are going to run one anyway?

We saw above in the 'yes' argument that it is a confidence booster. OK, but imagine if it does not go to plan. Your confidence would be shot. You would experience a massive dip in your mental ability to take this head on. It would be extremely detrimental to your ability to run the marathon on the day of the event. The positive attitude we are building, or have built, would take a huge hit. I have seen it before. With all the previous training you have done, you will have no problem completing a 20-mile training run. You will still be keeping it within the 'achievable' and safe guidelines – certainly, if you use a run/walk strategy. Running a 26.2-mile training run is quite different to what actually happens on the day of the marathon. The only similarity is the distance. On a training run, there is no atmosphere, no crowd, no aid stations, no heightened physical benefits that pre-marathon time and the day itself produces. I could go on and on. It is a training run – and a very long one at that! It may also just wear you out. It may affect your taper period because you would also be running another marathon-distance run on top of all the training you have done previously. The training schedule I have given you is to enable you to run 26.2 miles once, not twice! The taper period is your recovery time after your last long run. This may be compromised. You will effectively be running two marathons within a space of three weeks. You have been aiming mentally and physically for one. There is a very big difference between running your last long run of 20 miles, which is fine, and running the full distance. You will get all the benefits you need, pre-marathon, by sticking to a last long run of 20 miles.

I believe that for a very first-time marathoner with not much previous running experience for this venture, a last long run of marathon distance is a recipe for disaster. Is it worth jeopardising everything you have done because of over exuberance? Absolutely not!

There is, of course, also the risk of injury. By running anything longer than 20–22 miles, you push everything to the maximum. Your legs and muscles start to break down and fatigue. This increases every mile you run beyond 20 miles. Your skeletal muscles, tendons, ligaments and bones will also take a hit. To be honest, everything that happens in your actual marathon will happen here if you run the full distance in your training. So there is a chance that you will injure yourself. You may be able to handle this aerobically. But your muscles, tendons and ligaments may not – hence the dramatic increase in the risk of injury. The taper period will rectify all of this if done properly. By properly I mean sticking to a last long run of 20 miles. As I have said, I will explain all about the taper period in the next chapter.

Before we move on, the final thing I will say on the importance of *not* running 26 miles in your training is this: your last three training runs I have suggested in month 9 are 18 miles, 12 miles and 20 miles, so if you run 26 miles, rather than the suggested 20, there would be a massive jump in overall mileage in the last 1–2 weeks. Firstly, 12 miles to 20 miles is an 8-mile jump in mileage, bearing in mind you have run 18 miles in week 2, which is fine. This is totally structured and well within the guidelines that are underpinned by the months of training and building up you have done. But a jump from 12 miles to 26.2 miles as a last long run is a massive leap. This would be 14.2 miles if you run the whole distance. That is more than a half marathon distance. I think this speaks for itself. My advice to you as first-time marathon runners is this: stick with a 20-mile training run as your last long run. Anything longer and you are entering unknown territory for you. Please don't be tempted!

I always recommend taking at least one month off after running your marathon – and I mean at least! This is another reason not to run 26.2 miles in training.

Should you run for 3 hours or stay with 20 miles for your last very long run?

I have not explained to you yet that some coaches say running for three hours is more or less equivalent to running for 20 miles in your training. This is the case for some people. Matt again is a very good example of this. (I use Matt as an example as he is someone I helped to train and coach for his very first marathon – so very similar to you. Therefore, he is a great example of how you can successfully train to run this for charity and get round unscathed on the big day.) As I have said, Matt ran his last long 20-mile training run in around 3 hours and 5 minutes, which ticks both of these training boxes (give or take 5 minutes), so that is fine. However, I am not entirely sure about this rule because for many people the two factors (distance and time) may not equate.

Let's find out why this is the case by looking at the two extremes: competitive marathoners and first-time marathoners. There are two very quick runners at the Taunton Athletic Club whom I help Charlotte coach sometimes. I also run with them and compete alongside them. James Watson and Phil Burden are our two marathon speedsters. Both James and Phil have run the London Marathon in 2 hours and 28 minutes and come in the top 50 at London too. Both have also represented England as veteran runners because of their performances. So they are quick! I am sure they won't mind me saying this, but the fact they are both in their forties makes this even more impressive. So firstly, taking this into consideration, if I said that the 'running for three hours rule' was something they should do, as opposed to running for 20–22 miles, then the following would happen. At their standard of ability, if they went out and ran for three hours or more, they would run for well in excess of 26.2 miles. They would probably run for about 27–30 miles as a training run. Whereas if they ran for two hours, then they would probably cover about 20–22 miles at comfortable pace. The bottom line here is they would have to run very slowly to cover 20 miles in three hours. Of course, this can be done, but let us not forget that they are very quick and there is the danger that they would pick up the pace anyway. Even their very slow pace would be faster than most. I should also imagine a certain amount of frustration would also kick in at such slow running. Competitive marathoners would do something in between three to four and up to six very long runs (maybe even one or two more) in their schedule. Most of these runs would probably contain some faster stuff thrown in, such as race pace running or progressive running, or maybe even 3:1 running (running the last quarter of your long run at a much faster pace – another type of long run mentioned in Hal Higdon's marathon training book). Hence the danger for these guys of running too many miles. This may seem irrelevant to you as a first-time marathon runner who is not aiming to run your first marathon competitively. But this is vitally important in showing you the discrepancies in faster training paces and hours spent on your feet as opposed to sticking to running 20 miles.

Before I move on, let me say that I do not want to cause offence by comparing very quick speedsters to people running for the very first time. It is only to use as a comparison for your benefit. The term novice that I use in the book simply means someone who has never run a marathon before. It is not a condescending or arrogant term. I was a novice marathoner once, so were James and Phil!

Let's now consider the other extreme: a non-competitive runner who is just aiming to get round. If I asked you to run for three hours, then the opposite would happen. If you were hoping to get round the marathon in five hours (just for argument's sake), as regulated by your pace, then it is possible you would not cover anywhere near the 20 miles needed to complete your last long training run. So this would not work. To run a five-hour marathon your average pace per mile would be around 11 minutes and 30 seconds. If you were to run for three hours at this pace (what you run in your long runs and other training runs will be more or less similar to the pace on the day of the marathon – if anything you may run the marathon a little slower, but this will be explained later in the book), then you would fall way short of the 20-mile target for your last long run. You would probably cover 15–16 miles. If your marathon pace is slower than this, then you would cover an even shorter distance in your last long run. Basically, you would not meet the requirement of running 20 miles and all the benefits it provides before you start your taper. It's important to remember that the 20-mile training run is as near to being event specific as you can get, so falling short of your mileage is not recommended. As I have already said, this would work for someone like Matt whose average pace means he would run 20 miles in around three hours, at about 8 minutes and 30 seconds per mile. If this is you, then you are perhaps rather lucky. You are ticking both of these boxes and that, in this instance, is fine. Matt was just faster than the average time for his 2011 London Marathon effort. The average time for that year, I believe, was 4 hours and 37 minutes. But for the majority of you, I would really recommend that you stick to running 20 miles for your last long run – not the time of three hours as doing so would mean you may well fall short of your 20-mile target.

Final comments on the long run

I'd like to apologise to those of you who are governed by kilometres, and not miles, when you run. There would be equivalents here, which would equate in both time and distance. Personally, I love miles and really struggle with kilometres. Kilometres don't mean much to me, but miles speak volumes. My pace times are all in minutes per mile not minutes per km! I seem to remember James and Phil plus another of my running buddies Phil Roberts – another sub-3-hour marathoner that I regularly train with – having their GPS watches set to kilometres. It throws me out totally when they beep after every km as we are running. Whenever they start talking in kilometres, I have to ask them to speak in English! I guess it is just an old-school attitude that someone well on the wrong side of 50 hangs on to!

Phil Roberts has a personal best time of 2 hours 51, so we are of similar standard. The two Phils, James and I often run and train together. We are rather like a band of brothers. We have a lot of fun and banter. This is another reason why you might like to run with a group. It helps. The banter is fun. Hence why I am always complaining about their watches set in kilometre repeats and not miles. They certainly keep me on my toes. In fact, more often than not, I am trailing in their wake!

Use the long training runs as a bit of a dress rehearsal for the real thing. Experiment with fluids and food before your run. Find out what works and what doesn't. If you have porridge, bananas, water or a cup of coffee and it agrees with you, then stick with it. Don't change anything.

If something does not agree with you and you find you have stomach problems, then try something else. Acidic citrus fruits are not ideal, but experiment with gels and jelly babies. I'd recommend you take some with you as they will be your saviour if you do find the going tough. Your very long runs are not just for a fitness benefit. They also let you know what works for you and what doesn't. Once you have found a fuelling and hydrating strategy pre-run that works, stay with it. As a good post-run refuelling and recovery drink do not forget the chocolate milk drinks too. Before we finish this chapter on the long runs, I'd like to focus specifically on using gels for these long runs and during your marathon.

Gels

Earlier in this chapter, I briefly mentioned sports gels as a way of replenishing your carbohydrate stores. I use sports gels for my marathons. It is a good idea to buy a few sports gels and to experiment with the different types. I like SiS gels. They agree with me, and I find them less viscous than some of the other brands. Experiment with these on your long runs. Some people find they can cause stomach problems and struggle to get on with them, but this is not the same for everyone. I have never had this problem, but we are all different. So try out different brands to see what works for you. But make sure you try them out on your long Sunday runs. If you think they disagree with you, make sure that it is actually the gels that are giving you stomach problems and not something else. In my marathons I have a gel about fifteen minutes before my marathon starts, and then I have one every 45 minutes to an hour while racing. The longer you are on the road, the more you may need to have. So if you are taking four to five, you might want to consider using a gel belt. In smaller marathons it is quite possible to have someone pass you a gel en route as you are running. I know one or two people who do this. In bigger marathons this should not be so much of a problem as they have gel stations on the course. I have even seen gels pinned to people's shorts before. Refuelling is important, so try to get this right on your long training runs.

5 The taper

The final 3 weeks before the marathon

In the previous chapters I have given you some schedules for your training. These may be a little different from those you have seen in other books on running. In most other books the training schedules are often grouped together in one section, usually at the end of the book. I have treated the training schedules as part of your journey by presenting them in sections interspersed with advice and comments along the way. My way of doing it may seem a little disjointed to you, but I feel that covering everything as we go along is beneficial. It is a good way of explaining all and sundry as you progress through your training. There are probably many things that you, as first-time runners, may be unsure of. This is my way of ticking every box as we progress.

So this is why I have dedicated one chapter to this next part of your schedule: the taper period. This is vital and needs all of your attention. I'll say it again: the taper period of your training is extremely important. It can make or break everything you have done over the last nine months. Personally, I love this period of the training schedule. I hope you will feel the same way as me. During this period, I look back on all the hard work I have done over the past few weeks and months and really enjoy drastically cutting my mileage and easing off. I look on this almost as a winding down period within the schedule. And that is exactly what it is. During the taper, competitive marathon runners will cut their mileage, but keep up the intensity, for the last three to four weeks. But as first-time runners you will just be cutting right back on your mileage as there has been no intensity to your training. You will be continuing to run at the same pace you have been running at over the last nine months. There are some other important aspects of the taper period I will look at, but, as far as just the running and cutting mileage side goes, that is it. The miles are in the bank.

Now, it would be a fair question if you asked me: 'Why is there a whole chapter dedicated just to the last three weeks, and such a small part, of the training schedule?' And my reply would be: 'Because these three weeks leading up to the big day of your marathon are vital.' This is make or break time. This is not just a case of cutting your mileage. It is not as simple as that. Apart from the running aspects, there are many things in the taper period that we need to look at. We have to get this right. At the beginning of this chapter, I explained that I thoroughly enjoy the taper period. I love cutting the mileage, no longer having to grind out those extra hard yards. Does this surprise you? Perhaps so, perhaps not. I do have a rather unusual attitude here because, as a runner, I don't mind *not* running (either as injury prevention or as recovery time off after a marathon). I actually enjoying *not* running as much as I love running. Amusingly, this often has some people looking on me as being a little unconventional in my attitude. Don't get me wrong. I am passionate about what I do here. I am just at ease with my cutbacks and my time off. Many runners, probably most, have a real problem with not running. I do not! So this leads me nicely into the taper period. This is something many people really struggle with. Therefore, we need to get this absolutely right. Now, again, please do not worry. There are things I need to look at. But going through everything you need to do will have you lining up on the start line of your chosen charity marathon. The taper is not something to worry about. It should be a really nice time in your training. It is for me! I will take you through this and lead you along this rather pleasant path to the start line on the big day.

What exactly is the taper period?

To answer this question, let me take you to the 'building a house' analogy again. The taper period is the roof of the house. Apart from the marathon itself, the taper is the last piece of the jigsaw puzzle.

Easing off during these last few weeks before the marathon will give you a chance to recover from the months of training you have done and from the long mileage you've been doing recently. Remember, your last long training run was 20 miles. You need to recover from this. This happens during the taper. During your winding down period, you will cut your mileage each week from your 20-mile training run right up to the marathon. Actually, sometimes I wonder how many people have actually recovered as much as they should have when they line up on marathon day. I would not be surprised to know that quite a few people had not. I know of more than one runner who either did the whole 26.2-mile distance in their training or raced in another marathon during their taper period for the London Marathon. Seasoned marathoners, or ultramarathoners, with an excellent aerobic base may get away with this. But it could easily backfire. Use the taper sensibly to prepare you for the oncoming event. Along with needing to recover from your last long run and all the other training, you actually become fitter as you recover. And this process of you getting fitter during these last few weeks could be totally disrupted if you do too much now.

Why do you become fitter when you ease off during the taper period?

You may remember that in month 5, I discussed the step-back weeks as a form of recovery. The taper has the same principle, just on a slightly larger scale. There is something known as 'supercompensation' built into your training. This means that if you train hard and then rest appropriately, your fitness will return but to a higher level than it was before – that is, it supercompensates and prepares itself for a greater future training load. This happens after your heavy training load when you ease off the mileage. As far as you are concerned, it's your last few weeks leading up to, and including, your 20-mile training run. Quite simply, your body repairs all the muscle damage from your training. The muscle fibres repair themselves and become stronger than they were before. Hence, you get fitter. Basically, your muscle strength improves. Your bones, ligaments and tendons also get stressed by the long mileage and all the training, so your whole physiological system needs to recover. Resting during the three weeks prior to your marathon allows everything to repair and strengthen. You will go into your marathon fitter than you have ever been. As an aside from the taper, I firmly believe that running your marathon combined with all the months of training beforehand will cause your fitness levels to skyrocket in the weeks you have off after your marathon. If you decide to run another marathon, the rest period after your first marathon will hold you in good stead for another marathon training cycle if this is what you decide to do.

The psychological side to the taper

Even though I said I thoroughly enjoy the taper period prior to marathon day, I have to admit there are many people who struggle a little with it. One reason is this: after training runs of such high mileage (plus all the other workouts) there is quite a void all of a sudden in your schedule. You have, week in, week out, been churning out the miles, and now you are not. Your brain and body have got used to this large amount of mileage. Many runners find this a little difficult to cope with. There is the temptation to go out and do just one more long run, or do more than perhaps you should. You must resist this temptation. This is the time to do less, not more. It is a common mistake that is made in the taper period. Your brain tells you that you have not done enough. For some reason over eagerness can cloud your judgement. Be happy with what you have done. If you have successfully negotiated your 20-mile training run, you are there. It does not matter how long it takes you or how many times you stop and walk. You have been on your feet for a long period of time in your last long run and that is good enough. Take it ... and enjoy an easier final three weeks. As long as you keep things ticking over for the three weeks of the taper, prior to the marathon, you will benefit from a cut in mileage. Please do not think you will start to lose fitness – you won't. In the last week before your marathon, you do not gain or lose any fitness at all. The only reason you go out for any runs then is just to release some pent-up energy – and to keep you from going stir crazy if you are by now climbing the walls. As you will see in the training schedule I give you, the mileage in this final week is minimal.

Taper madness

This phenomenon is something that some marathoners suffer from in the taper period. It is not just about trying to convince yourself that the work you have done in the preceding months is enough to carry you round (and you don't need to grind out more mileage), but also about a few other things, such as:

- ghost injuries
- illness
- withdrawal symptoms

These three things can sometimes happen in the taper, so we'll look at some of the ways you can avoid these and get through the taper successfully. But please do not get anxious about it. I will say it again: I enjoy the taper and look on it as my best friend. Use it to your advantage and embrace it. It really is nice to start easing off. The hard work is in the bank, and you have a very special day in your running calendar to look forward to.

Ghost injuries

Ghost injuries are, basically, just that. They don't exist, but your brain thinks they are there, hence the name. They are a part of the taper madness phenomenon. Every little niggle, or ache, seems 50 times worse than it actually is. There is a fear of breaking down injured before the big day. After all the hard work done in your training schedule, not making the start line is just not an option, so every little ache or pain is amplified. It can become a vicious circle. The more you stress about it, the worse it seems to become. You start to believe it too, and you convince yourself that you are perhaps carrying an injury. Fret not, this is more than likely your brain playing tricks on you. Believe me, if you are injured, you will know. After all the mileage and training you have done, the chances of you really injuring yourself during the taper are extremely unlikely. You are cutting your mileage now, not increasing it. If you were going to succumb to anything (and I have tried to make sure you have trained in a way that avoids injuries), it is highly likely that it would have happened before you start your taper. Unless you totally broke down in your last long 20-mile training run, or you are carrying something that really is sore, then you are fine. If you ran your last very long run without any problems, what makes you think you are not going to be OK now? If you are really that worried, take two or three days off – remember what I said about not losing fitness over a short period of time, even a week, especially at this stage! I bet you find that when you go out for your next run this phantasm of an injury/ niggle will miraculously do a disappearing act.

Even competitive marathon runners, who have much more intensive training schedules, are not exempt from this ghost injury phenomenon. In fact, I have something of a ghost injury story of my own. In 2011, the same year I ran the London Marathon with Matt, I was at work on the Friday before the big weekend. I was crouched down on the back of a trailer, which was connected to another vehicle. From what I remember we were picking up rugby poles that had been left out from the previous rugby season and needed to be put away. I had crouched down in order to get off the trailer to keep it safe. We were actually very low to the ground anyway, but all of a sudden, the vehicle that the trailer was attached to moved a couple of feet. I fell, banging my knee on the trailer, and it actually did hurt. The marathon was taking place the following Sunday, and there was a lot of charity money riding on this, so I was quite worried. That evening at home I tried a very slow run. I made it to the end of the road but had to stop as it seemed too sore. To say I was concerned was an understatement. Anyhow, early on Saturday morning, Julia, Lucy and I met up with Matt, his wife and his daughter, and we travelled to Hammersmith on the coach provided by Weston Running Promotions as part of their London Marathon tour package. I was sitting with Matt on the journey, and I told him what had happened. I was still anxious but had decided to try to run as there was too much riding on this marathon. I know! One of the golden rules is don't run injured or ill, but I had to try. At the London Marathon expo, I bought a spray for my knee. I sprayed this on to a crepe bandage and kept the bandage on my knee until Sunday morning. I am an optimistic person and, as concerned as I was, at the back of my mind, I kept up a positive mindset hoping it may still be OK. Marathon day came. I handed in the official plastic bag containing my track suit and gear at the baggage lorry at the Championship start. I lined up with the other runners. The gun went off. And off we ran. I knew almost immediately – well, after the first ten yards or so – that I would be OK. After a mile, I could not feel the pain at all. It seemed I had dodged a bullet. I finished in 2 hours 37. It was the quickest marathon I ever ran. Please believe me when I say I am not trying to show off about my London time, but show you how sometimes when things seem hopeless, they actually are not. In fact, they can often turn out better than you could have imagined. I consider this to be the nearest thing I have had to a ghost injury. OK, I did bang my knee at work, but if it had been that bad there is no way I could have been able to run a marathon, let alone a PB. It just would not have been possible. The substance I put on it with the crepe bandage plus the day's rest it had after knocking it on the trailer may have helped a little. But a full-blown injury, or a really bad knock would have had me finding the St John Ambulance people en route. On the Friday night, I had almost convinced myself that all was lost, but it certainly was not. My brain had amplified the problem.

Please be sensible, but look on my story here as a case of mind over matter and an appearance of an injury that really wasn't there – or at least not nearly as bad as I made out.

Illness

The taper is a time when people tend to wrap themselves up in cotton wool. You will probably feel like totally quarantining yourself from anyone who even coughs! Sure, if you have a work colleague who comes in with a cold and cough, then you will probably want to keep out of their way. But a cold is just that – a cold! Nothing too serious. You would have to be incredibly unlucky to come up against someone who has such a debilitating illness that it would have you on your knees if you caught it. Even a sore throat or a few sniffles a couple of weeks out will probably have gone by the time of the big day. If you do have a few sniffles on the day and your temperature is normal, then go with it. You are aiming just to finish, so you should be fine. But never run if you have a high temperature and you are really suffering. However, as I said, you would have to be rather unlucky, indeed. Personally, with my work, I had my lunch breaks and teas breaks with the other guys I worked with in the same mess room. In the 42 marathons I have entered, I have never had to pull out because I've caught an illness from someone else. Of course, over the years, millions of people have run marathons, so there will be a percentage of people who have had to pull out because they have become ill. I have no idea what the percentage is, but I bet it is small. However, be on your guard just in case, but don't worry too much. There is an old saying: with a cold in the throat and above, run; below the throat, don't.

While we are looking at illness, it would be worth briefly considering the state of your immune system during the taper. Experts say that up to three days after your last very long run (that is the beginning of the taper) your immune system is at a lower point than normal. This is because after your last long 20-mile run, combined with all the work you have done preceding it, your immunity has taken a hit. These three days are probably the time when marathoners are more likely to succumb to illness. Perhaps be a little more vigilant during this three-day period. If, for some reason, you do develop the 'marathon sniffles' in the week before the marathon, do not stress too much. I know I have said this time and time again, but you are not there to run some stunning time. Your aim is to finish, get that medal round your neck and raise some money for your chosen charity.

As with the ghost injury situation I found myself in previously, I also have my one and only pre-marathon illness story. It's not a bad one, but one that I will mention anyway. It may help you make up your mind whether to run if you have something that is not too serious.

In 2014 I ran the Three Bridges Marathon in my hometown of Whanganui, in New Zealand. I have lived in England for over thirty five years, and it is always nice to get back to my home and my roots. I have some very fond memories of my life there and all the people and friends I grew up with. Sadly, a few of them are no longer with us, so when I had the chance to run a marathon in my own country – even better, my hometown – I grabbed it. It was going to be, and was, rather surreal in a way. Julia, Lucy and I had gone back for a visit. We don't get back that often, so it was perfect timing that the marathon was taking place at the same time as I was back home in Whanganui. It actually took place only two to three days after we arrived in New Zealand, and I was still a little jet lagged. I had also picked up a throat infection (in fact, I had totally lost my voice), but I ran the race. I ended up coming second, in 2 hours 52. So, considering the sore throat, I was fairly happy. However, please be careful if you are feeling under the weather. Run only if you think you can honestly get through it. My sore throat did not stop me. But, please, be sensible.

There are two ways to help fight against illness in the taper: eating a proper diet and getting enough sleep. Let's look at these in a bit more detail.

Diet

Yes, the diet subject again. It has been said that the right diet can have a big effect in fighting colds and viruses during the taper and after the marathon. As a rule, those who exercise regularly have a greater capacity to fight off viruses such as colds because of the presence of certain cells within the immune system that destroy viruses. However, as I mentioned before, there is an 'open window' period of between just hours to a few days at the start of your taper where illness could strike. A balanced diet, with the right amount of carbohydrates, is said to be a great help in boosting your immune system. According to research, carbohydrates help to keep the stress hormone cortisol at lower levels. Cortisol alters immune system responses. I make sure I eat my fair share of carbohydrates, without being too particular about it, and it works for me. Remember, a balanced diet will tick all the right boxes. This includes keeping hydrated. Make sure you get your fair share of protein too. This will help keep the vitamins in your body at the right levels.

Sleep

I am certainly raking over old ground in this section of the book, and sleep is no exception here. I know I have looked at this earlier, but as part of the taper it is still important. The taper period is vital, so these topics are definitely worth mentioning here too. As with poor diet, lack of sleep will also raise the cortisol levels, which will affect the immune system. Try to get eight hours of sleep a night. There is a saying: 'sleep yourself fit.' It is true. As you sleep, your fitness levels improve because the body releases hormones that aid muscle recovery and help to strengthen the bones. Getting a good night's sleep will also help keep illnesses and viruses at arm's length. This will help your immune system to recover after a long few months of training.

If you find you are having trouble sleeping, try not to exercise within a couple of hours of going to bed. Keep off alcohol, caffeine and eating heavily before you hit the hay. Smoking and nicotine are totally destructive to your sleep patterns. Smoking also raises anxiety levels, and this includes vapes as they still contain nicotine. However, as a budding marathoner, I would really hope smoking is not an issue for you.

There are also breathing exercises and relaxation techniques that can help if you are really having trouble getting off to sleep. This, however, is outside my comfort zone as I know very little relaxation techniques. But it may be something you want to follow up if necessary.

Withdrawal Symptoms

Yes, you read correctly. Some runners do get addicted to exercise and running. I often wonder why some runners, even when injured, still insist on running when it will be totally detrimental to their situation. Or why runners who should be resting up and taking it easy still insist on going out for a quick 10k or more because having a few days off is sending them stir crazy and up the wall, especially when it is not necessary. One rhetorical question for you. Why, after running a marathon, do runners hit the track or road for a session just days after, when their whole physiological system is in tatters and needs downtime? I have seen runners churning out a fairly hard session on the track two days after a marathon, when they have another marathon to run looming up in less than a month! I have often struggled with this question and have never really got it.

Runners do have a rather strange mentality at times. I have often wondered why I have the attitude of being very big on recovery and of not running when you shouldn't. In fact, I go to the other extreme and have months off at a time. I have often thought, am I really that different to any other runner? Another rhetorical question that I still don't know the answer to. Perhaps I am – who knows! What I do know is that one reason runners get that 'runners high' is because of something called endorphins. These are the natural pain relievers that the body releases during exercise. This feel-good effect is said to be very similar to the one experienced by opium and morphine users. So this is now starting to make some sense. It is also known as the 'legal high'. So, yes, exercise can be addictive. This is one of the reasons runners go out and run when they shouldn't. Perhaps this is one of the reasons why marathoners sometimes get the taper wrong. They feel guilty and actually become irritable, anxious or down in the dumps because they are not getting their running fix. This is certainly true for some marathoners in the taper period because the big reduction in mileage leaves them feeling empty and frustrated. You will remember me talking about the void in training earlier in this chapter. This is a classic case of the void, just more extreme. It is totally detrimental and can ruin everything, undoing all the previous months of hard work – and all in a brief moment of your training schedule. At this stage, just one more long run or the wrong type of training run can be all it takes to bring your whole marathon dream crashing down around you.

There is a difference in being a little nervous or restless prior to the big day – and thus feeling raring to go (that is actually quite normal, and fine) – and having a real all-consuming running addiction. By all-consuming I mean it takes over your life. If it is bad, it interferes with just about everything and clouds your judgement. This is a big reason why some runners run on niggles and injuries and then break down. It is really a type of withdrawal from an addiction. Do not make this mistake. What I have said here may seem very extreme and a little brutal, but you, the athlete, are the important person here, and your wellbeing is one of the main concerns of a coach. My aim is to get you through in one piece, so I have to cover all bases. I will also say that having a running addiction is extreme, and the majority of runners have a very successful marathon. If, in the very unlikely event, you do struggle with the taper, just think of the charity you are representing and the people who will be rooting for you. They need a healthy runner in a fit state.

Here are some things you can do to help you if you are finding the void in your training during the taper a little difficult. As a coach to some of our marathoners here in Taunton, I am always watching out for tell-tale signs of them doing a little too much in the taper. Occasionally, Charlotte and I have had to pull in the reins a little, but not often. You are no different and, as unlikely as it is, I just ask you to be aware of it. I am not saying you are suffering from a running addiction at all. But these suggestions should help if you do find you are struggling a little with a void in your training.

Keep running: Just be sensible and stay within the constraints of the taper. (In the next section, I will cover the taper schedule for your last three weeks of training before the marathon. This will keep you safely within the training guidelines.) Even though you still need to hit the road as part of your pre-marathon training, by continuing to run you will be releasing some pent-up energy as well. The taper will improve your fitness levels, but this is not its only benefit. It also is a form of recovery, it keeps your fitness levels up to standard and it is a good stress buster too.

Listen to your head, not your heart: Keep telling yourself 'less is more'. This is a common saying in marathon training. It is absolutely true. Remind yourself that you will get fitter by easing off – because you will not if you don't. Immerse yourself in the thought that you have done the hard miles. You do not have to get up next Sunday morning and run 20 miles. You have done it. Embrace it. When I walk through the door after my last long training run, I feel a real sense of self-satisfaction. You deserve to feel quite proud of what you have achieved so far. Enjoy this moment and know the next three weeks will be a lot easier for you. The marathon will look after itself. Try not to stress yourself about that now. I will guide you through this in the next chapter. Don't look too far ahead. Just enjoy the moment of getting through your training successfully. You deserve some praise, so reward yourself.

Keep yourself busy: Read running magazines for inspiration (but only if it doesn't add to your non-running frustrations). Go for walks. Go to the cinema. Start learning a foreign language or take up learning an instrument. Play video games. Go swimming or cycling. You may even want to contact the charity you are supporting and let them know how you are doing in your preparation for the marathon. Anything at all that takes your mind off going for another long run if you feel tempted. Don't forget you will need downtime after the marathon too. For some runners, this can prove as difficult as the taper. So the above activities may be useful for post-marathon blues. However, if you feel like me after running a marathon, you won't entertain any thoughts of running at all for quite a while until you feel ready to do so.

Schedule a sports massage on a non-running day of the taper: This has a physiological and psychological effect. If you are feeling a little pent-up, it will relax you. A massage also removes metabolic waste and helps blood flow. It will help to remove knots. I tend to get one or two of these, and Fiona has to dig a little deeper to try to sort them out when I am having my sports massage. I always get them in my calf muscles. 'Knots are muscles that become slightly constricted, and the muscle fibres have become stuck to each other. This makes the removal of waste from the area much more difficult, so it becomes a little tender and tight.' These were Fiona's exact words when I asked her to explain what knots in muscles are. Do not worry, though. They will not hinder you in any way. You may not even know you have them. I never do until I have a massage. A massage will also help keep your muscles feeling fresh and light, and psychologically it will help take your mind off running and keep you on track. But make it a light massage, not a deep one. Hopefully, some of the above should help you if you are really going stir crazy.

Month 10: the taper

In this section, I will give you a marathon taper training schedule to carry you through to the big day. I am giving you a three-week taper, rather than other options sometimes used, such as a two-week taper or a four-week taper (and I have also heard of people having up to five or six weeks). The length of the taper may be open to discussion, but I feel that, with the amount of training you have been doing, three weeks will be more than adequate. It is also the most common amount of time taken for a taper and will suit the training you have done. There is an argument that says, if you have been training for around six months to a year, then perhaps a four-week taper is a better idea. There is an awful amount of mileage in your legs. That would certainly be true for a competitive runner with their training schedule. Most runners still have a three-week taper, though, me included. So I will stick to a three-week schedule here for you. You will be absolutely fine with this. It will totally suit your schedule.

The schedule

	Sunday	Monday	Tuesday	Wednesday	Thursday	Friday	Saturday
Week 1	13.1 miles	Rest day	3 miles	5 miles	Rest day	5 miles	Rest day
Week 2	8 miles	Rest day	3 miles	3 miles	2 miles	Rest day	Rest day
Week 3	Marathon						

You might think that this is only a two-week taper, but your 20-mile run was three weeks before your marathon date. To make it a little easier to follow, here is your taper period in its entirety. It shows all the training sessions from your last long 20-mile run up to the marathon. It is exactly the same as above but also includes week 4 from month 9.

	Sunday	Monday	Tuesday	Wednesday	Thursday	Friday	Saturday
Week 4 (Month 9)	20 miles	Rest day	5 miles	8 miles	Rest day	5 miles	Rest day
Week 1	13.1 miles	Rest day	3 miles	5 miles	Rest day	5 miles	Rest day
Week 2	8 miles	Rest day	3 miles	3 miles	2 miles	Rest day	Rest day
Week 3	Marathon						

As you can see there is a big cut in mileage in your long Sunday runs. I have explained earlier in this chapter why you cut the mileage in the taper. Cutting mileage equals recovery plus a rise in fitness levels. A large chunk of your total weekly mileage volume is reduced through the decrease in mileage on your Sunday runs. It is also important to cut back on your other weekly runs, too. This is not quite so drastic, but important all the same for recovery purposes. However, overall, your mileage is reducing.

In the penultimate week of the taper, you will see your Sunday run is 13.1 miles. Does it seem a familiar distance? You may notice this is exactly half marathon distance. I usually find most runners and coaches suggest around 12 miles for your penultimate long run. However, I quite like doing the half marathon distance as my second-to-last long training run for one reason: it is a confidence builder. It is a psychological boost you can take into the last two weeks of the taper and the marathon itself. Even at this stage there is not too much of a difference between running 12 miles and running 13.1 miles. The difference in mileage is minimal and will not have an impact on your taper. It is well within the guidelines. For those of you who may think you have to keep up the mileage or are finding it a little hard to cut back, then this can help. In your mind you are tackling half the marathon distance, so psychologically you feel you are running further. Of course, it is further, but only by a mile. But I have to stipulate, this is optional, flexible and not imperative. Running 12 miles is still fine. It's your choice, and neither will have an impact on your taper.

In the last week of the taper – the week prior to the marathon – you will be running much less than you have been in some of the previous weeks' training. Just because this last week's mileage is quite minimal, it is no less important than any other week of your training schedule – far from it! Although minimal, it is a real 'ease off' week, and it is very important here to do very little. It is a known fact that, after all the previous training you have done in your schedule, you will not lose or gain any fitness in this final week. So, and this is important, there is no need to do any more than the recommended training in this week, or in the rest of the taper for that matter. If for any reason, apart from perhaps illness or injury, you find you cannot get out and run in the last week, DON'T PANIC! It will not matter one iota. As we have explained, the last few weeks of training runs are really just to keep things ticking over and to release a little nervous energy. So this is why I say it is no less important than any other week. It still has its purpose. Your actual fitness levels will not change.

Here is something for you to think about from a previous taper experience of my own. It should help put your mind at ease over fitness level worries in the taper weeks. A few years back I ran the Barnstaple Marathon in North Devon, and pre-race, in the first week of my taper, I did not run from my last long 20-mile training run on the Sunday, until the following Friday. So that was four days of no running. My run on that following Friday went very well, and I ran with a renewed sense of vigour. Because of work and various other things happening that week, I was unable to run. I ran a very successful race at Barnstaple and that gap of four days of no running did not matter at all. Obviously, I would have preferred to have kept things ticking over for that first week of the taper, but it was not possible. It is fair to say a good aerobic base helps here, and with all the miles you have been running up until now, you will be fine if you have a little hiatus in your training. So take my experience as the proof that you don't need to do too much in the taper, and also to relieve any fitness concerns you may have you if you cannot get out on the road for a few days. It will not matter. DO NOT try to play catch up on any days and miles lost through not being able to run in the taper. Just go with it. As Adrian Marriott, the ex-GB marathoner and fellow coach I have previously mentioned, used to say: 'The hay is in the barn.' Believe it – it's true.

Lastly, in terms of your training, I want to take a brief look at the day before your marathon – in this case the Saturday of month 10, week 2. I will look at other non-training aspects of what to do the day before in Chapter 6.

There are one or two things people say you should and should not do on the day before a marathon. One is staying off your feet as often as you can. That is not a bad idea. In a big city marathon, you will have to go to the expo, or place of registration, to pick up your number and other things. You may find there is a fair amount of walking around to be done. Some expos are big and there is a lot happening. However, there are plenty of eating and drinking places, so you can always find somewhere to take the weight off your feet. The London expo, for example, is open three days before marathon day, so you could pick up your number on either the Thursday or the Friday to avoid the rush on the Saturday. But, if you are concerned you are spending too long on your feet, do not worry. It will not matter too much. Whether you are at home or staying in a hotel pre-marathon day, the following may help. Once I have picked up my number and found a place for an earlyish tea later on in the evening, I spend the rest of the afternoon just chilling in the hotel. I go through all of the paraphernalia I have picked up from the expo and just relax. If I am running London, we have an Italian restaurant that we go to, which is just over the road from our hotel in Hammersmith. So not too much walking. Just take it easy and, if you are concerned that you have done too much walking, enjoy some downtime time later on in the day and just relax. I honestly don't think a little walking about the day before will impact on your marathon. Unless you are walking a silly number of miles, don't worry too much. But all the same, enjoy just chilling.

Should you run the day before?

I have not included going for a run the Saturday before your marathon in the schedule (or whatever day your marathon may be on), so you may be surprised to have me tell you this: yes, you can run. OK, this may sound totally contradictory. I am telling you to chill and relax, but now saying you can run! It is actually a good idea. However, this must be minimal and be very slow. By minimal I mean 1–2 miles and absolutely no more. Apparently, the Kenyans go out for a couple of very slow easy miles the day before, but they are running practically at walking pace. That to me says it all. If you do run, keep it slow and minimal.

Why can you run the day before?

A good question. It will help you to run off any nervous energy and help any pre-race nerves. It also helps to get blood flowing around the body and to the muscles. It stimulates the nervous system, which improves brain to muscle communications. So it is certainly beneficial. But please do not feel this is absolutely what you have to do the day before. This is not a rule that is written in stone. I will leave it up to you to decide what to do here. Personally, I do not run the day before. I certainly experience a feeling of nervous excitement, but I do not suffer from anything more than that. I am quite happy reading up on all the pre-marathon information I have collected. I find this quite stimulating anyway, and I get into the marathon zone this way. Even in smaller marathons far removed from the likes of Berlin or London, I am happy going over race day tactics at my leisure and making mental preparations in the confines of my room. I regard my pre-race warm-up as an adequate way of ticking all the boxes mentioned above apart from the one about running off nervous energy, which I am fine with. The body adapts very quickly. This is personal and works for me. Do what you think will benefit you most. It is entirely up to you. It is totally optional. Either way, you will not be jeopardising anything by running or not running the day before.

What next?

From a training point of view, that is practically it. You have done the work out on the road and had a good taper. The only thing you need to do now is run the marathon. I said to you earlier, in the Introduction, that once you step up to the plate on marathon day the chances of you finishing are 99% in your favour. In many ways the hard work is done. The marathon itself is the final push.

Now, it is absolutely fine to be a little self-congratulatory. You have successfully negotiated your training and your runs are done. In the next chapter I will look at some non-training aspects of your marathon preparation. Well done, you have every reason to be proud of what you have achieved so far.

Pacing

Before we move on to the non-training aspects of your pre-marathon preparations, it is worth having a look at your pace. This also may sound a little contradictory as I have continuously said that you do not need to worry about how fast you run your marathon and training runs. This is still the case. However, it is also a good idea to use the pace that you run most of your training runs at as something of a guide. This is certainly the case on your long runs as these are actually the most event-specific runs you do. Take note of your pace just out of interest. Again, don't be concerned at all about intensity. You are not racing. I know I keep banging on about how you are not racing but just aiming to finish. This is because it is important, and it is a trap many still fall into. It is human nature to worry about pace and how fast you should be going. I am no different to you here. I still need to pull the reins in on some of my long runs. I am always having to tell the marathon runners that I help coach to try to keep to their pace and not go too fast. Even with experienced runners I help, it can still fall on deaf ears. I find that youngsters we coach often struggle with pacing. But adults can be just as bad. Do not fall into this trap. I must add here, though, that the younger runners we coach do not run marathons. This is entirely aimed at the adult runners we coach.

The pace you have been training at (or at least the average, as it will fluctuate a little) is a good guide to what your finishing time will be, give or take a little. There is no pressure here; it is merely a guide. The reason

I have included a section on pace here at the end of the chapter, and not alongside the training schedules, is because I wanted to make sure that you did not focus on, or stress too much about, how quick your pace is. Just go with the flow and run at your own comfortable pace. Once you have some sort of an idea about your predicted finishing time, then, if on the day it feels a little too quick or uncomfortable (there are often other variables here, such as weather conditions, terrain and the likes), aim to finish anything from 10–20 minutes slower. If, for example, you run at 11 minutes and 25 seconds per mile (this would give you a 5-hour finishing time), then slow down to a 12-minute mile. This would mean your finishing time would be between 5 hours 15 and 5 hours 20. The 99% chance you have of finishing has now been reinforced even more. You may find your pace is faster or slower than this. You will all have different personal paces and finishing times. Nobody is any better than anyone else. We all have personal benchmarks and times. Again, take this on board now. Never compare yourself to anyone else or try to race other people on the day. Stick to your pace and never be afraid to be conservative with your aims – this is very important!

6 Last-minute preparations

The week before

From a non-training point of view, there are a few things to think about in the week before you run your marathon – mainly diet again, but there are other pre-marathon preparations, too. Most of these need to be done the day and night before, but it is not a bad idea to start thinking about getting your head round certain things in advance and not leaving things to the last minute.

Let's look now at the things you need to think about and do during this final week so that you can make sure all the boxes are ticked:

1. Get the balance right with your nutrition and hydration
2. Get enough sleep
3. Don't change anything
4. Have a sports massage
5. Give your feet some TLC
6. Sort out any pre-marathon tasks
7. Contact your charity

Nutrition and hydration

This is a recurring theme, but a very important one. In the week before your marathon, keep to a balanced diet and make sure you take protein on board as well as carbohydrates. You need to let everything rebuild in the taper period, and a balanced diet with the right food will help here. If you are drinking plenty of fluids – that could be tea, coffee, squash, fruit juice or water – then great, but do not be too obsessed about it. Remember that fruit and vegetables are full of water, and you'd be surprised at the amount of water you consume through eating these foods. Remember, the colour of your urine is a great guide. If it is dark, you need take on board more fluid. If it is light or pale-straw coloured, you are OK. The body does not lie. Also, make sure you do not take on too much fluid as this can be detrimental. Rehydrate at a sensible rate, only when you need to, and you will be fine.

I used to have a totally different attitude to this. I would pile on the carbohydrates a week or so before. I would eat jacket potatoes for lunch and pasta for tea. I would attempt to consume around two litres of water a day (I did not find this easy, and imagine how many times I was running to the loo!), and this was on top of what I was already taking on board in terms of fluid without realising it. I hasten to add, I was not obsessed by this refuelling and rehydrating strategy. It was just what I thought I had to do. But after attending Renee McGregor's nutrition workshops, I came out with a totally different and far more relaxed attitude. For my last four marathons, I have drunk and eaten sensibly during the last week, without being too particular about it, and I've had very successful races.

Carbo loading in the last week

Carbohydrate loading is something that many marathon runners do a few days before the event. Done in moderation this is fine. I have already said that I used to eat far more carbohydrates than I really needed to. Some people starve themselves of carbohydrates, by using the carb-depletion theory, then pack the carbs away a couple of days before. The thinking behind this is that the body will soak them up like a sponge and be more efficient in turning the carbohydrates into glycogen to fuel the body. I am a little uncomfortable with all of this. It can cause a few problems and there are side effects. I do not think there is anything wrong with adding a few more carbohydrates to your diet if you feel this is what you want to do. But starving yourself of carbohydrates is not good practice when you are hoping to get to the start line firing on all cylinders. For one, your brain needs carbohydrates and nutrients. Starving yourself of these will compromise the functioning of the brain. Having no carbs for two to three days can make you feel sluggish and slow. This is totally opposite to the 'caged animal, raring to go' feeling that you should be experiencing leading up to the big day.

One thing I have not mentioned that can happen in the taper, especially in the week before your marathon, is that you may gain a little weight. Please do not worry, this is quite common with some runners before a marathon. This happens because you are cutting right back on your training, but still taking on board carbohydrates. You do not have the same intensity or mileage in your training, so the extra carbs will not be burned and this may make a little difference to your weight. But most of this weight is water. Yes, absolutely true! For every gram of carbohydrate there are three grams of water, so the weight is the stored water. This is not a bad thing. You will need this stored carbohydrate when you run your marathon. Do not think for one moment you need to go out and run some of this off! You may think that being three or four pounds heavier will impact on your marathon. This is not the case. It won't. Go with it and look on it as an important part of your refuelling process that will help you to get round on marathon day. Believe me, after burning around 3,300 calories on marathon day, you will lose this extra weight. Here are some side effects of not eating enough carbs:

1   Your immune system will take a hit and be much weaker.

2   You can become irritable.

3   You may feel more hungry than usual.

4   You may feel mentally and physically drained.

5   You may have trouble sleeping.

5   You may experience lower self-esteem.

Don't forget that your taper period is the time you spend recovering from your overall training load. So the body needs carbohydrates to help keep your immune system strong.

As a first-time marathoner, you may not have thought about, or even heard of, carbohydrate depleting and loading. I think it is a good idea to consider this as a very important part of nutrition in the taper, particularly in the final week. The safe way to approach this is to keep things balanced. There are too many things that would negate all your hard work if you were to use the carbohydrate depletion theory.

Sleep

A few years ago, I ran the Amsterdam Marathon. I became quite friendly with many of the other runners when I was there. Some were doing the half marathon and some doing the full thing. On the morning of the races, one of the marathon runners I had got to know came down for breakfast having not been able to sleep a wink the night before. This can be quite distressing – obviously, many people think it will have an impact on their performance. However, it is not so much the sleep you get the night before that is important, but the sleep you get each night in the previous few days to a week before. Those are the nights that really count. Now, don't get me wrong, no one wants to have a sleepless night on the night before a marathon – this is of course not the ideal scenario. But, if this happens to you, please do not panic. It is extremely likely you will be OK. This runner still ran a successful marathon. I will go over this in a little more detail when I look at what you need to do the day and night before. This should also help you to relax. The thought that it will not matter too much if you do have a little trouble sleeping should help you to feel less stressed about the situation. But the bottom line here is to make sure you get a decent night's sleep over the previous week.

Don't change anything

This may seem a little trivial, but it is very important! Now is not the time to try out a new pair of trainers or have a change of heart in what you run in and try that new vest and shorts. Wear what you have been training in. You must adhere to this. Your long runs have been a dress rehearsal for the day itself. Wear the same kit you wore on your last long run. Hopefully, you will have been wearing the same outfit for most of your other long runs, too. Perhaps you have a vest or T-shirt advertising the charity you want to represent. Obviously, if people are running for charity they may dress up in all manner of different outfits. This is your call if it is what you want to do. It may be an idea to run in something a little more practical. Remember, you will have to do some of your training runs in your outfit. My marathon-running buddy James Watson and I often use a canal path to train on. It's popular with runners and right on the doorstep of his business. Logistically very handy and a good base to start and finish. A while ago we saw a runner training in her full firefighting outfit, so training in your full charity outfit can be done.

If the shoes that you have successfully trained in up until now are looking a little ragged, wear them on the day. Don't try a new pair now. If they have lasted this long, they are still wearable. They will get you round. When I ran the Barnstaple Marathon, I wore the same shoes that I'd worn during all my training plus my previous two marathons. My shoes had two holes about half an inch wide in the area near my big toes. The sole was also getting a little worn under my big toes. But they got me round the marathon no problem. I have a new pair now. But the old ones are absolutely fine for wearing on the track or for doing minimal mileage training such as hill reps. So they do not need to be retired entirely just yet.

Sports massage

I have already covered the benefits of a sports massage in Chapter 5, when we looked at the taper period. It is beneficial to have sports massages anytime in your training schedule. Do not have an aggressive massage as this may leave you feeling a little sore – make sure it is a gentle one. You may have one or two stubborn knots in your muscles, and the massage may have to be a little deep to remove them, but having this done three to four days ahead of your marathon will not affect you at all. It will relax you and help to get the blood circulating around the system. I try to schedule one with Fiona a few days out.

Give your feet some TLC

By this I mean your toenails! Seriously. We are leaving nothing to chance, and this means making sure this part of your body (your feet) that will carry you around the 26 miles and 385 yards and something like 35,000 steps are in working order. You need to make sure you do not damage your toes. I have a problem sometimes with the corners of my toenails digging into the side of my adjacent toe. I have often come back from a training run with a bleeding toe because it has been punctured by a sharp toenail. Just be aware of any sharp edges and spikes that could be a problem. Remove these and check them again the day before the marathon. Your feet are an intricate part of your body. There are something like 25–27 bones and over 100 ligaments and tendons in your feet, and these have taken you through the whole training schedule. After all your hard work, it would be a real shame to succumb to something as simple as a sharp toenail stabbing you as you are running on the day.

Sort out any pre-marathon tasks

These tasks include things such as picking up your race number, registering, deciding how you are going to get to the start line and by when. If you plan to drive to the marathon, plan your route and work out where you are going to park. If you are staying away from home the night before the marathon, you should have sorted your accommodation by now, but if you are staying in a town or city you do not know, then you still need to start to plan your route from your accommodation to the start of the marathon. Aim to get to the start line in plenty of time. I have sometimes cut it fine, and it just adds to stress levels. It is important to be organised because, on the day, you do not need or want any last-minute hassles. You want the day of the marathon to go as smoothly as possible. If you are running a big city marathon, the expo will be open a few days before. You will have enough time to pick up numbers, other marathon-day information, goody bags, etc. At the London Marathon, the expo at the EXCEL Centre opens on the Thursday and closes on Saturday evening. Berlin is similar. They can be very busy and crowded so get there in plenty of time. If you get there a day or two early, you will give yourself more than enough time. Just don't leave it until four o'clock on Saturday if it shuts at five!

A few years ago, I arrived, with Julia, at the London Marathon expo, at the EXCEL Centre, at around one o'clock on the Saturday afternoon to register and get my London Marathon championship number. I realised I had left my registration letter on the couch back at the hotel in Hammersmith. You cannot pick up your number and run without it. It was an hour (and a couple of journeys on the tube) back to Hammersmith. It is a bit like leaving your passport behind when going to the airport. Without it, you're going nowhere. By the time we went back and got it and returned to the expo it was three o'clock. I still had a couple of hours to spare, but it was cutting it a little fine. If we had left it any later, I would have been struggling. Don't leave it too late. Julia was very patient with me that day. It was my fault entirely. We got away with it. Unlike me on that day, keep a checklist of everything you need to do.

Contact your charity

To keep you focused and enthusiastic, contact your charity and let them know how you are doing. They will be very keen to hear you are doing

OK. You are supporting them, and they will support you too, making this a two-way thing. If your marathon is a big city one, then the expo will have an area for your charity, and you can visit them there. Pop along and tell them you are representing them. The NSPCC area hands out banners, rattles and all the paraphernalia for your supporting loved ones to make a row with as you run past. It is all good fun. The charities like to include your supporters as well so they feel part of your venture, too.

The day and night before

You are nearly there. However, there are still a number of things to be done the day before your marathon. Depending on the size of the event, you may have been to the expo and registered as well as picking up your number if it is a big city marathon. For much smaller marathons, you will either get your number on the day or have it sent to you. Some coaches believe that you should not spend too much time at the expo. They say: get there, get your number and leave. OK, that is a fair comment to a certain extent. However, the big city expos can be very interesting. I usually buy my race gels there. I often check out the NSPCC area. I say hi to the people there and let them know I am running for their charity. There are plenty of eating places and cafés where you can get some decent pre-day food and refreshments. I buy a bottle of water there and slowly hydrate over the day. (If you are really particular about getting more fluid on board, do it the day before. Keep it to a minimum on the actual day of the marathon.) You can always find a place to sit down and eat if you are worried about spending too long wandering about. Julia, Lucy and I probably spend a couple of hours at the expo before heading back to Hammersmith or, if we are in Berlin, to our hotel in Alexanderplatz.

If you are worried about eating and hydrating over the course of the day, then just keep it simple. I buy a couple of bottles of water and just sip on these during the day. Anything like sandwiches (bread is carbs) and fruit (not citrus and preferably bananas) will be fine. Just avoid anything spicy. Do not stress about it too much. Just keep yourself topped up. Once you have had a good look around the expo, head back to your hotel or accommodation and relax. It is a good idea to think about your evening meal. Over the road from our hotel in Hammersmith there is a nice Italian restaurant. We book a table for about 6.30–7 pm and have a pasta meal (nothing too much, just a nice average plateful and nothing spicy) and are normally back at the hotel by about 8.30–9 pm just to chill for the rest of the evening. It is best to avoid prawns and shellfish as they can give you gastrointestinal problems if not cooked properly. For the last couple of years, I have had a spaghetti carbonara. A nice mix of protein and carbohydrates and nothing that will cause stomach problems the following day. Pizza is another good idea. But don't overdo it. Just a nice comfortable meal. If you pack it away and eat a huge amount the night before, it takes longer to digest. This can also cause gastrointestinal problems the next day. This may surprise you too: if you think you may have a little trouble getting to sleep and feel a little wound up the night before, it is well within the rules to have a pint of beer or a glass of wine. It may just help you to relax and help you to drift off. As long as it is only one! This will not impact on your performance at all and will calm you if you need relaxing. But, as I say, just keep it to one drink.

Before you go to bed, get your kit ready so that you do not need to sort it out on the morning of the marathon. Pin your number to your vest, tie your timing chip to your shoe (if you have one, but not every marathon does) and get everything you need laid out ready to put on in the morning. Put your gels out ready to take in the morning, pre-marathon, and get the gels ready that you will be taking with you on the run. The fewer things you need to do and worry about the following morning, the better. You want to keep this as stress-free as possible. I suggest keeping a checklist of things you need. Just make sure your shoes, socks, vest (with number attached if you have it), shorts, gels and anything else are all ready. It can be beneficial to apply Vaseline to minimise the risk of chafing. If it is hot, or at least quite warm, then put a little Vaseline over, or just above your eyebrows. Yes, seriously. Some people who sweat a lot can have problems with perspiration dripping into their eyes. This is salty and can sting a little. The Vaseline will help keep this at bay.

I find it quite helpful to go to bed a little later rather than earlier. I have heard many people recommend getting an early night. That is, perhaps, the obvious thing to do, but remember the story I told you of a runner who could not sleep a wink the night before. Rather than go to bed early and lie there wide-awake thinking about the following day, go to bed when you are starting to feel tired. I have often left it to between 11 pm and midnight before putting my head down. I just lie on the bed with the light off and the TV on. It is not long until I start to succumb to tiredness. It is better to hit the sack a little later feeling tired rather than early when you are still buzzing and wide awake.

Can you run the day before?

Actually, yes, you can! It is not a bad idea to go out for a very easy jog of about 1–2 miles (but no more) if you are feeling a little wound up or anxious as it will help you to release a little pent-up energy. You may be feeling like a caged animal raring to go, so don't go mad. It is just, as I say, an easy jog, and when I say easy, I mean very easy! Apart from being a stress buster, a slow jog the day before also has a neurological benefit and other physiological benefits too.

Firstly, it is important to let you know that a very easy jog of 1–2 miles the day before your marathon will not have any impact on your performance the following day. It will not tire you out – just the opposite. It will help focus your mind and body and prepare you for the upcoming event. It will get the blood flowing around the body and fuel the muscles with nutrients and oxygen needed for the event itself. You may also think that a run the day before will use valuable glycogen stores. It won't, as this is minimal, and you will be taking on more carbohydrates through your diet in what you eat the day before and on the day itself. If you do decide to have a light run the day before and are visiting the expo too, then probably keep your expo jaunt a little shorter. But to be honest I would not stress about it too much. Remember you are aiming only to finish the marathon, and getting round with a run/walk strategy if need be, so the pressure is right off you. Try to enjoy the build-up and atmosphere as much as the day itself. This will be the case especially if you are running a big city marathon. Much smaller marathons may not have the same big city marathon razzmatazz. However, they still have every right to be part of the marathon-running circuit as any others.

Every time you run you open up the neural pathway. This is where the messages travel to and from the brain and the muscles. This helps to activate the muscle fibres. The more you activate, the better you run. A pre-marathon-day run will help you to be up to speed on the day. You will be opening up the neural pathways. By up to speed, I do not mean you are aiming to pick up the pace in your slow pre-marathon-day run. I have already discussed this. I mean you will be fully primed and ready. It also serves as something of a shake-up run. If you have travelled the day before on the coach or car for a few hours, then a very easy 10–30 minutes can help loosen everything up and stop you feeling so sluggish the next day. All of the above will help you. But it is not compulsory. If you want to run the day before, then run. If you don't, then don't. It's your choice entirely.

The day of the marathon

Once you get up, it is a good idea to get yourself sorted and get down to breakfast. Make sure you eat at least two to three hours before the marathon. On the morning of the London Marathon, I am up by 6 am. There is an early breakfast for the runners from 5.45 am. The marathon does not start until 10 am, so it gives me plenty of time to get there. However, the company we used to use for London – the excellent Weston Running Promotions, which was based in Weston-Super-Mare here in the South West of England and the brain child of John Joiner (a former London Marathon runner himself) – not only provided us with the hotel in Hammersmith, but also took us to the start line by coach (again, everything is stress free). The coach left at 7 am prompt, getting us to Blackheath Common by 8 am. I would then have two hours to get myself into running mode, have that last cup of coffee, sip on a little water if I wanted it, and go to the loo. There was also, of course, a warm-up to do. Even though we were a little segregated, we were in the same warm-up area as the likes of Wilson Kipsang, Kenenisa Bekele, Abel Kirui and, in 2019, Mo Farah and Eliud Kipchoge. Yes, I am name dropping, but just because I want to say that watching these magnificent runners go through their paces right in front of us was extremely humbling. Before too long we needed to get out to the start line, too. So the two hours after being dropped off by Weston Running Promotions gave me plenty of time to get myself ready and to focus on what lay ahead. (Unfortunately, due to the coronavirus pandemic, Weston Running Promotions do not operate anymore.) If I appear to be digressing here, I am just saying having plenty of time to get things done pre-marathon helps to make it stress free.

Before we move on to looking at what you should eat before your marathon, I have another slight digression, as I want to put a positive spin on the whole marathon-day experience. During these few hours before the marathon starts, I also find it interesting to hear other people's stories. In 2019, having been taken down to the start line of the London Marathon by Weston Running Promotions, I had a few moments to talk to Roland Gibbard, who was a representative of the company. Roland has run the marathon in 2 hours and 20 minutes, so he is very fast indeed. He told me of the time, a few years back, when he was running London and at one stage he found himself to be in the lead. It was only a quick story, but as we were walking across Blackheath it was just the sort of thing I needed to hear before racing. I loved the positivity. In a way, his story gave me a real lift to go out and run my best. It may seem a little irrelevant to you and perhaps a little pointless, but I fed off this. You may start talking to many people beforehand. Feed off any positivity, try to block out the negative stories of woe people may talk to you about. I do not want to sound arrogant or mean, but you will get stories from people who have had a cold, not been well, have got a niggle, and so on. To me, this is a negative way of thinking, one that some people use to cover their fears in case the marathon doesn't go according to plan. This is almost a defeatist attitude. When hearing these stories, these tales of woe, I am never dismissive or rude because people react in different ways. Sure, listen to them, but block out the negativity. I really mean this; a positive attitude helps considerably. Remember the chances of you getting from the start line to the end are in your favour by 99%. Nothing will go wrong: no one is there to judge you, you will be proudly wearing the vest representing your charity, and you will have a good amount of support and a tremendous amount of admiration both from those running with you and from those watching you. All of these things are massively in your favour. Feed off this.

What to eat before the event

This is up to you. But it is important to eat foods that contain slow-release carbohydrates. The favourite pre-race food for most marathoners is porridge. Wholemeal bread is also classed as a slow-release food, and my favourite pre-race food, bananas, are excellent. I have covered the benefits of this fruit as a pre-marathon breakfast before (see Chapter 4). By now you should have been eating a pre-long-run breakfast when you have been training. So stick to what you have been doing previously and do not change it on the day of the marathon. This is very important. I will usually eat a couple of bananas and maybe a piece of bread plus drink a cup of coffee or two. I will also have a small glass of water, and then I am ready to rumble. As far as caffeine is concerned, if you are a regular tea or coffee drinker, you will be fine. If not, don't experiment with this now. Just stick to water. Peanut butter is another good thing to eat. I tend to steer clear of any fruit juices as they are acidic and can cause stomach problems. The long Sunday runs you have been doing in your training have been the dress rehearsal for the big day. So, stick to what you have been eating for your long runs. A sudden change in diet may have a detrimental effect on your marathon. You may suffer from gastrointestinal problems or perhaps nausea, or both. Just go with what has been working for you previously. I remember Adrian Marriott telling me that before a race he used to eat a pot of cold porridge. He said it was pretty unappetising, but it worked for him. I have also had quite a few discussions with Adrian about eating food containing refined sugar before your marathon. It is quite an interesting topic, so let's look at this now.

Is sugar in your pre-marathon diet beneficial or not?

Well, it depends on what type of sugar. Your body needs sugar to run. We have already looked at how you can use carbohydrates – which convert into glycogen – to fuel the exercising body. Without getting too technical, glycogen is known as a polysaccharide. It is a complex carbohydrate, and it takes longer to break down. This means that it suits long distance running. Table (white) sugar is known as a simple sugar and is a disaccharide. This is the sugar that Adrian and I discussed at length as we talked about the risks of eating it before a marathon.

Many runners believe the theory that eating this refined white sugar for breakfast (e.g., in tea, coffee, jam and cereals) on the morning of a marathon will cause you problems. It was widely believed that if you ingest white refined sugar beforehand, then, when you start to run your marathon, the body will target this sugar as a readily available source of fuel. It will burn this with gay abandon, and once it has used this up, your body will immediately tap into other fuel reserves. It thinks, oh, lovely sugar, then rapidly burns up your other body fuel. When this happens, you get a sugar spike that causes you to crash and burn. This would happen fairly early on in your marathon, and then, as you could imagine, things could get ugly! This is probably the case for competitive marathon runners who up the pace a bit. But it is still worth looking at anyway. This theory makes perfect sense to me; however, there are more recent research articles that say refined sugar is actually OK. As usual with research, once you think you have got your head around one fact, a new theory emerges and everything gets turned on its head. To help us think about this, it is useful to consider the glycaemic index (GI) of foods. This is a tool that helps measure how quickly the body responds to different types of carbohydrates in foods. It is a relative ranking (from 0 to 100) of how the carbohydrates in these foods impact your blood sugar levels: low GI foods (0–55), medium (56–69), high (70–100). While delving into this topic, I have found that anything with a low GI is slow-release and will not cause a sugar spike (e.g., the GI of porridge is low, around somewhere between 40-55). Foods with a high glycaemic index will cause a spike (e.g., the GI of a baked potato is around 90 and the GI of jelly babies is around80). Normal table sugar has a medium GI of 65, so it does not have as high a glycaemic index as many other things that you could eat before you run your marathon (e.g., the GI of white bread is 70 and the GI of cornflakes is around 77-79). So table sugar is perhaps a bit of an anomaly here as it supposedly causes a sugar spike but has a medium GI index. I am not a scientist or nutritionist, so this takes me a little bit out of my comfort zone as my knowledge is not as good as these experts. So will not dwell on this too much and tie things up in knots. My way of thinking here is, again, to carry on as normal and do what has always worked – that is, to avoid simple sugar pre-long run and marathons. Perhaps one day I will experiment, test the theory, and see what happens. But for the moment I won't confuse things by trying this theory out. I do not want to confuse things for you, either. Therefore, carry on as normal and do what has been working for the past few months. My bananas have never let me down – and Adrian swears by his cold porridge. So, to briefly recap here, until more research from the experts proves otherwise, I will continue on as normal and keep refined sugar out of my pre-marathon breakfast.

Foods to eat and avoid on marathon day

Foods to eat:

1. Bananas
2. Bagels
3. Porridge
4. Wholegrain bread – toast it if you want too, but if you have gastric problems, it is best to avoid wholegrains

5. Peanut butter – this contains the right sort of fat, provides protein and is slow-release (excellent for runners!) so spread it on wholemeal bread, toast or bagels

6. Poached/scrambled eggs on wholemeal toast – this provides a nice mix of protein and carbohydrates, but eat three hours before as eggs take longer to digest

Foods to avoid

1. Anything spicy (probably unlikely for breakfast)

2. Sugar in tea or coffee

3. Jam

4. White bread – unlike wholemeal bread, this is a quick-release carbohydrate with a high GI

5. Fruit juices (too acidic)

6. Citrus fruit (again, too acidic)

7. Fatty foods such as sausages, bacon and fry-ups

These lists are a guide. If you have been eating anything else before your long runs, and this does not cause you problems, then stick to what you know. Don't forget to eat at least two to three hours before you run as, depending on what you eat, it could take this long to digest.

I will now look at important last-minute things to consider before you head off to run your chosen marathon.

Pre-race checklist

Your running kit

Make sure you have all of your kit on. This means everything. Track suit, shorts, vest, shoes, socks, and make sure everything is in a good state of repair. I am serious. I am not trying to treat you like children. I know of runners who have had elastic go in their underpants. You can imagine how disruptive and humiliating this could be. This is your big day. You do not want to be a source of amusement for others. I know of shoelaces that have snapped – and no spares! Things like this can ruin your day and certainly add to the stress levels. Tick every box. In some marathons timing chips are provided – as they are in the London Marathon. No chip means no official time. If you have a timing chip, it needs to be tied to your shoelaces, so make sure this is done. Some timing chips are already in your race number. You will have been told this information by the organisers, so make sure you know where your chip is if you have one. Make sure your number is pinned to your vest. Again, no number will mean no marathon. This is obviously a last-minute check as all of this should have been done the night before. However, it makes things foolproof by going through everything again. When your mind is focused on the event itself, it is easy to get a little side-tracked and forget other important pre-marathon things.

As for your running vest, if you are representing a charity, put your name on it. This is a massive tonic. It makes the event personal. When people are supporting you and yelling out your name, it really is an uplifting experience. It does not matter whether you know them or not. You will still get many people cheering you on. Sometimes you will make eye contact with one of the spectators and, when they yell out your name, for a very brief moment in time, they become your best friend. Supporters of marathon runners are very encouraging, and there is a great deal of respect here. So get your name on your vest!

When I ran my first London Marathon a few years ago, I had a championship start. I was raising money for the NSPCC and was wearing the green NSPCC vest. But unlike the people who had a place through a charity, I was racing as a championship runner because I had gained the London Marathon championship qualifying time in another race, the Gosport Half Marathon. As I was heading through to the championship runners' zone, two officials asked me to show them my running vest. They looked at me and started to shake their heads. I asked them what was wrong, and they told me that I was not permitted to wear anything else other than my club vest – after all, we were not charity runners; we were racing. There was not supposed to be any advertising on our person and we had to be wearing our club vest. With all the money I had raised riding on this, I was a little concerned to say the least. I thought I was going to be disqualified before I had even got to the start! However, they did let me through with a little wrap on the knuckles – but next time I had to be wearing the Taunton Running Forever Running Club vest. I did explain to the officials that I had been totally oblivious to this rule and it had been a total oversight. It was actually in the rules of the championship start; I had just not seen this. Luckily, I got away with it. I got to the start wearing my NSPCC vest (with my name on it), and when we were running, the support I got was a huge pick me up. Now when I run London, I do not get the same buzz from the charity supporters because I have to run in my club colours. On the day, the NSPCC do not know I am representing them, even though I am fundraising for them, because I am running in my club colours and not my charity vest. Don't get me wrong, I love running for my club, but from a charity point of view I run past the NSPCC supporters unnoticed. I slip through the net. When I ran in my charity vest by accident that first time, the support I got through their yelling and cheering was totally uplifting when the going was getting a little tough. It would be the same for Cancer Research UK, or whatever you choose. Take my advice, wear your name on your vest, make it personal and you will feed off the incredible support you get.

Check on the weather. London can be warm and sunny, so avoid wearing a black vest on a hot day as this will attract the heat. On the other hand, New York can be cold. Many runners wear gloves – for example, Paula Radcliffe. I am not saying that you will be running these two marathons for your first one (if you are, then that is fantastic), but wherever you run, just be aware of the weather. If it is raining, then you may need Vaseline. I mentioned chafing earlier, so apply Vaseline to areas that may rub as this will help prevent it. I have found that wet conditions once did make me susceptible to chafing, so I make sure I have a jar with me. It is best to put it on regardless. And remember to put a little Vaseline on your eyebrows to help stop your salty sweat from dripping into your eyes and stinging them.

If it is cold or raining, it is a very good idea to take an old throwaway top or even a bin liner – you can make holes in it to poke your head and arms through. You can wear these to keep warm and dry before you start. When the marathon begins you can discard them.

Your gels

These will help you to replenish some of the glycogen stores as you run your marathon. Take one about fifteen minutes before the marathon starts and then take them every 45 minutes to one hour. But do not forget to take them with you. If they are a little viscous have a little water at the next water stop to help wash them down. One of the reasons I like SiS gels is because they are not too thick.

Jelly babies

Yes, that's right, jelly babies! These are little power packs, jammed full of carbohydrates. I believe there are 5 grams of carbs in just one jelly baby. Remember they have a high GI of 80, so they will give you energy instantly, whenever you need it. It is a great idea to put half a dozen or so in your pocket and chew on one in between having your gels. They are small, easy to eat and will help to keep you topped up.

Remain calm

Try not to stress too much about the start and the marathon itself. You can use up energy by getting stressed out about the pending event. Just relax and enjoy the atmosphere. Keep telling yourself you only need to finish, no matter how long it takes. You will take a lot of pressure off yourself with this attitude. You can walk if you want to and run if you want to. You are in control here. You call all the shots. It is under your control, so take it easy and enjoy the moment. To get a little nervous is fine, but relax, take a few deep breaths and try to focus in a positive manner. You have made it this far, so you will get round and finish. Also remember there are many others here in exactly the same situation as you, so there is a wealth of camaraderie and support out there. You are amongst friends – all trying to do their bit and possibly raise money like you. Embrace this as it will help. I personally have run enough of these marathons to know that the support you get from other people is a massive help. You will talk to people en route that you have never met before, but at that moment in time you will feel as if you have been friends for years. The banter and chat are very uplifting. Also, think of that finishing medal you will get as a memento of what you have just done. It will be worth its weight in gold in terms of your achievement. Treasure it! It is a testament to your efforts over the last few months and the marathon itself. It is the icing on the cake.

The warm-up

It is a good idea to think of a warm-up as you head for the start line. Give yourself plenty of time and don't cram it in last minute. Keep it stress free.

145

Do not do static stretching either. If you want to do arm swings, leg swings and so on, then fine. But I think some gentle jogging will do it. Find an area on the road and just jog for about 50 metres – a few gentle runs up and down, nothing too strenuous.

I was watching the elite runners (Wilson Kipsang and Stanley Biwott in particular) warming up on the same area of road we used before the 2015 London Marathon. I was interested to see them do nothing else but just jog steadily up and down the stretch of road. They did not do anything too technical, but just kept it simple. So I did the same – and have done ever since! For races of much shorter distances, a good thorough warm-up is imperative (5ks, 10ks, etc.), but perhaps not here so much. The reason for this is you really do not want to start tapping into your fuel reserves too much before you even get started. Anything too vigorous will start to use up your stores, so just some light jogging and a few strides will suffice.

GPS watch

If you are using a GPS watch for your marathon, turn it on about 15 to 20 minutes before as there is nothing more annoying and frustrating than a watch that has not logged in before you start. (Some watches have longer battery lives that others, so the amount of time depends on what type you have.) It has happened to me before. Using a GPS watch is useful as you can keep an eye on your pace and aim to run a little slower than the time you may have predicted. If this is the case, you are increasing the very large odds of you getting round even more. I still say to you, though, do not be too concerned about your pace; just aim to finish. Sometimes running without any time constraints is a very good idea. This is certainly the case for you.

Last-minute checks

You are about to make your way to the start line. Double check that:

- your shoes are tied up in a double knot (not too tight, just comfortable)
- you have been to the loo
- your GPS watch is on (if you use one)
- you have your gels/jelly babies

- you've had a last little slurp of water if needed
- you have your water bottle (if you want to take one)

You are now ready to hit the road!

The start

You are now lining up and ready to go. Go through the positives and mentally focus on these. Use this following list in the form of mental notes to take with you when you are lining up and when you are running to keep you in a positive frame of mind.

1. Remember the fact that you are now lining up at the start means you are 99% likely to finish.

2. You are not at all worried about how fast you run this – 2 hours 30 or 6 hours 30, it does not matter. It is still a good idea to run slower than any predicted time, if you have one, but this is just to make it easier for you. You do not have to adhere to any set pace if you don't want to; just run at a nice slow pace.

3. Feed off the support, not just of your supporters and the spectators, but also of the other runners around you. Remember, you are not the only one here. There will be many others like you who are just aiming to get round with no added pressure. There will be lots of camaraderie, and you will probably meet up with other runners and make new friends both during the marathon and after it. You will probably also find that you will be the support that others may need – it works both ways.

4. Think of why you are doing this – for your charity (or if it is just for yourself then that is of course fine too). This is no way an added pressure; this is a tonic. The fact you are running for a chosen cause for whatever reason will drive you on. You will have the support of the charity you are running for. They will be behind you 100%.

5. Think of all the miles and hours you have spent on the road. This is the pinnacle of all your hard work. This is your moment. It is a very personal thing. This is a very special moment. Embrace it, hold your head up high and feel very proud indeed.

6. Do not in any way be afraid of this moment. Respect the marathon, but do not be in awe of it. I have said earlier in the book that millions of people have run marathons. Why are you any different? You most certainly are not in any way!

7. Lastly, don't forget that by running this marathon you are part of an elite group. Only 1% of all people will have run a marathon in their lifetime, making you very special indeed.

On the move

Once the gun goes and you have started moving, there are some things you can do that will help you:

1. It may not be the case so much in a smaller marathon, but in the bigger city marathons it can take a while for you to get over the start line. In the London Marathon, it can take 15 minutes or longer just to reach the start line after the gun has gone, so do not panic. The bigger marathons are chip timed. So you will get an official time from start to finish. This will be your actual marathon time, not the time you get after the gun has gone. However, remember, you are not too worried about what time you run it in. Just run to finish. I know I keep reiterating this fact, but it is very important that you adhere to this. It is very risky to get carried away and go too fast. Save more competitive and quicker stuff for future marathons if you decide to do anymore, not your first. I make no apology for repeating this time and time again in this book. It is extremely important, so please try to stick to it.

2. Your first mile should be slower than normal. I say this because with the atmosphere, nerves, excitement, camaraderie, the whole shebang, it is very easy to get carried away. Everything is heightened (mentally and physically), your heart rate is up, the adrenaline is pumping when you first start and there is a danger you may start off running too fast. You will probably not realise it until it is too late. You may pay for it later on. Your pace for the first mile should feel unnaturally slow – and that is fine. You will also find that the first mile seems to pass very quickly. Just go with the flow, chill and kill your pace.

3. Play mind games with yourself. Have milestones along the way. I do this in all my marathons. I tick off certain distances. First up it is 5k – just think: that's 3 miles completed already. Do not look at how far you have to go; look at how far you have run. Never look too far ahead – it is the same in training. Look at what you have done, not so much what you still have to do. That will come. Take it one step (or mile) at a time. The next milestone is 10k. You have completed nearly one quarter of the marathon at this stage. Then it is 10 miles, and by then you have completed over a third of the marathon. After this the next milestone is halfway: 13.1 miles. After the 13.1-mile halfway mark, the next distance I make note of is 16 miles. Why 16 miles? Because this is where you start to use up your available glycogen stores. Perhaps after running around 90 minutes will equate to this too. But certainly, I have found with my competitive running if I reach 16 miles and I am feeling OK, then I will be OK overall. It is just something to be aware of. I am not trying to put you off, but this is where things, perhaps, become more of a grind as your fuel supplies become low. Again, you may be absolutely fine, but if you feel you want to stop and walk, then do so! I also find, though, that once I have gone beyond 15 miles, then mile by mile, it is not so much of a jump from 16 miles to 20. I actually find these miles pass by more quickly than I thought they would. This leads me to the next milestone: 20 miles. When you have run 20 miles, look on the final 6 miles as just 10k. Once you get to 23 miles, then it is only 5k to go. You are so nearly there now. So you are breaking down the last 6.2 miles into bite size chunks. I also have one last little thing I do when I am running and counting down the last few miles beyond the 20-mile mark: I do not count the last mile. It may sound silly to you, but I tell myself once I have reached 25 miles I am there. It just makes the last few miles so much easier to manage. The last mile, from 25–26.2, just happens and looks after itself. For the last mile, picture in your head a running track. Think, that is four times around the track. That is all you have to do now. Then you have done it! When you have reached mile 25, then the last 1.2 miles is a mere formality. Try these mind games as you run to help you tick off the miles. This works for me. It is worth trying.

4. It is also a really good idea to put your name on your vest. This makes it personal, especially if there is eye contact with the supporters. It is a real tonic and helps tremendously. I can't recommend this enough.

5. It is great to get support and encouragement from any of your supporters. I find that it really helps nearer the end. In the London Marathon, my wife and daughter are usually waiting around the 24-mile mark. I am so near the end that it just helps to give me that little push to the finish line. But this is personal. It often depends on your supporters being in a location where they can get to see you. It is entirely up to you where you would want them, but seeing them and receiving their support certainly helps.

7 The finish and beyond

You are now running down the road and the finish line is only metres in front of you. You are just a few steps away from conquering the asphalt beast. This is a very special moment. You will then run over the finish line. Absolutely embrace this very special occasion. You have worked very hard over the last few months, maybe even years, for this moment in time. This is personal; take it on board and let it soak in. You will have the finishers medal put around your neck. It may not be made from a valuable metal, but it is worth its weight in gold. You can also celebrate the fact you have put your marathon to good use by raising money. It is a great feeling to think that all the money you have raised is going to a good cause. There is no better feeling than being able to contact your charity to say 'I have done it!' It is highly likely that your charity will have been watching out for you too. This is all very special. Once you have composed yourself and enjoyed the plaudits of those watching and supporting (nothing wrong with this, you have totally deserved it), delve into the goody bag you will have received at the finish and grab the bottle of whatever recovery drink you have been given. Have a few sips of this and kickstart your recovery process.

It doesn't finish here: post-marathon recovery

Your marathon has been run, and you are soaking up the atmosphere and ambience of the whole event. However, there is still a lot of work to be done. It goes beyond the 26.2 miles. You need to recover, and this starts the moment you place your feet over the finish line. I have just mentioned that you need to get some fluid on board. You need to start replacing everything that has been lost en route. Do not guzzle down large amounts of water or recovery drink at the finish line. This could upset your stomach, and there is a big chance it may come straight back up again. Just have small sips at a time.

Do you remember me telling you about the conversation I was having about chocolate milk drinks curing my post-marathon nausea? This type of drink is the best thing you could have as a recovery drink. The discovery came out of a very interesting conversation Fiona and I had. I was suffering quite badly with post-marathon nausea and wanted to find out what I could do about it. I was not happy with the idea of it being 'just the nature of the beast' or the theory of 'it goes with the territory'. I wanted to sort it. During our conversation, we discussed her brother Alec, a 2.49 marathoner, and why he (and others) did not suffer, but I did. Sure, everyone probably has a little nausea, maybe some more than others, but mine was so unpleasant that on occasions I thought I was going to keel over. Trips back on the underground to the hotel after the London Marathon were pretty grim when I was feeling like this. So we came up with the theory that, as I have no meat on me at all, my body was struggling to cope with the refuelling process later in the race. I did, of course, eat and drink sensibly before running London, but my skinny frame struggled. My body was actually eating itself. We concluded that, because my available fuel stores are depleted, my body goes into shock and in a way shuts down, thus causing feelings of nausea and feeling faint. I am basically running in what is known as a catabolic state. This is where the body uses muscle as a fuel basically to survive. But where does Fiona's brother Alec come into it? Well, he is of slim build and very athletic. However, I am slimmer. So after a marathon I am going to suffer more because I am leaner and have far less muscle mass – which, we've just seen, the body starts to tap into as a means of survival. Hence my feelings of extreme nausea. Fiona told me that Alec, even though slim, still has more meat on his bones that me, so this is why I suffered. Now, this is not meant to scare you off running marathons. My case was extreme. I am just over 5 foot 11, and after a marathon and all the training I dip to under 10 stone. I am also running at pace as we are racing; you are not. However, I would recommend you have a chocolate milk drink to consume after you have finished. For me this drink has sugar to get glucose back into my body and brain, and protein to get me back on my feet again. As I said, it killed my nausea. I would totally recommend you have the same. Julia and Lucy have one on them ready for me to drink, when we meet after the marathon, and by drinking this I can restore everything back to its normal state. I should also tell you that I have never, ever, felt nauseous while running the marathon; it was only after I had finished.

What do you eat after the marathon?

To be honest, as soon as I have finished, food is the last thing I want. I am thirsty so will have my recovery drink. You will probably find something in your post-marathon goody bag to restore protein and carbs. So when you feel like it, eat this. I already said that bananas are a very good food to have before you run. They are also very good to have afterwards, too.

After running London (and we are back at the Hammersmith underground station) my first port of call is Starbucks. By now I am ready for a coffee (with sugar) and some type of muffin or cake. Just enough to get something back into the body. It is your call, but try to get something on board as soon as possible to stabilise your sugar levels. Once we were back in the hotel in Hammersmith, Weston Running Promotions used to put on an excellent spread and buffet for runners and their supporters. There was everything from soup to sandwiches, fruit juice, crisps and so on. By this time it was about 2–3 hours since finishing. I was always ravenous, so it went down very well indeed. I have already mentioned Weston Running Promotions. They were the brainchild of John Joiner. He and his WRP partner Roland Gibbard and their team were a godsend when it came to running the London Marathon. We used them for 11 years, and they made the whole venture stress-free, which was extremely important for all the runners. I have already mentioned that Roland has run the marathon, but John has also run London. So they knew how to look after us. I used to sit down and have a chat to John afterwards and just 'pig-out'. By now my recovery process was in full swing.

Keep on the move!

One thing you should do after you have finished is keep moving – seriously! You may think this is not the thing to do; in fact, you may want just to collapse somewhere in a crumpled heap. Not so. The worst thing you can do is sit down for long periods or be totally inactive. The more you move about, the more you will minimise the DOMS (delayed onset muscle soreness) the following day and for up to 48 hours afterwards. Actually, it is a good idea, once you have recovered from the marathon and feel more composed, to walk about as much as you can. Use the stairs, not the lift, in your hotel. This may seem crazy to you, but believe me, this is the best thing to do, and you will benefit from less muscle soreness in the following days.

A few years ago, I ran the Amsterdam Marathon as one of Malcolm Hargraves and Running Crazy's tours. The following morning I was, as you would expect, a little sore, so I decided to go for a walk around the area of our hotel. I wandered along a main road to a canal. I then got a little lost and mistook one main street for another and had trouble finding my way back to the hotel. I was out and about for around three and a half hours. I was not too concerned as it was quite nice to take in the atmosphere and just walk. But after all of this time I was starting to get a little tired. I walked into a street cafe and, after ordering a coffee, asked the way back to the hotel. It was just a short distance away, so I wandered back. The following day my muscle soreness had all but gone. This walk, although a little accidental, was a massive tonic towards curing my DOMS. I can also remember the half an hour or so after running the Romantic Castles Marathon in Füssen, Bavaria, a few years ago. My daughter, Lucy, had seen a McDonald's and asked if we could go there after the marathon. It was about a half-mile walk. I had just run 26.2 miles and that half-mile walk was a bigger challenge than the marathon itself and about all I could manage! But it was just what I needed. So keep on the move afterwards. Of course, there will be times after the marathon when you just want to chill and sit or lie down. That is fine, just try not to do this immediately afterwards. Try to remain as active as you can within reason.

Post-marathon stretching

Normally, with races of shorter distances and training sessions, it is very important to stretch afterwards. By this I mean static stretching. However, after a marathon, I personally never do. Now, with some coaches, this may open things up for me to cop a little bit of flack. But I am sticking to what I am saying here. My way of thinking here is that, after running a marathon, your legs are absolutely shot. If you will excuse the pun, your legs are on their knees. The muscle-fibre damage is as bad as it is going to be. You have run 26.2 miles, not 6.2 miles, or even 13.1. I do not believe in stretching already badly damaged muscle fibres. I totally recommend stretching after your training runs. Even after your longest 20-mile training run. But not after your marathon! Remember, you have previously run no further than 20 miles. The last 10k of a marathon is uncharted territory. This is when you call on all your reserves. This is also the stage when you have recruited all of the muscle fibres possible to get you round. They are taking an absolute hammering. Both fast-twitch and slow-twitch fibres are now being used and are really getting battered, especially in the last 10k of the marathon. So, when you finish, your legs, muscles fibres, tendons and ligaments have had the most brutal and extensive workout, so why try to stretch trashed legs? I have never stretched after a marathon. I let the body do its own recovering. I walk around and remain as active as possible without overdoing it. But no stretching. Think about it, you are not running again now for weeks – the job is done. You do not have to recover more quickly to get another training run on board. You do not have another race coming up. That is it – marathon over! Let the recovery process begin and let the damaged legs heal without extra extensive stretching of already heavily damaged muscles. They will heal themselves soon enough. I have always let my muscles recover over the following days by themselves. They start to feel OK after 3–4 days. Do not run on them either; let them mend.

Ice baths

This is a hotly debated topic. There are many scientists and coaches who say ice baths are the way to go, while others say a warm shower is the best thing to do. There is also an argument for cold/heat treatment – that is, alternating the temperature of your shower from hot to cold. The theory behind the ice bath treatment is that it constricts the blood vessels and suppresses inflammation. After the bath, when the body warms up, the blood flow increases and targets the damaged areas more quickly with nutrients. It also helps flush toxins out of the body. OK, that is fine. I honestly don't see any harm in taking ice baths. I know rugby players have them, as well as athletes and other sports men and women. However, I have always looked on ice baths as a quick way of speeding up recovery, which it is. Perhaps, they are used in other sports because people need to be ready to take on another match or training session in a shorter space of time. This is not the case with the marathon. You will not be running again for weeks. Personally, I have never had an ice bath in my life. It comes across to me as some kind of medieval torture. You can, of course, run a bath and gradually add the ice to lessen the pain! If you really want an ice bath, it won't hurt you. This is up to you. There is also another good argument for ice baths if you want to go down this road. The cold will numb muscles and help relieve the post-marathon muscles soreness. But bear in mind by keeping on the move you will be helping to minimise soreness anyway, and you do not have to be ready to do any exercise for a few weeks. I am more than happy to have a warm shower after my marathons. Unlike some of my other competitive marathon-running buddies, I have no problem taking a decent amount of time off after running a marathon. Therefore, I am in no rush to get back out on the road, so I strongly recommend you have this attitude, too.

A warm shower

This is more me! After every marathon I have run, I have been more than happy to have a warm shower. I have the attitude that, after running a marathon, my muscles are going to be sore and tired anyway. To repeat what I have said above: I will not be running for at least a month or more. I am more than prepared to let my body work its magic and recover naturally. I still maintain that, after all of my 42 marathons, I found keeping on the move was the best tonic for easing DOMS. A warm shower will, say the experts, help stimulate muscle recovery like the ice bath. Do not have your shower/bath too hot; otherwise, something called vasodilation takes place – if it is too hot, it can cause light headedness. The warm water will help to pump the blood and nutrients around the body to the affected areas through vasodilation. Vasodilation is the technical term for dilation of the blood vessels. Vasoconstriction is the opposite. This is what you will get when taking ice baths. After running a marathon, everyone wants to have a nice shower or bath to get themselves clean after sweating it out for running 26.2 miles. That goes with the territory. One little piece of advice I can give you is this: I have found showers much easier to step out of, rather than struggling to climb out of a bath, especially if you are pretty sore and have been lying more prostrate. Just a little tip that may help!

Contrast shower

A contrast shower is simply alternating between the two treatments above. It is alternating cold water and then warm water. So what is the effect of doing this? Just the same as the above. It will help to force oxygen-rich blood and nutrients around the physiological system to help aid recovery. If it appeals, then do this.

I have found that, as with an awful lot of scientific research, there are so many positive and negative points for and against any theory or argument. What one person will say is right, another will say is wrong. It can be a little frustrating. As far as post-marathon recovery treatments are concerned, just do what appeals most. I do not think any of them are any better, or worse, that the others. They will all help. I just fancy a normal shower after my marathon, and I let the body do its own recovering. You are just giving it a slight helping hand here. Is all of what I have said trivial? Perhaps. But it is my job to help you through every aspect of marathon running and that includes recovery processes. However, do what works for you.

Post-marathon massages

This is an interesting one. More often than not, you will find massages are available at the end of most marathons. Is this a good idea? I have told you that I do not stretch my already trashed muscles after running this distance. But there is a difference between stretching and having a post-marathon massage. I asked Fiona for advice on having a post-marathon massage, and this is what she said:

> A light massage is a good idea as soon as possible after a marathon. The idea here is that it will keep blood pumping through the muscles and will aid in getting the blood flowing with all the nutrients to the affected areas to help recovery. It will also deliver oxygen to assist the recovery process.

But, as Fiona said, and I agree, it is a light massage. So, really, the principle of getting blood flowing around the body is the same as having your post-marathon shower. Do not, though, go for anything that is deep tissue or aggressive. Remember, you have put your legs through the ringer. Keep it light! To answer the above rhetorical question: yes, a light massage after a marathon is a great idea. If there is one available to you, and you fancy it, then by all means have one. I have.

The days and weeks after the marathon

You have just pushed your whole physiological system to its max, so recovery is of the utmost importance. Here is a list of some of the things that happen to your body after a marathon:

1. Microtrauma to the skeletal muscles
2. Tendon and ligament damage
3. Oxidative damage
4. Cellular damage
5. Weakened immune system
6. Cardiac muscle damage (possibly)
7. Mental exhaustion

I will look at these now in more detail. Firstly, though, I do not want you to stress. These things do happen; it is just part of running a marathon. However, they all rectify themselves as the recovery process kicks in and come right. The human body is an amazing thing. Let it do its work and within a month you will totally be back on the road to normality and, believe me, fitter than you have ever been, so stress not.

Microtrauma to the muscles

Somewhere around two weeks after running your marathon, your muscles will be well on the way to repairing themselves after having been traumatised from running 26.2 miles. Even though they may be starting to feel OK after a few days, that does not mean they are back to normal – far from it. There will still be some muscle-fibre tearing. Give them a fortnight (at least) to totally knit back together.

Tendon and ligament damage

The training you have been doing for the last few months or years has meant that your tendons and ligaments are now tuned in and toned for the marathon. So what about afterwards? Having done some research into what happens to tendons and ligaments after a marathon, I must admit (to my frustration) that I have found very little information. There is the usual damage that we would expect – that is, inflammation. But, unlike muscles, tendons and ligaments are made of collagen. This means that tendons and ligaments take longer to recover from any damage, so this is another good reason to have a decent recovery from your marathon. We know that ligaments and tendons take a hammering, just like every other part of the physiological system. Like your muscles, continuous stretching and overuse of your tendons and ligaments leads to inflammation. On the other hand, though, ligament and tendon tissue has evolved over time in a way that they can take an awful lot of punishment. The Achilles tendon is the strongest in the body; it can stand up to a lot of stress and has fatigue resistance. So even though tendons and ligaments have evolved over time (hunter gatherers were chasing down prey through running long distances around two million years ago or more – hence a reason they needed to evolve), they still have their breaking point. A marathon is fine, but overuse is not. If they become inflamed and damaged, and you do not give them time to recuperate, in time you could run into problems. So make sure you rest up after running a marathon.

Oxidative damage

When we carry out exhaustive exercises, we produce unstable molecules in the body. These are known as free radicals as they are molecules that have one or more unpaired electrons. This is linked to the oxygen we breath in – hence the term oxidative stress, or damage. Of course, everyone needs to breathe, but there are things you can do in terms of diet to neutralise free radical damage. Free radicals are produced naturally anyway, and the body has defences (antioxidants) to fight these. But when running a marathon, we produce additional free radicals that overwhelm the body's natural defences. Free radicals attack cells and are detrimental to your health. So is running a marathon going to be that bad for you? I have run 42, and I am fighting fit. Marathon training need not be extreme if done properly. I regard it as average exercise as it comes within the health and safety guidelines and constraints and the human body's capabilities. So average exercise is fine, and by eating a good diet and getting proper rest you will be covering yourself, so don't worry. Free radicals are the reason your immune system takes a hit after a marathon – they also cause inflammation. However, there is an easy fix: your diet (yet again) and total recovery. Food that has a colour to it – that is, carrots, berries, tomatoes, green vegetables, oranges, or any other naturally coloured foodstuffs – have all the antioxidants you will need to neutralise free radicals and the damage they may cause. Lycopene is a very powerful antioxidant that is found in tomatoes. So after running a marathon, I hit the tomato juice. It is also an excellent source of vitamin C and many other nutrients. Lycopene is responsible for giving tomatoes their red colour. It can also be found in watermelon, pink grapefruit, apricots and many other fruits. If you want to mop up free radicals, hit the lycopene and tomatoes. If you do not like tomatoes, any fruit or vegetable I have mentioned above will do the trick. Just get the antioxidants on board after your marathon and rest up. It takes something like 4–5 days to for oxidative stress to return to normal levels after running a marathon.

Cellular damage

The topic of cellular damage after running a marathon is perhaps quite generic. There are a colossal number of cells in the human body. Research suggests that there are tens of trillions of cells that make up the organs in our bodies. So cellular damage means damage to all the organs affected during the marathon. It also means damage to the muscle fibres, kidneys, tendons and ligaments, which I have already covered. It includes oxidative stress, too. They all come under the cellular damage umbrella caused by running a marathon. So this is quite generic.

Weakened immune system

In Chapter 5, when we looked at the marathon taper, I explained that the immune system is at a lower ebb as a result of all the training and long runs you have been doing. This is the same after your marathon as you have pushed and stressed everything far more than ever before. I can count the number of times I have had a cold on one hand, but, if I am going to get one, it is highly likely to be in the days after running a marathon. The immune system has been temporarily weakened. The reason for this is because when you push yourself hard the body produces cortisol – yes, the same stuff that is produced when you do not get enough sleep. Skimping on your sleep puts stress on your immune system, but the same thing happens after running the marathon, too. It is also responsible for cellular damage. Experts say that in the three, or so, days after your marathon, you are susceptible to ailments such as colds. So eating a proper diet and getting sufficient sleep are imperative after your marathon as these will help to strengthen your immunity and lessen the chance of you catching any post-marathon illnesses. But don't be surprised if you do get a cold!

Cardiac heart muscle damage (possibly)

When researching and reading about the possibility of damage to our bodies when running marathons, one of the first things I looked at, certainly from a health and safety point of view, was just how dangerous is it. In regard to everything else I have covered, we seem to be in safe hands when exercising. I must admit to being a little loath to go on too much about the detrimental sides of marathon running, simply because this may cause anxiety and concern. Obviously, this is what I do not want. Marathon running is still incredibly safe if done properly. But as our safety in running is paramount, I feel compelled to look at this. Everything in the list of seven things that can happen to your body when running a marathon is important in terms of recovery and wellbeing post-marathon. But, if you think the same as me, as soon as a major organ is mentioned, then the red flag is raised. I do not apologise for saying this yet again, but do not get stressed or worried about this. Just be aware that recovery is important. At the end of this list I am going through, I will again try to alleviate any concerns about marathon running by giving you some very interesting facts and figures to mull over if you get a little concerned.

Back to the major organs, let's look at the heart. As a seasoned marathoner myself, I am familiar with the usual muscle soreness that accompanies training for and running marathons. But when I was doing some reading and research into the possible damage associated with running marathons, as soon as the word 'heart' was mentioned, I really took note. There are many articles in magazines and online that look at what damage there is, or may be, to the heart. I must admit, because it is such an important organ, I was determined to find out how bad (or good) marathon running is for the heart. I have yet to find a definitive answer aimed at the negative side of this question! I have to say again, I am not a doctor, so compared to the experts my knowledge is, of course, minimal. But I am still a marathoner, so I'm interested to read about and research the subject. I have spent hours and hours reading about the risks of running and whether it has a detrimental effect on the heart. Firstly, I have noticed that there are a large number of variables here: whether there is a pre-existing heart condition (that may not be known to the runner), a lifetime of smoking or drinking, poor diet, lack of sleep and so on, all need to be considered. Any of these, of course, would be detrimental and may be unhealthy to your heart. Throw on top of this a marathon-training regimen and you may have to look at what you are doing. You may have had a lifestyle that includes the above, but you want to get fit and have kicked some of your vices into touch. So you may be OK, or you may not – it is perhaps up for debate. Your doctor will certainly point you in the right direction here.

One other topic that is up for debate is the possibility of heart muscle scarring. It has been suggested that over time (that is, not just running one marathon, but multiple marathons and ultramarathons), you may eventually contract some heart muscle scarring. If you are interested in finding out more, there was an article published by the Mayo Clinic (Rochester, USA) in June 2012 with details of the research carried out by Dr James O'Keefe. It suggests that there may be some heart muscle scarring. I have yet to find an article, though, to say that this has been proven. Another interesting article was published more recently by the *New York Times* in 2017. They tested a number of runners for signs of scar damage and these runners showed quite varied results. So as far as I can see, the jury is still out on this.

I would like to put my own little piece of possible reassurance in here for you too. After taking my running to the highest possible level I could at school, I had a break from running, not just for a few years, but for nearly three decades. I took up smoking for a few years and spent an awful lot of time in the pub socialising and spending far too much money. I have already told you I ran my first marathon in my 40s, and now, at the age of 58, I have run and raced in (and done all the thousands of miles of training for) 42 marathons competitively. I had my most recent health check at my local clinic and my heart age was comparable to that of a 51-year-old. There was not a mention at all of any possible heart damage, just the opposite. I am not trying to sound high and mighty and show off. Of course, I was delighted with the results of my health test, and I know we are all different to a certain extent. But this, I hope, is of some comfort to you – it certainly was to me. You are training for and doing your first. So, unless the doctor tells you otherwise, rest easy and crack on with your marathon quest.

The bottom line is that your heart will probably be under some strain when running a marathon. But anything that happens here is temporary and will go back to normal within a few days, according to the experts. There is the fact, also, and I repeat it again, that you will be running your first-ever marathon. You may decide to run another in the future, but you are not a multiple marathoner or churning out hundreds of miles month in month out in training for events of very long distances. This is all very much in your favour. I may be being repetitive here, but I do not want you to worry and concern yourself over this. Look again at Steve Boone and his wife Paula in Texas. They have run hundreds of marathons between them (and getting near the 1,000 mark now. A few days ago Steve told me he has run 799 now and 4 in the last 2 weeks – and they are still churning them out!) and, as far as I know from the last time we were in contact, they are fine.

Mental exhaustion

As you may appreciate there is a reason to recover physically. But it does not stop just with the physical side of marathon running. Months of training can take its toll – this means mentally too. It is highly likely that after the months of training and the marathon itself you will feel mentally drained – this is normal. The last thing I want to do after running a marathon is think about running again anytime soon. And I'm not talking about just for a few days, but for at least a month or more. I think that one of the reasons people are too eager to hit the road is because afterwards there is a void. You have been training for months and churning out a lot of miles. Once the marathon has been run, that is it, nothing more to do. Your brain and body get used to running long distances. It may even feel a little abnormal now to be doing nothing. Some people struggle with this. Some runners even feel a little down in the dumps afterwards. There is a lack of purpose, and perhaps focus, as the deed is done. This does not happen to everyone, of course, and this may not happen to you. Just be aware that there may be a bit of a void after your marathon. We coaches and runners call it the post-marathon blues. However, this is nothing unusual, so try not to be too concerned if you feel a little like this afterwards. If you do feel a little flat, try to do what I do. Revel in the fact that you have just achieved something momentous. Think that every day you have off afterwards is vital in terms of your body's recovery. You are actually getting stronger physiologically as your body repairs all the damage, so this is good. Be proud of the amount you have raised to help support a good charity that is important to you. There is a bit of an endorphin come down as such, too. Your body has been through a lot. Just accept the fact that this is normal. This post-marathon blues will pass. It is only temporary for a couple of days or so. Try to occupy yourself with some of the things you have not been able to do before you took on this venture. Get plenty of sleep, eat well and contact the charity with the good news that you have a nice cheque coming to them. Pat yourself on the back and be proud of what you have achieved. If you are hooked on what you have just done, you may want to look at doing the same thing in the future. If this is the case, then do not be in too much of a rush. Give it six months at the earliest. Remember, recovery is extremely important, especially as this is your first marathon.

On top of finishing and revelling in what you have done, reward yourself. Go for those couple of pints and a burger. You have earned it; it doesn't matter now.

Interesting facts about marathon running

As promised, to help alleviate any concerns you may have, I have compiled a list of facts about marathon running that you may find interesting if you have found the above list on recovery a little worrying. Can I also mention that, in this chapter, I have brought the importance of recovery to your attention for a very good reason. It is for your own good. But this is not so much to let you think that marathons are bad or dangerous in anyway – they are not. It is purely to give you a grounding on what happens to allow you to get back to a normal, healthy physical state afterwards. I have said already that the body is fantastic at repairing itself, and it is. You can just help it along the way by doing everything I have suggested. Look on the plus side of the following list, not the negative.

The main reasons for fatalities in marathons are hyponatremia, heart disorders and heatstroke. I have yet to hear of, or find any information on, any deaths caused by dehydration.

1. There have been just 52 deaths (if you include Phedippides) in all the marathons ever run.

2. The chances of dying from a cardiac problem in a marathon are around 1 in 100,000.

3. The odds of being killed by a sky dive are the same, around 1 in 100,000, as are the odds of being killed by a bee.

4. It is safer running a marathon than travelling by car. The odds of being in a fatal car crash are around 1 in 115.

5. Fauja Singh ran the Mumbai Marathon at the age of 104.

6. Female runner Harriette Thompson ran the San Diego Rock and Roll Marathon aged 94.

7. Humans can outrun almost any other animal and are amongst the best long-distance runners around. The top two animals that can beat a human for distance running are the ostrich and the pronghorn antelope.

8. There is a higher chance of being struck by lightning than dying in a marathon – around 1 in 85,000.

9. The chance of succumbing to a major natural catastrophe courtesy of mother nature is about 1 in 3,500.

10. In 2004 Xu Zhenjun broke the world record by running the Beijing Marathon in 3 hours and 43 minutes, backwards!

11. A charity record: the most money raised by an individual in the London Marathon £2,330,159 by Reverend Steve Chalke in 2011.

12. Matt Gunby broke the world record as the fastest superhero in the 2016 London Marathon running it in 2 hours and 27 minutes. It was his first-ever marathon, and he was dressed as Wonder Woman. The record had previously been broken by Paul Martelletti in 2015, dressed as Spider Man. Paul is a former Whanganui boy like me.

13. In 2012 Lloyd Scott MBE broke the world record for the slowest ever marathon time. He walked it in a time of 6 days, in a deep-sea-diving costume! Lloyd was diagnosed with leukaemia in 1989, and since then has raised a huge amount of money for many different charities by running a number of extreme marathons and other events, some of them quite phenomenal – very inspirational.

14. British astronaut Tim Peake broke the world record for running a marathon in space. He ran the 2016 London Marathon in a time of 3 hours and 35 minutes, orbiting the earth on a treadmill (in the space station, that is).

15. In the 2016 London Marathon the millionth runner crossed the line.

16. The 2019 New York Marathon is the largest ever run. There were 53,627 finishers.

17. Top marathoner Hugh Lob became the first person to beat a horse. This was in the man versus horse marathon in Wales. A horse had won for the first quarter of a century.

18. The most disturbing outfit to be worn in the London Marathon must surely be a mankini!

19. The world's fastest Elvis was Nikki Johnstone in the 2018 Berlin Marathon. His time was 2 hours and 37 minutes.

20. Finally, I have to throw this one in here too. This is about Raphael Igrisianu, an excellent marathoner from Romania. Raphael previously ran the Dusseldorf Marathon (Raphael resides in Germany) dribbling a basketball. It was a new world record run/dribbled in a time of 3 hours and 25 seconds. Raphael has a number of quirky world records to his name.

An aside

I first met Raphael a few years ago. We were both running the 2014 Cyprus Marathon. I was there with Malcolm Hargraves and Running Crazy again. As the race progressed, we were both out in front of the rest of the field. As we were running we started chatting and found we got on very well. We shook hands and totally gelled. However, as the race progressed, we realised this was still a race after all. I made my move with just a few miles to go, establishing something of a lead. However, I had made my break too early and broke myself. Raphael caught me, and even though Malcolm was encouraging me all the way to the end, I was done in. Raphael caught me and won the race. I came in second, one minute behind him. So another learning curve for me. Raphael was more tactically astute on the day. Our paths met again the following year at the World Masters Champs in Lyon.

As we were running around the marathon course, I heard a voice call out 'Hey, Gerry' from the runners on the other side of the road. It was Raphael, and he beat me again, by one minute! I have only met up with Raphael twice, but we have become very good friends on social media and often keep in touch. If you are interested, you can look him up on DONmarathon. de.tl. He is a very good marathoner and very popular in running circles. He also is a coach and a great inspiration to anyone who runs marathons. It is worth looking at some of his inspirational marathon-running efforts. He is a real character and a thoroughly nice guy.

Figure 7.1 Raphael on his way to breaking a new world record, running a marathon while dribbling a basketball.

Figure 7.2 Raphael at the end and the holder of a new world record time.

There are literally thousands of marathon-running facts out there, but the ones listed above are just a few to help reinforce how safe it is and to give you a brief insight into what some people have done. For many of us, marathons are a competitive thing. But they can also be fun and, by using them for fundraising, can help others.

8 The end of the road (and more on fundraising)

By now you have run your marathon. It is in the bag. With a bit of luck the challenge has been successfully negotiated and you have tamed the beast. So what now? You will be well into your recovery – which should have started the moment you finished your marathon. Day by day your body (and brain) will be getting back to its normal physical and mental state. As the weeks and months progress you may decide you never want to run another marathon, or that this is not the end. You may have run, or may be thinking of running, another. Perhaps, you have been well and truly bitten by the charity-fundraising bug. If so, then great. I target the London Marathon every year as my big fundraising event. Now that you are, or should be, in full recovery mode, it is a good time to focus on your charity. Now that you have run your marathon, you will be going around everyone who have said they will sponsor you to collect the money. This can prove a little challenging at times. After I ran the 2019 London Marathon, it took seven months before I had all the money in, including all the money I raised online. If you have not raised money through something like this before, then you may not have heard of 'Just Giving'. It is a fundraising page you can set up online. It is linked to a social media page, and people can contribute funds by submitting money online. I have used this for my last three London Marathons. It is a very good way of collecting the fundraising money as it takes away the work of having to chase everyone after you have run the marathon. You can leave your Just Giving page open for a few months following your fundraising challenge – I leave mine open for around six months – then when it is closed your charity will take the money you have raised. They should inform you once they have collected it. It does take a lot of the stress out of chasing people who have said they will sponsor you.

If, like me, you have worked in an establishment with a large number of people, you may find that you are lucky enough to get some help and support from your colleagues. In the past, I have been lucky enough to have had the help and support of the staff and students at Queen's College here in Taunton.

Before I ran my first London Marathon I was talking to Dave Cook, a biology teacher and the head of the sixth form at Queen's, and when he realised I was fundraising, he told me that the school could help. After talking to the school's chief executive, Dave and another teacher who ran the sixth form with him, Laura Schofield, we got the sixth form students on board. Over the next five years or so, we raised thousands of pounds for the NSPCC. We worked alongside Donna Statham of the NSPCC, and we made quite a good team. Donna came in to the school several times to talk to the students. I circulated sponsorship forms around the school. Dave and Laura collected money that was raised through school events such as barbecues and functions. They even raided the money in the sixth form pool table to help with the fundraising. It was all passed on to Donna and the NSPCC. Dave has now retired, and Laura has gone back up to Scotland to teach at Gordonstoun, but we still keep in touch. I have also been grateful for the help from the school's chaplain, Tim Aldridge. He set up an 'own clothes' day where the students each pay £2 so that they can wear their own civvy clothes instead of school uniform. Again, the proceeds went towards my London Marathon fundraising effort. Tim highlighted the importance of what we do in a recent school chapel service. So I am very grateful to the likes of Laura, Dave and Tim. They have supported me with what I do, and this helps fly the flag for the cause. Very sadly we also lost Tim through illness. He was a constant support to everyone at Queens College, and a fan of AC/DC's music like me. This was often our topic of conversation. He was with us at the school for 5 years and will be greatly missed, RIP Tim. The school's deputy head, Andrew Free, also uses a lot of resource material from the NSPCC. He is in charge of child protection within the school, so there has been a lot of contact between the school and the NSPCC in the past. Andrew is also a keen sportsman, and he runs, so we have some common ground in more than one area.

I also get a lot of help from another Queen's College staff member, Margaret Forshaw. For years, Margaret has taken one of my sponsorship forms around all of the school's domestic staff. Margaret has been a star and has saved me a lot of work by covering this side of things for me.

Figure 8.1 Me with Queen's College students Arthur Banks and Holly Brown (left). Holly and Arthur represented the school as we handed over a cheque for £693 to Donna Statham (right) of the NSPCC, back in 2013. Holly was a very fine runner. She was one of our athletes down at the Taunton Athletic Club. She and her older brother, Blair, also a former student at the school, ran to a very high standard.

This is my story involving the school. It may seem a little irrelevant to you, but it is just something I can write about which just may help to give you a few ideas if you have worked in an establishment like I have. The idea of this book is not just to negotiate you through all the training and your marathon. It is also about raising funds and supporting good causes through your running. If you want to try again in a few months' time, then put it out there. You will find that most people are often more than willing to help any good cause.

Here are a few more ideas that may help, and some brief stories of what others have done to raise money. You may find this gives you an idea or two if you are struggling with how to go about raising funds. It is often a good idea to 'pick the brains' of others who have been here before. I have to admit, of all the long distance and marathon runners I know, most of them have used their running as a means to raise money for charity at some stage. These stories are from some of the runners I know, both locally (from my running clubs) and further afield. I hope this helps.

Denis's story

While I was running for the Trull Troggers here in Taunton, I got to know one of the runners very well. His name is Denis Violet, and I contacted Denis recently to ask him if he would mind me writing about how he raised the required amount to get into the New York Marathon. His charity was the British Heart Foundation.

Denis and his brother, Chris, who was also involved in helping, raised a tidy sum for this cause. If you are interested in running for this charity, or any others for that matter, then you may find the information Denis sent over to me recently very useful and full of ideas. The British Heart Foundation put Denis and Chris in touch with 2.09 events, a company similar to the one I use (Running Crazy) who provide a service that takes runners to events all around the world. It is the brainchild of Mike Gratton, the 1983 London Marathon winner. Denis and Chris met up and trained with Mike and Keith Anderson (10th in the 1998 Kuala Lumpur Commonwealth Games Marathon). This was part of the pre-marathon preparation provided by the British Heart Foundation, or BHF as Denis refers to it in the text to me. Here is Denis's story, in his words:

> The BHF put me in touch with 2.09 events to arrange a race entry and travel package. The BHF provided fundraising support and online pages, free training day hosted by Heart runner team coach, Keith Anderson, who provided us with a 16-week training plan. I found this invaluable, providing an excellent opportunity to learn about every aspect of the challenge.

Dedicated BHF and 2.09 events tour leaders while in New York, a pre-marathon familiarisation run into Central Park to see the finish line and the last mile of the route were on offer. On the day before the marathon there was a Heart runners pre-race briefing, which gave us an opportunity to ask any questions and provided us with the full race information. Both the pre-race run and the briefing the day before the race were a great opportunity to meet fellow Heart runners.

Having set myself a target of £2,650, as well as the Just Giving website, I arranged through the local authority to have street collections for a couple of hours on a Saturday morning in both Taunton and Wellington (Somerset, UK), wearing my Heart runners top. This involved filling out a lot of forms for the local authority, but it proved to be well worth the effort as the people of Wellington and Taunton in Somerset gave very generously.

When I approached the local shops for their sponsorship, the manager of one store suggested that I hold a raffle as he could not make a financial contribution but would be able to supply a number of prizes. I received one very generous offer from one of the well-known jewellers in the town of either £100 or a piece of jewellery worth £350, which became first prize in the raffle. After writing to the chief executive officer of a very famous high street store, I received a £100 gift voucher, which became the second prize. I received a number of very generous donations from other companies, all of which helped to boost my sponsorship effort.

The raffle itself took place after one of the Trull Troggers' Thursday night club runs, in the local pub in the Somerset village of Trull. The raffle was very well supported on the night, raising over £950 together with tickets already sold. There were a number of additional prizes for those attending on the night.

Figure 8.2 Chris (left) and Denis Violet at the fundraising raffle evening in the Winchester Arms in Trull village, Somerset.

The majority of the marathon training was done with the support of fellow Troggers and under the guidance of Brian and Sandra North (founder members of the Trull Troggers). I was very fortunate to run on a Saturday morning with a group of Troggers with a vast amount of marathon-running experience between them. We gradually built up the mileage by a mile a week until we reached a target of 20 miles, which was considered the maximum required in order to feel confident of completing the marathon distance. This was in May of 2008, and the New York Marathon was on 2 November. We tapered off the distance of the runs for the rest of the summer, building up to a second 20-mile run final taper nearer the day.

Denis successfully ran the New York Marathon in a time of 4:35.08 – a great time. He also raised £3,500 for the British Heart Foundation – a tremendous effort!

Denis said: 'I'd hoped for a quicker time, but I helped another BHF runner to finish the marathon. She wanted to drop out of the race just before the 17-mile point, but I managed to get her to 25 miles, at which point she told me to go on. I found out later she finished the marathon only 5 minutes after me.' Another great example of the support and camaraderie of others doing the same thing as you in a marathon. Believe me, there are plenty more stories of support and camaraderie like this.

I must add that Denis was already an experienced runner. I have raced more than once alongside Denis in many races around this part of the country, so he has a good foundation in running, and his training would be a little different to the schedule I have written up in this book, which is aimed at first-time marathoners with less experience. I was also in the pub in Trull that night. It was a very successful night.

That was Denis's story, and it shows you what can be achieved and how to go about things when aiming to raise funds for charity. Denis can be extremely proud of his achievement.

Nick and Mark's fundraiser

Another runner from Taunton, Nick Cutler, who has always run for Running Forever Running Club (the same affiliated club I run for), decided to dress up as a banana. He was joined in this fundraising quest by Mark Fisher, another very talented local runner. I know Nick and Mark well. The first time I teamed up with Nick was when we both got our Somerset vests representing the county at the Dartmoor Vale Half Marathon. I have trained with, and raced alongside, Nick more than once (including in the London Marathon). They both ran the Taunton Half Marathon in these banana outfits to raise funds. I remember watching the race from the sidelines. Nick and Mark led the race at the start for a couple of hundred metres – a great way to gain publicity as there are normally many photos taken at the beginning of any big enough race, press and all. Nick and Mark eventually completed the race in a time of 1 hour and 27 minutes. I know this was a half marathon and not a full marathon. But that is irrelevant as I am focusing on the charity side of this just to show what others do. They raised money for a charity called Escape. This charity helps families who have children with special needs. Like Matt Murray, who I have mentioned earlier in this book, they chose to support a smaller local charity. Nick and

Mark are both very good runners, hence their quick time dressed up as the marathoners' superfood.

Figure 8.3 Nick Cutler and Mark Fisher running the Taunton Half Marathon for Escape.

The Taunton Marathon and Half Marathon are run on the same day. They are organised by John Lewis. If it were not for the London Marathon being run at roughly the same time, then I would run it every year. It is a shame they clash as it is a very well-organised event indeed. I know how much trouble John goes to in order to get the day to run smoothly. He should be commended for organising such a great local event. I have told you of my very first marathon experience, which was here at Taunton. The year after, having not been put off by my experience, I had a far more successful race in the Taunton Marathon. I have always said that the year I do not get into London, then Taunton will be my focus for an April or spring marathon. It is on the doorstep for me, and anyone who lives in the Southwest of England could do an awful lot worse in choosing this for their fundraising marathon or half marathon. As I have said, it was my first.

Dave's fundraiser

The general committee member of Running Forever Running Club in Taunton is Dave Marshall. I have known Dave for some time, and he has also run for charity. His chosen charity was the Freya Foundation. It is named after a little girl who was born with PDHD (Pyruvate Dehydrogenase Deficiency). Before contacting Dave, I had never heard of this illness nor the charity. So I was quite keen to find out more about it, especially since it is diagnosed in small children, usually just after birth. PDHD is a life-threatening build-up of lactic acid that leads to many metabolic and neurological problems. Dave sent me a link to the Freya Foundation. There is a website if anyone is interested: www.freyafoundation.co.uk. Dave ran the South Devon Marathon. This is a coastal race, which is organised by Endurancelife. This particular one was held near Kingsbridge in South Devon. This marathon is 27.5 miles, slightly longer than the usual 26.2 miles. Dave ran this in 2015, raising somewhere between £100 and £150.

Scott's fundraiser

Many of the runners at Running Forever regularly run marathons and ultramarathons. A lot of these are off road and far more challenging than any of the flat marathons I run. So I admire the determination and the efforts put in here. One of these runners is Scott Weetch. Scott is one of our Running Forever Running Club members who runs further than 26.2 miles ... much further. In 2014 Scott ran the Thames Trot 50 miler, raising money for cancer research. He told me he had lost his nan to cancer, hence why he chose this cause. He raised a tidy sum of around £600 through support from family and friends, a cake sale, etc. He ran the race in 10 hours. This is, indeed, a very long way to run, so total respect here to Scott.

Peter's fundraiser

Like Dave and Scott, Peter Hall is another of the club's committee members. Also, like many of the Running Forever runners, Peter is also a keen long-distance runner, often running further than 26.2 miles. However, his very first marathon was London 2007. That year, he ran London for Help the Hospices and raised a tidy amount of £1,500. It was very hot, so times were not as quick as normal. His time was 4 hours 50 minutes, which is still very good considering the hotter conditions. Peter entered the ballot again in 2008 and got in. This time he ran it in 4 hours and 15 minutes. A tremendous improvement. He also raised money for charity when he ran his second ever ultramarathon. This was the Classic Quarter 44-mile race from the Lizard to Land's End in Cornwall. This time he raised £450 for Cornwall Hospice Care. He ran it with two of our other Running Forever Club members, Lynn Cunningham and Richard Staunton, in a time of 12 hours and 50 minutes. A long time to be on your feet, so again, respect! Peter ran this event because a work colleague had recently died of cancer and had spent his last days in St Peter's Hospice in Bristol. We all have our own personal reasons for raising money, and this was Peter's.

Tanya's fundraiser

It is not only the male members of Running Forever who have been fundraising. One of our ladies, Tanya Lewis, a keen long-distance runner and a triathlete, competed in the 2018 Ironman Wales competition in Tenby. She explained that she had received 13 hours of amazing Welsh support' while competing in this event. This event includes a cycle and a swim as well as a run of marathon distance. Tanya raised funds for Macmillan Cancer Support. Obviously, you do not have to enter an ironman competition to run your marathon, but this shows you what another athlete has done to raise money to help others. By successfully competing in an ironman, Tanya has incorporated two other disciplines, in addition to running, into her competitive fundraising venture.

Steve and Paula Boone

I have left this story until last as I think it is a good place to finish off this section on people's fundraising efforts. It takes us over the Atlantic to the USA. This is a little different. It involves fundraising, but it is from a slightly different angle. You may remember me saying in the Introduction that I ran the 2009 Texas Marathon on New Year's Day. This marathon is the brainchild of Steve and Paula Boone.

Back in 2000 they founded The Sawblade Texas Marathon to help a local runner called Rick Worley. Rick was aiming to get into the Guinness Book of World Records. He wanted to set a new world record for running the most marathons on consecutive weekends. Rick's record attempt had him running 200 marathons in 159 weekends. Unfortunately for Rick, there were no marathons taking place over the Christmas weekend in 1999, so his running streak would have been broken; however, Steve and Paula came to the rescue and created the Texas Marathon to enable Rick to keep his marathon-running streak going. Rick went on to run the Texas Marathon four times and also ran one in every state in the USA. Sadly, Rick was tragically killed in a traffic accident in 2010. This race has now been held every New Year's Day up until the most recent race, in 2022, in his memory. When I was in Texas, and ran this race, I got to know Paula and Steve for the few days we were there.

Just to show you how dedicated they are to their marathons and the causes they represent, after our most recent correspondence, Paula had completed her 369th marathon and Steve his 799th and counting. Steve has competed in all the 50 states of the USA eight times now. This, of course, includes Alaska and Hawaii. They have also run in many of the continents around the world.

I quote what Steve shared with me about Rick when we were recently in contact: 'Rick was one of our best friends and set a Guinness world record by running 200 marathons in 159 consecutive weeks. Rick was a character. Always had a big grin on his face and would love to know he is still remembered.' Steve also explained that he used to run for charity around 25 years ago. But now he and Paula use the proceeds from the Texas Marathon to fund their Marathon Challenge running programme for elementary school children. This year will be the 27th year of the programme. It has grown from 14 students in one school to over 10,000 in 26 schools. The idea is to encourage students to complete the marathon distance in a school year. They give T-shirts to anyone who completes this challenge. It is about helping students to learn about long-term goals. It is also about motivating others to take up running. They thought of this when their own children were attending Pine Forest Elementary school in Humble, near Lake Houston. The programme has grown in stature and is very popular within many of the schools in the Houston area. It has been praised by PE teachers and health co-ordinators alike. In a nutshell, it encourages fit and healthy lifestyles for elementary school children and is proving very popular.

When it comes to raising money for charity, the Marathon Challenge programme is a little different than a one-off event. But it is the Boone's way of helping others and at the same time putting something back into the sport and their community. It was only a few days ago that Steve told me all about their Marathon Challenge programme. I am glad he did as it has shown me another way of putting one's marathon running to good use and it allows us to look at fundraising from a slightly different angle.

You may remember me telling you earlier in the book about Lucy McAlistair and how she had helped a blind runner to run the London Marathon. I have mentioned already that Lucy won the 2008 Austin Marathon. Steve was also running this race at the same time as Lucy. The other day Steve messaged me, joking that when Lucy came over the finish line in first place, he was passing the halfway mark. Steve is only one of three people to have run every Austin Marathon since it began. Paula and Steve are very inspirational, and I wanted to include their efforts in this book. Like me, I hope you get something out of their enthusiasm and total dedication.

Figure 8.4 Paula and Steve Boone, multiple marathoners, founders of the 50 States Club and the Marathon Challenge Programme for elementary school students in the USA, and also founders and organisers of the Texas Marathon.

Final thoughts

I guess there is not much more to say or do here. The race is run, and we are at the end of the road. There are a multitude of very inspirational stories about what people have achieved in their charity-marathon-running quests. Some are extremely inspirational, some are really quite sad and sobering, some are downright crazy if not bizarre. But there is a common denominator here: charities. People just want to do their bit for a cause that means everything to them.

By running in marathons and other distances and by joining various clubs, I have met so many great people with this common goal, regardless of which cause they run for. I find them inspiring, and they help keep me focused on using my running to help those less fortunate than myself.

I have also been very lucky to meet and work with a number of people (runners and non-runners alike) who have been instrumental in helping me with this project. This book would not have been possible without them, their stories, their knowledge and expertise, and their overall generosity in letting me use their experiences in this book. I have thanked them in the acknowledgement section. I feel it is the least I can do to repay my gratitude.

I am completing this book during the COVID pandemic. We are in difficult times now and running has taken a hit. Things are improving and races are happening again, however, charities did not receive the normal funding from our sport. Let's hope for better times ahead.

My final thoughts are stay well, look after yourselves and good luck in your marathon-running quests. Once things stabilise, I look forward to meeting up with you one day on the running circuit. There is a very good Maori saying, from back home, that means 'stay strong'. Use it – it works: *Kia Kaha*.

Ingram Content Group UK Ltd.
Milton Keynes UK
UKHW040809290323
419346UK00001B/5